Repeopling Vermont

The Paradox of Development
in the Twentieth Century

Repeopling Vermont

The Paradox of Development in the Twentieth Century

PAUL M. SEARLS

Vermont Historical Society

BARRE AND MONTPELIER

Copyright © 2019 by Paul M. Searls

Library of Congress Cataloging-in-Publication Data

Names: Searls, Paul M., author.
Title: Repeopling Vermont : the paradox of development in the twentieth century / Paul M. Searls.
Description: Barre : Vermont Historical Society, [2019] | Includes bibliographical references and index.
Identifiers: LCCN 2019017141 | ISBN 9780934720700 (alk. paper)
Subjects: LCSH: Vermont--History--20th century. | Vermont--Population--Economic aspects. | Vermont--Population--Environmental aspects. | Landgrove (Vt.)--History. | Immigrants--Vermont--Landgrove--History--20th century. | Swedes--Vermont-Landgrove. | Ogden, Samuel R. | Economic development--Vermont--History--20th century. | Social change--Vermont--History--20th century.
Classification: LCC F54 .S43 2019 | DDC 974.3/043--dc23
LC record available at https://lccn.loc.gov/2019017141

Printed in the United States of America

22 21 20 2 3 4

Designed by James F. Brisson

ISBN: 978-0-934720-70-0

Second Printing, January 2020

DEDICATED
TO THE MEMORY OF
ROBERT L. SEARLS,
SAMUEL B. HAND,
AND
LIONEL J. PALARDY

CONTENTS

ACKNOWLEDGMENTS

M Y FIRST DEBT OF THANKS is to Duncan and Sally Ogden of Peru, Vermont. They welcomed me into their home, and into their collection of material that Duncan's father Samuel accumulated over the course of his life. They were tirelessly patient, polite, and generous with their time, and this would be a very different, inferior book without them. Other members of the Landgrove community treated me with equal generosity and patience. The genesis of this book was a meeting I had with Priscilla Grayson at a Vermont Historical Society history fair in Tunbridge, and in the ensuing years Priscilla acted as tour guide to Landgrove, opened the town's archives to me, and fed me a delicious lunch. I am indebted also to Robert and Carolyn Badger for the illuminating tour of Landgrove Village they provided, and for responding to many emails requesting clarification or confirmation of facts.

I am greatly indebted to the descendants of Major Valentine's Swedes who helped with this project. Robert, Helen, and Travis Tifft of Arlington gave me invaluable information on Lottie Nyren and her family. Earl Cavanagh of Brattleboro graciously supplied me with a wealth of knowledge about the Andersons. The late Lillian Fellows Abbott and her son Kyle Fellows of Wilder provided me with information on Lillian's mother, Anna Nyren. I received further assistance from Heather Snow on the Neilsons, and from the late Leslie Westine.

I will be eternally grateful to Alan Berolzheimer of the Vermont Historical Society for his careful and insightful editing of the text, and for his encouragement and enthusiasm for the project at times when those things were very much needed. Gregory Sanford read an early version of the manuscript and provided excellent comments and suggestions for improvement. Dr. Ellen D. Searls also read the manuscript and gave me many helpful comments. I am very grateful for the help of Sam Boss and the staff at Lyndon State College's library, Prudence Doherty and the staff at the University of Vermont's Special Collections, and Paul Carnahan and the staff at the library of the Vermont Historical Society. I received advice and encouragement from Tyler Resch of the Bennington Museum and Walloomsac Review, Blake Harrison, Bruce C. Post, William Graves, Steve Gold, Ruth Barton, and Neal Wells. I am grateful for the resources and support provided by the members of the Center for Research on Vermont, and especially its directors Cheryl Morse and Richard Watts. I am very grateful to the students who have taken my course on Vermont History in the last couple years, with whom I worked through much of this material. They are a big part of this book. Shouts to my brother Tim for letting me use his Ancestry.com account.

This project greatly benefited from a grant supplied by Lyndon State College's Structure and Welfare Committee, and I am grateful to its members: Brandon Stroup, Janet Bennion, Donna Smith, Deb Hughes, and Phil Parisi. Thanks as well to Grant and Jo Reynolds. I'd also like to say hello to Jason Isaacs.

Portions of this book appeared in an article written for the journal *Vermont History*, 81 (Winter/Spring 2013): 139-69, and I am grateful for the use of that material here, and for the excellent editing work on the article provided by Michael Sherman.

Thank you for reading this book. If you helped me with this project and I did not thank you here, get in touch and I'll apologize. Everything else, once again, is for Andrea. Sending signals that sound in the dark.

INTRODUCTION

S AM OGDEN BEGAN HIS BEST-KNOWN WORK, the 1946 back-to-the-land how-to guide *This Country Life*, "In writing this book I have been motivated by a single purpose, and have hoped to accomplish one thing." This book attempts something similar. Its purpose is to tell the story of Vermont in the twentieth century, and seeks to accomplish that by tracing two distinct but interrelated stories. If this volume presents a narrow window into the state over a long period of time, from the 1890s to the 1970s, it seeks to examine the large forces at work throughout that era, and illuminate the fundamental contradictions and ironies that defined Vermont in the twentieth century.

The wellspring of those contradictions and ironies is a central paradox that matured over the course of many decades. In the late nineteenth century, the predominant feeling among the state's leaders was that Vermont's overwhelmingly rural character—its heavily agricultural economy, its declining rural population numbers, the insular and traditional way of life found in its small towns—was a distressing problem in need of a solution. Gradually in the decades that followed, however, that same class of people came to see Vermont's rural character as the state's greatest asset. They also concluded that this rural character was endangered and in need of action if it was to be saved. To them, Vermont's traditional landscapes, physical and human, increasingly distinguished the state amidst a nation growing ever more modern. Tourism, first in the summer and then year-round, became a crucial part of the state's economy and was dependent on that pastoral character. Perceptions that the state had a high quality of life were marketed to attract business. And those in positions of power came to appreciate the state's aesthetics and way of life as having their own intrinsic value.

Thus, the focus of both public and private efforts in the twentieth century was increasingly to attempt to preserve those things a certain class of people thought best about Vermont tradition. Along the way, however, those engaged in such efforts encountered a complex paradox. Not acting would result in the despoilment of Vermont's natural environment, its scenery, and its small-town character. But acting to save those things imperiled tradition in other ways. Efforts to preserve Vermont's perceived way of life and scenery altered both, especially because they were often undertaken largely to meet the expectations and desires of people like the reformers themselves. "Preservation" necessarily could not mean keeping things the same. Instead it required managing economic and environmental change intensively, often in ways that marginalized whole sectors of Vermont's population. Preservation endangered such aspects of the "traditional way of life" as affordability, small-scale democracy, local control, the independent use of one's resources, and strong communal bonds.

This book traces this process through two stories. One is that of a group of immigrants referred to here as "Major Valentine's Swedes," and their descendants. In 1890, at the peak of concern about the "decline" of rural Vermont, and on the cusp of the dramatic growth of summer tourism, a handful of Swedes were recruited by the state purportedly to become farmers and help "repopulate" rural sections of the state. The story of this program has been told in brief by a number of recent historians.[1] These narratives generally tell the same story: The state legislature established a new appointed office, Commissioner of Agriculture and Manufacturing Interests, in 1888. Creation of the position was a response to widespread concern among state leaders about the apparent decline of rural Vermont, both in population numbers and in the quality of its inhabitants. The man who occupied this position, Major Alonzo B. Valentine of Bennington, largely devoted his two years in the office to recruiting Scandinavians. Valentine focused on Scandinavians because he considered them superior to the "undesirable" people, many of French Canadian heritage, who at the time were often the ones settling on available farms. The product of his labors was a handful of Swedes who moved to three Vermont towns in 1890.[2] The state legislature judged the program to be an expensive failure and ended both the program and the position of commissioner in its 1890 session.[3]

2

Despite historians' interest in the story, a great deal of confusion exists about it. There is uncertainty about how many Swedes came to Vermont as part of the program; recent accounts range from twenty-three to fifty-five families.[4] There is also uncertainty about what happened to them after the cohesive Swedish colonies that Valentine envisioned supposedly failed to materialize. In one account they moved to "industrial centers," while another depicts them as being drawn away to work "in lumber camps, quarries and factories," with only some remaining in Vermont.[5]

The origins, execution, and consequences of Valentine's Swedish recruitment project are complex and fraught with irony. The program, as measured by the lives of five families of Swedes who settled in the small town of Landgrove and its surrounding area, has much to say about the political, social, and ethnic dynamics of Vermont. It illustrates many of the tensions that existed between the state's tradition of local control and the movement toward increased centralization. Valentine's immigration program sheds light on the origins of the boom in summer tourism that Vermont experienced in the 1890s, and, through the lives of its recruits, the long-term evolution of the state's economy. The lives of Valentine's Swedes in the decades after they arrived also make clear the ironies of the program's intentions and results. An attempt to engineer Vermont's human landscape, the program was founded on the premise that Scandinavians would prove themselves superior to most rural Vermonters. In an America in which "whiteness" was a fluid, dynamic concept, and people of Northern European ancestry were inherently superior to others, Valentine saw his Swedes as deserving privileged treatment. But it was instead largely characteristic of the Swedes settled in Landgrove that they fit right in with the class of people they were intended to replace. The program was also premised on the idea that Scandinavians would be accepted as community members in small towns much more quickly than Catholics; that they would find it relatively easy to become "Vermonters." Valentine's Swedes became Vermonters, sure enough, but not in the way that Valentine predicted. They instead became part of their human landscape in ways that made it progressively more difficult for them to remain in the places they were intended to regenerate. This book follows the story of these five families from the 1890s to the 1970s as a means of tracing the state's social and economic evolution.

The second story is that of Samuel R. Ogden, who along with his wife and small children entered into Landgrove's story in 1929. In that year Ogden, a resident of New Jersey, bought most of the structures in Landgrove's principal village, which was largely unoccupied. Within a year he established permanent residence there and commenced a project to renovate the buildings for resale as summer homes. Ogden arrived to a town that most certainly had problems. It had a declining, elderly population, a poor school, and a minimal tax base made worse by many delinquent taxpayers. Ogden set out to revive first the village and then the town as a whole. Within a few short years Ogden was well on his way to turning Landgrove into a thriving summer community that attracted artists, musicians, architects, and other professionals. All of Ogden's exertions were rooted in the fact that he found in Landgrove the life he sought as an antidote to the cosmopolitan world he held in contempt.

Ogden's endeavors took him well beyond the borders of Landgrove, however. He became a leading public figure in the state in a number of areas. Over the subsequent forty years Ogden was at the center of many of the most significant efforts to simultaneously preserve yet improve Vermont. Like the story of Major Valentine's Swedes, Sam Ogden has been treated briefly in a number of scholarly works of history.[6] Ogden became best known as a prominent proponent of the "back-to-the-land" ethic, albeit with a less ascetic vision than many other advocates. He also became an important public servant to Vermont, both in elected office and through service with various state and national organizations and panels. In his time he was acquainted with essentially all of the state's most important figures. He was instrumental in the growth of the ski industry. He worked to improve Vermont's cultural life in a number of ways. One of the founders of *Vermont Life* magazine, Ogden for many years filled its pages with articles extolling the state's values and attractions. These activities were rooted in his belief that the way of life represented by Landgrove, and by the state as a whole, in its human-scale social and political aspects, constituted a precious heritage in need of saving. But the process of saving that heritage, including actions Ogden personally took or supported, put that same way of life in peril. Over the years of his public life, the state became ever more dependent on large-scale, bureaucratic solutions to the challenges facing it, and its attractiveness caused an influx of outsiders who remade the state in their own image, an influx Ogden endorsed and encouraged, but also came to dislike and regret.

This book uses these two stories as a window into Vermont's journey through the twentieth century. Their subjects experienced joy and tragedy, success and failure. In many ways the characters in the two stories wanted very different things, and in other ways they very much had similar goals. Together, the two stories illustrate the paradoxical nature of the state. Vermont had been established in 1777 as a place that would reconcile the most fundamental contradictions of the human experience—the place where, as the state's motto promised, the competing attractions of freedom and unity, the needs of the one and the needs of the many, would be reconciled. As attractive as that sounded conceptually, bringing about such a perfect balance proved fraught with challenges and conundrums, leading to individual frustration and social conflict between groups of people. Such conflict ran throughout the nineteenth century, but took on new dimensions and heightened complexity after 1900. All Vermonters wanted to preserve those things they saw as best about life in the state. All Vermonters wanted to embrace the changes they felt would improve their lives. The question of what and how to preserve, and what and how to embrace, was the challenge around which the state's twentieth-century history revolved.

CHAPTER 1

Alonzo Valentine's Plan

Major Alonzo Valentine

IN THE 1880s ALONZO B. VALENTINE, the owner of a successful knitting mill in Bennington, was one of Vermont's most esteemed citizens. In 1884 he was a delegate to the Republican National Convention.[1] Two years later he was elected to the state senate. After serving one term in the senate, Valentine was appointed commissioner of agriculture and manufacturing by the legislature in January 1889.[2] The position was a new one, established by the legislature in the autumn of 1888. During the two years granted the commission, Valentine was charged with addressing what many state leaders saw as some of Vermont's most profound problems. The minds behind the commission believed that Vermont in general, but especially its rural sections, had been in a state of decline for roughly half a century. With each passing decade the problems associated with this decline were becoming manifestly worse. Finding evidence that rural Vermont was in a state of crisis was as simple as examining population numbers, which were decreasing in most small towns. The commission's supporters also perceived a decline in the quality of Vermonters. Emigration, they commonly believed, had disproportionately taken away the most energetic, intelligent, and talented, leaving behind the less capable. Compounding this situation was the ongoing arrival of immigrants who many state leaders considered inferior to the departing Yankees: people of Irish and French Canadian heritage. Something needed to be done.

The commission's devisers intended it to gather information on the condition of Vermont. It would also make suggestions about programs and strategies that might remedy the weaknesses its data revealed. But as the bill to establish the commission made its way through the legislative process, it was apparent that the belief that something was deeply wrong with rural Vermont was not universal. The one-vote, one-town apportionment of the General Assembly gave small towns representation vastly disproportionate to their population, and small-town representatives were at best skeptical about the commission. As consideration of the bill advanced, the originally proposed number of commissioners was cut from five to three, and then to just a single commissioner. The commission was given two years to justify its existence, a budget of only $2,000, and the limitation of not being able to engage in advertising. Accumulating data and making recommendations were the commissioner's sole responsibilities. The act provided that, should the two-year position prove its worth, it might be renewed in the 1890 legislative session.[3]

The task of justifying the commission's existence fell to Valentine. Born in 1830, he was the son of a prosperous Bennington mill owner. After the completion of his education he went into business with his father. In 1852 Valentine moved to California, chasing the Gold Rush. After two years engaged in mining and trade, he returned to Bennington, whereupon he took over his father's mill. In 1856 Valentine married Bennington native Alma Park, whose brother Trenor was finding great commercial and political success after moving to San Francisco. Valentine sold his interest in the Bennington mill to a partner in 1856 and moved to Wisconsin, where he engaged in the lumber business, but returned once again in 1858, when he repurchased the mill. Valentine thereafter began to establish himself as one of the most important public figures in Bennington County.

By the late 1850s Valentine was very much the ideal emulation of a certain type of "typical Vermonter": an ambitious, ostensibly self-made, independent, public-spirited man. The narrative that Vermonters were a particularly energetic and entrepreneurial people was rooted deeply in the state's founding experience. In its early years, the relative openness of Vermont's frontier conditions and its wealth of waterfalls convinced many that Vermont would become a great industrial center. By the 1850s, however, there was good reason to doubt that future for the state. The evolution of Bennington County was emblematic of how Vermont appeared to be headed in quite the opposite direction. The county's population as a whole dropped between 1830 and 1840. It recovered somewhat in subsequent decades but that growth was attributable to the county's larger towns; most small towns continued to lose population. The coming of railroads after the 1840s accelerated the trend in which big towns gained population while most small towns shrunk.[4] This pattern was largely replicated across the state, but in that era was especially true of southern Vermont.[5] The region's economy increasingly favored large towns with railroad depots, which continually acquired more economic and cultural clout. Meanwhile, the volume of emigration from the state made it seem as if Vermont had become quite the opposite of a land of opportunity: By 1850 more than 40 percent of Vermont's native population lived elsewhere.[6] As commerce centralized in increasingly fewer Vermont towns, the children of small-town merchants and tradesmen were especially likely to emigrate.[7] But rather than being seen by state leaders as the logical evolution of local economies, this process led to a gnawing fear that Vermont was falling behind and losing too many of its best young people, leaving behind only the enervated and unambitious.

As Valentine edged toward the age of thirty, he expanded his range of contacts with other ambitious young men in Bennington County. One of these was Silas L. Griffith. The product of a poor family from Danby, about 30 miles north of Bennington Town, Griffith had gone west to teach but had been ruined by the Panic of 1857. Moving back to Danby, he established a general store. Griffith catered to families in nearby towns, as well as those in Danby, including the adjacent town of Dorset. Among his customers from Dorset was a circle of humbly situated families who typified what state leaders saw as wrong with rural Vermont: families with a lack of ambition and excessive adherence to tradition. One of these was a numerous farming family named the Tiffts. The Tiffts and their friends may have lived relatively near Valentine, but they existed almost in another world.

The World of the Tiffts

Dorset Village is tucked into a valley, below a mountain ridge to its east that divides the town. To the east of Dorset is the town of Peru, which is mountainous and historically sparsely populated, even as in 1850 it reached its all-time largest population of 567. On the opposite side of Peru from Dorset sits Landgrove, a thin sliver of a town that in 1850 was the home of only 337 residents, a loss of about 40 over the previous 20 years. These towns are located where four counties come together: Abutting Landgrove to the southeast is Londonderry in Windham County, to the northeast is Weston in Windsor County, and to the northwest is Mount Tabor in Rutland County. Landgrove will become the main focus of this book, and when it does it will be the home of many who were born, or whose families originated, in Dorset, the Tiffts among them. The members of the Dorset community of which the Tiffts were a part are an important part of this story, as a number of them will intermarry with the Swedes recruited to the state in 1890. They are also a usefully representative example of the kind of families, and the communities they collectively comprised, in which the Swedes would become immersed.

The patriarch of the Tifft family in the 1850s was Rufus, born in Smithfield, Rhode Island, in 1801. Rufus's father Elisha moved to Vermont with his wife Thankful Bishop in the same year that Rufus was born. The family lived briefly in a number of Vermont towns before settling in Dorset in the 1820s. Elisha Tifft and his family were relative latecomers to the town. A number of families that arrived early in Dorset's history had come to dominate its economic life through ownership of the best land and by capitalizing on local natural resources, especially the town's marble deposits. Prominent among these were the Farwells, Baldwins, Sykeses, and Kents.[8] The Kent family was perhaps chief among these; the tavern owned by Cephas Kent was the site of the Dorset Conventions in 1775 and 1776, at which preliminary moves were made that directly led to the establishment of Vermont. By the time Elisha Tifft arrived in Dorset, many of the young members of these families were leaving, seeking their fortunes in what were seen as greener pastures elsewhere. Cephas Kent, for example, had five grandsons by his son Cephas Jr. By the 1830s all five lived in the Midwest.[9]

Living in the midst of these landed and professional families, and particularly clustered in the northwestern part of Dorset, were farming families with fewer resources and more in common with the Tiffts. Like the Tiffts, these families had generally arrived in Dorset after the frontier period had passed. Among such families were the Crandalls, Reeds, Wilkins, and Hazeltons. Over the first half of the nineteenth century these families became bound together by interdependence, familiarity, and a complex multitude of marital ties.

Elisha and Thankful Tifft settled among these families in a small house near the village, next to the town's poor farm, where they raised seven children. Elisha Tifft was never prosperous; his death certificate listed him as a farm laborer rather than the owner of a farm.[10] But while the family lived humbly, it achieved success defined in other ways. Elisha's children began to intermarry with Dorset families that were in relatively the same station of life. Son Rufus Tifft married Jane Lillie in 1823 in nearby Danby. Daughter Hannah married Stewart Lillie, Jane's brother. Jane and Stewart were children of Emmons Lillie, a Revolutionary War veteran who had served as a private on the continental line of Massachusetts and then moved to Vermont.[11] The Lillies, too, had come late to Vermont and struggled to establish themselves. Rufus and Jane moved to the nearby town of Rupert in the 1820s, and then back to Dorset, while producing six children between 1824 and 1841. In 1850 Rufus owned $450 worth of real estate, $50 more than his next-door neighbor Worthy Crandall, but barely a tenth as much as either of two Farwell families nearby.[12] Up the road from Rufus Tifft's house was the modest farm of George Reed, who had children roughly the same age as Rufus. The Crandall, Reed, and Tifft children grew up together, compounding the bonds of interdependence that their parents shared with each other. These people occupied a different Vermont from that of Alonzo Valentine and those like him. Valentine's world was relatively cosmopolitan, with a variety of educational and employment opportunities and easy access to the outside world, whether by the news available in publications, the commodities available in stores, or the railroad that ran through the center of Bennington. The Tiffts occupied a parochial world of diversified agriculture, local institutions, neighbors, friends, and relatives. There were challenges to living in Dorset for these families, to be sure. But the solution was not massive change to the town, but instead achieving stability and continuity.[13]

Dorset was a reasonably prosperous town in the 1850s. Unlike many of its surrounding towns its population continued to go up, from 1,426 in 1840 to 2,090 by 1860. For other small towns in Bennington County the story was very different. The population of Landgrove peaked in 1830 at 385 and then fell each decade to 1860, when it was 320. Rupert, Sandgate, and Peru peaked in population in the 1840 census and declined thereafter. It was that type of population decline that stoked concern about the "decline" of rural Vermont, in Bennington County and statewide. By the 1850s rural out-migration and depopulation had become an issue of serious public concern, but neither state leaders' exhortations to farmers to stay nor the formation of local agricultural societies stemmed the migratory tide. Rural Vermont at mid-century was clearly on its way to becoming one of the first agricultural regions in the nation to, in the words of historian Hal Barron, "grow old."[14]

The way people like the Tiffts would have seen it, though, those who stayed behind were the winners and not the losers, no matter how modestly they lived. The children of Rufus Tifft and Jane Lillie intermarried with a few local families that tended to be, like the Tiffts, on the lower end of Dorset's economy. Rufus Tifft's three daughters, Amy, Mary, and Martha, married brothers Ebenezer, George Jr., and Simeon Reed. They remained living close together: In the 1850 census Amy Tifft Reed and her husband George Jr., who was listed as a farm laborer rather than a landowner, lived with their two children next door to Mary Tifft Reed and her husband Ebenezer. Similarly, in 1852, Rufus Tifft's son Henry married Harriet Crandall, who had grown up next door to him. Henry's brothers Moses and James would also marry Crandalls, sisters Sophronia and Adeline, who were Harriet's cousins.

These families farmed small plots, supplemented by seasonal employment and odd jobs. This was made easier by the rise of Dorset's marble industry. Dorset was the first town in the United States to have a commercial marble quarry, which had opened in 1785, and by the 1850s there were a number of quarries in operation. In the neighborhood where the Tiffts, Crandalls, and Reeds lived was the Kent Quarry, owned by Juba Kent, a grandson of tavern owner Cephas. By the 1850s the quarries had attracted a substantial Irish population, which accounted to a great extent for the growth of the town's population. Census records indicate that many poorer Dorset breadwinners rotated between being farmers to farm laborers to marble work and back. The town was modestly prosperous as a whole, and those for whom persistence was a goal were largely able to hang on. The Tiffts and their friends and relatives may not have intermarried with the Irish before the Civil War, but certainly they grew accustomed to living in a multiethnic environment. They were not entirely isolated from the outside world, to be certain, but in the face of the changes and disruptions of the antebellum decades they crafted a world based on interdependence and cooperation.

In 1860, Rufus and Jane Tifft lived with Jane's widowed mother. They owned $100 value of real estate and $30 more of personal estate. They were not the poorest residents of Dorset, but certainly on the low end. Rufus's mother Thankful lived next door with Rufus's daughter Lydia, in possession of a personal estate of only $75. All six of Rufus's children lived nearby. His son Henry, along with wife Harriet and their three young children, moved the farthest, one town over to Peru, where Henry was a farmer with a personal estate of only $25. Henry's younger brother Moses lived with them. When in 1861 Moses married Sophronia Crandall, his marriage certificate listed him as a "day laborer."[15] Life in Dorset for the Tiffts and those in their circle had its difficulties and tragedies, of course. Sophronia, for example, died in December 1861, after only five months of marriage to Moses. Mary Tifft Reed gave her husband Ebenezer three children before dying in 1858 at age 30. Suggesting quite how parochial this world was, Ebenezer Reed remarried the next year to Louisa Lillie, Mary's cousin. It was certainly a different world from that of Alonzo Valentine, living in Bennington with his wife and two young children and working to make a success of his grist mill. But there was nothing fundamentally wrong with Dorset for the Tiffts, Reeds, Crandalls, and other families in a similar position.

The worlds of the Tiffts and Alonzo Valentine were disrupted when the Civil War began. Valentine entered the Union Army as a lieutenant in 1862. It was common that successful, educated Vermonters like Valentine tended to become officers.[16] The young men of Dorset responded to the call of service, as well. Moses Tifft enlisted as a private in the 7th Vermont Regiment in 1862, serving for nine months. His younger brother James enlisted in the 14th Vermont later that year. Listed as a musician, James was injured at the Battle of Gettysburg facing down Pickett's Charge. Serving with him in the 14th were a number of men with whom he had grown up in Dorset, including his brother-in-law Daniel Crandall. Alonzo Valentine, meanwhile, finished the war as a brevet-major. That experience, and the connections he made with other officers from across the state, would be an asset to his postwar ambitions, both commercial and political. The Tiffts and their friends were simply glad to return home.

The Tiffts After the War

It is a famous fact of life about the Civil War's impact on Vermont that it took away a great many young men from the state, either by death or by choice. But Moses Tifft, James Tifft, and most of their circle of relatives and friends who fought in the war returned home and resumed their lives. In 1864 the widowed Moses married Sarah Hazelton, a member of another extensive Dorset family. In the years that followed Moses and James began families, following their older brother Henry, who had begun his own family before the war. In 1866, Henry's wife gave birth to a son Edward, the fourth of their eventual seven children.

Dorset generally weathered the Civil War era well. Its population increased by about 100 people between 1860 and 1870. In 1870 Rufus Tifft, at age 69, lived with his wife and granddaughter Betsy. The census of that year listed him as a "farm laborer." He may not have met great financial success, but he was surrounded by relatives and long-term acquaintances. Living on one side of his house was son Moses and his wife Sarah, with many other Hazeltons residing nearby. Next door on the other side of Rufus's house lived Aaron Reed, three of whose brothers had married daughters of Rufus. Aaron was employed as a carpenter. Another house down lived Daniel Beebe, a farm laborer from another long-term Dorset family. Among Daniel's eight children, ranging from 14 to infant, was 12-year-old daughter Agnes, who went on to play a role in this story.[17] Some members of this tight circle of families left in the years after the Civil War. Rufus's sister Hannah and husband Stewart Lillie moved to Iowa, for example. For a great many Vermonters in those years, migration was a sign of ambition and success, in contrast to the supposedly dull and despondent people who persisted. A different definition of success characterized the Tiffts: It could be measured by whether one stayed, despite all the obstacles, even if staying consigned one to the humble life of a farm laborer.

Fortunately for those determined to stay, employment opportunities in Dorset were not limited to agriculture. The marble industry experienced a resurgence in the years after the war. The industry slumped in the mid-1870s, but business rebounded and during the 1880s the volume of business was better than ever.[18] Lumbering also thrived in the area, led by the local "lumber baron," Silas Griffith. Griffith had taken over a sawmill as payment for a debt in 1865, and over the next twenty years he acquired more than 50,000 acres in Bennington and Rutland counties. He owned a very profitable operation that produced charcoal in Peru, and purchased property in North Dorset in 1869, where he located a mill.[19] Griffith hired some local men for the mill, but also had a special fondness for Scandinavians: He employed a number of Finns at that mill because of how well behaved he perceived them to be.[20]

As Griffith's business ventures expanded, so did his connections to other enterprising men in the area. Among these was Eugene McIntyre. Griffith had first become partners with McIntyre in a lumber mill in Mount Tabor in 1872.[21] In 1888 the two of them, along with three other partners, purchased 1,400 acres on Peru Mountain, where they erected a steam mill. The leading businessmen of the area were intent on exploiting its natural resources, with little thought given to the environmental costs. The marble industry befouled local streams, and the harvesting of trees led to such a scale of deforestation that, by the late 1880s the lumber business was beginning to decline.[22] For the time being, though, it provided much-needed jobs for local men; in the late 1880s, Griffith's various lumbering operations had a reported 500 employees.[23] As Griffith and McIntyre's operation in Peru expanded, more men from surrounding towns were drawn there and to neighboring Landgrove, from which there was easy access. Lumbering, especially in the winter, was one more way that local citizens could succeed in remaining among their family and friends.

With a combination of farming small plots, working as farm laborers, and taking non-agricultural, often seasonal jobs, the Tiffts hung on. After the death of Rufus, his widow Jane lived in Peru with her daughter Amy and son-in-law George Reed. Henry Tifft lived a short walk away with wife Harriet and five children. He was listed in the 1880 census as a farm laborer. His two oldest sons, 21 and 17, were also farm laborers, while 14-year-old son Edward was still at school. James and Adeline Tifft lived in Dorset with their seven children; James too was listed on the census as a laborer rather than a farmer, as was brother Moses, who also lived in Dorset. None of Rufus Tifft's sons or daughters had prospered, but they had stayed. They were able to construct the rules and customs of their society around the fostering and maintenance of strong communal bonds. This path, as historian Hal Barron has written of similarly situated Vermonters, "diverged considerably from the prevailing tenor of contemporary urban and industrial society."[24] It was most certainly a departure from the world that Alonzo Valentine knew.

Alonzo Valentine Becomes Commissioner

After the war Valentine returned to Bennington and opened a successful knitting mill, specializing in women's underwear. He was an energetic and confident man. One obituary described him as "a strong man, a kind friend, a vigorous fighter and possessing a virility of both body and mind that would have brought him to the front anywhere."[25] He became president of the Bennington County Savings Bank. He threw himself into public service, particularly school reform; he worked ardently, and successfully, for the introduction of a graded school system in Bennington Town. Civil War service enabled him to expand his network of business, political, and social contacts throughout the state. He was a chief figure in the veterans' organization the Grand Army of the Republic, serving as state department commander in the early 1880s, and for a time was the president of the smaller, more elite Vermont Reunion Society of Officers.[26] Tragedy struck Valentine's family in 1882 when his son and daughter-in-law were killed in a well-publicized train accident in New York City while returning from their honeymoon. Valentine recovered from his grief and returned to public life. When elected to the state senate in 1886 he focused on education reform, and particularly improvement of the state normal schools.[27]

Valentine was not especially identified with agricultural issues, but he shared the consensus among men of his class that rural Vermont was in crisis. The average value of an acre of Vermont farmland in 1870 was $37.21; in 1880 it was $26.79.[28] Wool production shrunk to virtual irrelevancy, while commercial vegetable production fell as prices declined.[29] The era was rife with dolorous descriptions of rural decline. Frequent reports on the topic appeared in the Vermont State Board of Agriculture's reports, such as an 1878 article titled "The Depopulation of Our Rural Districts."[30] The publications of the Vermont Dairymen's Association similarly decried the state's moribund character, especially the failure of too many farmers to adopt the latest agricultural technology and practices. But if many state leaders felt glum about Vermont's prospects, the state was coming to occupy a special place in the American mind. In a nation being transformed by immigration and urbanization, northern New England was increasingly prized for its imagined Yankee purity. As they watched the cities of the East Coast become progressively more industrial and ethnically heterogeneous, successful city dwellers constructed a narrative about the past based on visions of a better, purer "Old New England" free from the poverty, disharmony, and confusion around them.[31] Prior to the late 1880s, however, there was little conception in Vermont that that narrative could be employed to remedy the failings of rural areas that state leaders perceived.

For many of Vermont's leading citizens, the unique place in the American mind occupied by the state was endangered by the fact that Vermont was mainly attracting what they saw as the wrong kind of immigrants. By 1890 about one-third of Vermont's residents were either first- or second-generation French Canadians.[32] Governor William Dillingham, under whose watch the Swedish program was launched, was among those with a strong anti-Catholic bias. Dillingham's inaugural address called for legislation to correct the many social ills that he ascribed to immigrants.[33] He was hardly alone; in an 1889 article titled "Regenerating Vermont," the Boston *Evening Transcript* called it a common complaint in Vermont that "a considerable proportion of the hired men have of late been French Canadians" who had taken up "some of the disused back farms" and occupied "slab shanties which are an eyesore and a menace to the thrifty native farmers." The *Transcript* concluded that, "For a variety of reasons, the Vermonters regard the occupation of the land by French-Canadians and Irishmen as undesirable."[34] In addition to prejudice against various Catholic groups, state leaders also sensed a decline in the quality of the rural Yankee population. In an 1890 letter to the *Deerfield Valley Times* of Wilmington, attorney L. H. Wiler summed up the feelings of many elite Vermonters by writing that emigration had taken away "those with the most energetic push," leaving behind a dissipated population that merely lived off the work of previous generations. Lamenting that no effort had been made to "keep up the grade" of rural Vermonters, Wiler frowned that "cousin has married cousin until the race has about run out."[35] For many observers of rural Vermont, not just its economy needed to improve, but also the quality of its residents.

With all that in mind, there were many ideas about how to fix rural Vermont. One thought was that it was essential to encourage the right kind of immigration. An ambitious young lawyer in the state senate named Hosea Mann led a discussion in the mid-1880s about establishing a program to attract English farmers, but it went nowhere. Mann then was the chief force behind the creation of the office of Commissioner of Agriculture and Manufacturing in 1888. Governor Dillingham first offered the position to Mann, but he declined on account of other pressing political obligations. The offer fell to Alonzo Valentine, who accepted it in February 1889.

Soon after his appointment, Valentine gave an interview to one of the state's leading papers. A reporter called on him at a Burlington hotel to learn of his proposed course of action. Valentine told the reporter that he had prepared questionnaires to be sent out to the listers of towns, and to farmers and manufacturers, in order to gather information. Valentine planned to send out 65,000 forms, and optimistically expected to receive at least 40,000 back. It would then, Valentine said, take 400 days to arrange the information he gathered "in proper form for use." Among the questions Valentine said would be on the form was, "How many abandoned farms and acreage of same?"[36] Describing Vermont farms as "abandoned" was an odd choice. There were farms that had been consolidated, and farms going back to woodlots, and there were farms for sale, but no evidence of farms from which owners had simply walked away without compensation of some kind. Valentine could not have known it, but making the phrase even odder was the fact that, according to a 1960s calculation of the historical number of Vermont farms, they peaked in 1880 at 35,522.[37] Valentine might have been using the word metaphorically, meaning that the farms' former residents had given up trying to make a living on them, or he may have used the word simply to refer to houses and barns that had been left unoccupied when two or more farms were consolidated. Whatever he meant by it, it would become a constant refrain of his, and then a part of the state lexicon. Whereas the phrase "abandoned farm" rarely appeared in print prior to 1889, it would occupy a prominent place in the public discussion about rural Vermont for decades to come.

Valentine went on to promise the reporter that he would gather hard information on the state's natural resources and agricultural production, and answers to such questions as the "disposition of your young men to settle in or leave the State." He also hoped to ascertain whether those completing the forms had any suggestions for legislation that would induce more Vermonters to remain, or encourage immigration to the state. On that last note, the *Free Press* asked Valentine if he himself had any ideas about how to address population decline, and the problem of Vermont's "abandoned farms." Valentine replied that he "had in mind the operations of a rich Swede in Nebraska," who "buys all the unoccupied land along the railroads that he can lay his hands upon. He then goes to his native land and forms a small colony to whom he sells this land, bringing them back with him." This plan, Valentine said, was "a good one." With a mandate merely to gather information on Vermont and make suggestions about how to improve it, Valentine had clearly gotten out of the gate quickly. The *Free Press* noted at the end of the article that Valentine had accepted the position of commissioner reluctantly, "but with his energy and executive ability there is no doubt but he will fill the position ably, and render valuable public service in it."[38] The kind of "valuable public service" that Valentine had in mind likely would have made little sense to rural Vermonters like the Tiffts. But in the coming decades Valentine's work as commissioner would paradoxically enrich the lives of some of the Tiffts and their neighbors in the short term, and in the long term make their position in the state increasingly marginal and precarious.

CHAPTER 2

The "Weston Colony"

Alonzo Valentine Sets to Work

VALENTINE THREW HIMSELF INTO the commissioner's work vigorously.[1] Prohibited by the legislature from spending any of his commission's allowance on newspaper advertisements, Valentine had to seek other ways to reverse the "decline" of rural Vermont.[2] In March 1889, he printed the 65,000 copies of his first circular as he had promised, distributing packets of them to listers in each town. These were to be distributed to taxpayers, who would list on them the value of any agricultural and manufacturing enterprise in which they were engaged. The circulars were then to be gathered by listers and returned to Valentine by June 1.[3] To Valentine's disappointment only about half of the towns returned any circulars at all, and even fewer provided information that he considered of any use. Undeterred, Valentine sent out a second circular in July seeking similar information. Even though this time he included return postage, the response was again, as Valentine wrote later, "very meager" and of "little value."[4]

Even as the circulars continued to trickle back into his office, Valentine had already set his mind upon a course of action: recruiting farmers from Scandinavia. Valentine later wrote that in the course of his "extensive" travels in the West, his attention had been called to "the thrifty, hard-working, honest Scandinavian, especially from Sweden," a place he had never been but imagined to resemble Vermont in climate and physical conditions. In Valentine's opinion Swedes were attractive immigrants because, as he wrote later, they "Americanize sooner than any other class of immigrants."[5] In particular, Valentine thought Swedes would naturally become good Vermonters. In the coming year, he and his supporters continuously attached to Swedes in general such "Vermontish" characteristics as frugality, honesty, industriousness, and independence. Valentine wrote in the magazine *The Quill* in 1890 that he pursued Scandinavians because they were Vermonters' "cousin with like instincts of freedom, secular and religious."[6]

Beyond assigning such character traits to Swedes, there were obvious racial components to Valentine's scheme. America in the late nineteenth century teemed with complex and evolving conceptions of what constituted "whiteness." American Irish, for example, were commonly referred to as a separate race of people. Immigrants were categorized on a relative scale of whiteness. Tracts such as Arthur Comte de Gobineau's *An Essay on the Inequality of Human Races* decried how Anglo-Saxons were being overwhelmed by "the most degenerate races of olden day Europe. They are the human flotsam of all ages: Irish, cross-bred Germans, and French and Italians of even more doubtful stock." Such ideas about scientific racism greatly informed the everyday thinking of middle-class Americans with northern European ancestry.[7] Such people perceived Scandinavians as a superior stock. In other sections of the country, Scandinavian immigrants found themselves placed in positions of racial privilege, and generally avoided the stereotyping and prejudice encountered by other groups.[8]

Such racially privileged people were Valentine's target. A Pittsburgh newspaper in August, in dismissing the scheme as folly, challenged Vermont to recruit African Americans instead. Reminding Vermont that since it purportedly "has always been so devoted to the colored race, and radical in maintaining their 'rights' and asserting their 'equality,'" it suggested sarcastically that with an outbreak of an "exodus fever" among blacks in North Carolina, "here is a chance for a good class of immigrants to fill the vacant farms of the Green Mountains." Neither Valentine's detractors nor supporters would have countenanced a scheme like that, Valentine never would have pursued it, and the Pittsburgh *Daily Post* did not actually expect Vermont to consider it, as, it agreed, "the negroes, the French Canadians, the Italians, Hungarians, Polanders, Bohemians, Russians, and of course the Chinese" did not meet "the requirements of a thrifty and pushing community."[9] A man harboring the common prejudices of his era, Alonzo Valentine was not just trying to repopulate rural Vermont. He was attempting to engineer its racial landscape.

Valentine first acted on his Swedish idea by distributing a new circular at the beginning of August soliciting opinions on the advisability of recruiting Scandinavian farmers. Valentine announced that he had been in correspondence with the Swedish friend he had mentioned in March, John G. Nordgren, a farmer and land speculator who had recently published a pamphlet in Swedish promoting emigration to Nebraska.[10] Nordgren had agreed to tour Vermont to assess the suitability of its available farms for Swedish immigrants. But according to Valentine, even without having visited the state, Nordgren had assured him that, given the proper funding, he could easily bring a minimum of fifty families from Sweden to Vermont.[11] The circular requested from town listers information on the availability and price of land on which Nordgren's Swedes might settle. It also requested citizens in each town to volunteer to serve as contacts for the potential settlement of Swedes, and more generally for inquiries about land for sale.

As Valentine himself wrote, this new circular "seemed to excite much interest through this and neighboring states."[12] Reporting on the situation in Vermont, the Troy (NY) *Weekly Budget* described Valentine's announcement as provoking a "general and spirited discussion."[13] The Boston *Evening Transcript* called the proposal very interesting and noted that Swedes were "not unlike...the people of New England; they are Protestants, and thrifty and peaceable. Moreover, they assimilate more readily than any other emigrants who come to us."[14] Like many newspapers, the Cleveland *Plain Dealer* focused on the ethnic dimensions of the program, reporting that the Swedes would find the climate congenial and be happy in places "which the Irish and Canadian French invaders have so far spared."[15] The *Register* of New Haven, Connecticut, guaranteed that, should the first Vermont colonies succeed, other Swedes would flock to the state in large numbers.[16] Newspapers in Baltimore, Detroit, Chicago, San Francisco, and Macon, Georgia, among others, also reported on the plan soon after the circular's appearance.[17] The interest of these far-flung newspapers was mainly stimulated by a combination of ethnic prejudice, disdain for Vermont's agricultural economy, and the sheer oddity of the scheme.

Valentine provoked another wave of news and debate by releasing a new circular on August 28 that concluded that the plan to establish colonies of Swedes in rural Vermont was viable. Whether it had been by design or not, Valentine by then could point to results of his work beyond the potential recruitment of Scandinavian immigrants. In a round of interviews that followed the August 28 circular, Valentine told newspapers that agitation on the topic had already resulted in a "boom" for Vermont land sales, and that his office was "flooded" with inquiries from residents of other states.[18] Whether it was viewed positively or negatively, the Swedes program was certainly bringing Vermont a lot of free publicity.

In mid-September Valentine hosted the tour of the state by Nordgren. By this time Valentine had settled on the towns of Wilmington and Weston as the locations for two Swedish colonies. This decision was based on tours of the state he undertook during the summer, and on correspondence with leading citizens of those towns. Wilmington possessed a particularly ambitious set of businessmen and lawyers who, already heartened by completion in 1889 of a new hotel on the shores of the town's principal lake, were planning a public celebration in the summer of 1890, and were eagerly anticipating the imminent extension of a railroad line to town. Wilmington's local business community, led by Hosea Mann, assured Valentine that all recruited Swedes would receive the support they needed. The location where Swedes were to be settled in Weston was planned to comprise of a few farms in the district of town adjacent to the neighboring town of Peru. In his travels in the summer, during which he had been accompanied by Governor William Dillingham and the leading citizen of Peru, Marshall Hapgood, Valentine had been impressed by the farms available in the towns of Weston, Peru, Landgrove, and Mount Tabor. He often touted the area as a shining example of where good farms had been "abandoned" and could be had cheaply.[19] In addition to good prospects for farming, one advantage of the area was that the Peru lumber operation owned by Silas Griffith, Eugene McIntyre, and their partners could supply immigrants with immediate employment. Nordgren's visit generated another round of publicity and debate, in and out of the state. By all reports, Nordgren was impressed by the farms available in both Weston and Wilmington, and also with available farmland in Orange County.

He left Vermont assuring Valentine that he would bring back from Sweden a minimum of fifty families.[20]

Valentine's Plan: Reception and Rejection

As the story of the Swedes scheme spread around the country, so did confusion about the exact nature of Valentine's job. A North Dakota newspaper called him Vermont's "land commissioner," while one in West Virginia gave him the title "State Commissioner of Immigration."[21] But it was clear by the fall of 1889 that word was getting out in the United States about the availability of cheap Vermont farms. Articles in the largest New York City newspapers, such as the *New York Times*, were reprinted around the country.[22] Stories about the colonization plan appeared in newspapers as far away as the *Grey River Argus* of Greymouth, New Zealand, which reported that the Swedish colonies were a response to the "incredibly large" number of "vacant" Vermont farms.[23] The Bennington *Banner* reported in November that Valentine's correspondence had reached "worldwide proportions," specifying a letter of inquiry about Vermont farms received from an officer of the "agricultural department of the British Empire in India."[24] Valentine did not have to pay for this coverage, and if one essential message was getting out, it was that, as the Boston *Daily Journal* reported in October, in Vermont "lands are good and cheap."[25]

Much of the press coverage outside the state of the Swedes scheme was negative. The Macon (GA), *Telegraph*, commenting on an article about the program in the *New York Post*, ascribed Vermont's abandoned farms to the high tariffs protecting its manufacturers, concluding that preference was being given to Swedes only because they were accustomed to hard work and poor living.[26] Most articles that autumn, however, tended either to treat the plan as a curiosity or were favorable. Much of this positive coverage seems merely to have resulted from the idea's exotic nature, but it was by no means treated as a joke. So seriously was the Swedes idea taken in New Hampshire that, having created its own commissioner of immigration in 1889, the state legislature pondered pursuing a similar program, thereby launching what the Boston *Herald* predicted would be a rivalry between the two states for

Scandinavian farmers.[27] The Boston *Evening Transcript* typified the positive press that the scheme was receiving when it commended Valentine on pursuing "judiciously chosen Swedish agriculturalists" who were sure to prove "a class of hardy, thrifty, and Protestant citizens." Valentine's many critics in Vermont, the *Transcript* declared, were just a bunch of "shouters."[28]

In Vermont that autumn the reaction to the proposal was deeply divided. There seems to have been little pattern to the opposition, with newspapers in both cities and smaller towns in disagreement. Many newspapers were very enthusiastic about it, not just in support of recruiting Swedes but also in light of the interest in Vermont that Valentine had provoked elsewhere. Ludlow's *Vermont Tribune*, for example, reported that agitation over the colonization project had already resulted in a "boom" that had left Valentine overrun with inquiries from citizens of other states about farms for sale.[29] But a significant portion of the state's press was either skeptical or hostile. In particular, there was a widespread perception that Valentine's repeated description of Vermont as a place where farmers had simply "abandoned" land did great harm to the state's reputation. Montpelier's *Argus and Patriot*, which was particularly contemptuous of the program, insisted that there was no good land in the state that had been abandoned.[30] The West Randolph *Herald* similarly called talk about abandoned farms "wild" because there was no such thing, only "tracts on steep hill and mountain sides which have been allowed to grow into forest."[31] The Brattleboro *Vermont Phoenix* complained that Valentine's efforts had given outsiders "false impressions" of the state as a deserted and desolate place.[32]

For decades afterward, the poor impression of the state purportedly created by Valentine's emphasis on "abandoned farms" and "deserted land" remained the chief memory of the scheme to many. The St. Albans *Messenger*, recalling in 1921 the "tremendous controversy" over the program, wrote that "the discussion led the press of other states to speak of our commonwealth as a state of abandoned farms, and no end of damage was done as a result."[33] Why Valentine chose to persistently refer to some Vermont farms as abandoned is unclear. Using the term certainly brought him a lot of ill-will in the state. In December *The Earth*, a weekly paper in Burlington, summed up the sentiments of many Vermonters who had a closer attachment to Vermont's rural economy than Valentine: "Much has been said and written about abandoned farms, and much of this is the sheerest nonsense; in fact there are no abandoned farms in Vermont. True there are some farms on the mountain sides that are more profitable for grazing than tillage, and so have been purchased by the neighbor in the valley and now support his dairy...This indiscriminate talk about 'abandoned farms' in this State conveys a wrong impression, and is doing great injury to our farming interests."[34]

Valentine's supporters did not apologize for the phrase "abandoned." Some insisted that Valentine's description was perfectly accurate.[35] Others argued that he was using the word metaphorically. Wilmington's newspaper urged readers to see that "when farms once successfully cultivated by sturdy yeomen, occupying comfortable dwellings, are now given up to weeds and encroaching forests...if there is any word other than 'abandoned' which will give an idea of the desolation existing, the commissioner does not know what that word is."[36] By late autumn of 1889 it was even possible to dismiss use of the word as unimportant; the Burlington *Free Press*, in an article titled "The Best Kind of Advertising," argued that "In spite of the talk which has been made in some quarters about the injury to Vermont which Mr. Valentine's circulars in relation to 'abandoned' farms have done, the State is getting the best kind of advertising out of the colonization project."[37]

There were other objections to the scheme beyond the feelings of insult to the state's reputation. Many Vermonters wondered why state government was pursuing a program that appeared to favor immigrants over native-born Vermonters. One paper, granting that "there may be one hundred or ten thousand abandoned farms in Vermont," asked "why go to Europe for occupants when there are plenty of honest industrial Vermonters that would be glad to take the chance, if they could be helped at the start, as is proposed to do for the Swedes?"[38] Members of the Democratic Party circulated a conspiracy theory that state leaders wanted to attract Swedes because they were certain to vote Republican.[39] The scheme particularly provoked opposition to its premise that Scandinavians would seamlessly blend into rural communities, becoming Vermonters in ways that Catholics could not. The West Randolph *Herald* wrote that it did not want "the Swedes or any other foreigners to colonize the state," though Swedes were "generally admitted to be better than Italians or Bohemians."[40] The president of the state's Dairymen's Association, F. D. Douglas, spoke for many rural Vermonters in October when he sharply criticized the idea that Vermont could benefit from "calling on the heathen from the old world to come and occupy our so-called deserted lands," which Douglas emphatically denied existed in the first place. "The so-called desertion," Douglas continued, "is but a conversion of the soil to a more rational use." Dismissing Valentine's contention that Swedes were the excellent raw material of state residents, Douglas concluded, "Let Vermonters still occupy Vermont."[41] In this discussion, the fundamental differences of perception between cosmopolitans like Valentine and residents of small towns were laid bare. Where the cosmopolitans saw emigration as a crisis of abandonment, locals saw natural and rational evolution in the use of local resources. Farms that had proven unable to support families had been sold and the land put to other uses. Where cosmopolitans saw gradations of "whiteness" as a determining feature of the ease of assimilation, locals rooted community in long-term, interdependent relationships. Ethnicity most likely mattered to them to varying extents, but familiarity far overrode it in significance.[42] Asserting that there was "no such thing" as an abandoned farm in Londonderry, a town adjacent to Weston, its local paper, with what would turn out to be some irony, declared "We have no room for Swedish colonists."[43]

Valentine pressed on despite the opposition. In October he settled on Vershire as the location for a third Swedish colony, announcing it at a public meeting in the town. In Vershire, as with Wilmington, Valentine's project stimulated the town to act on its own to publicize further its land for sale. After Valentine's announcement, Vershire's town clerk issued a free pamphlet combining a list of available farms with general descriptions of the town's appearance and services.[44] Valentine, meanwhile, moved the process along in November by issuing a new circular for town clerks titled "Schedule Relating to Unoccupied or Abandoned Farms" that requested information on the number, size, and price of farms available for sale in towns.[45] This was the first effort to make available to the public a comprehensive list of farms for sale across Vermont.

In preparation for Nordgren's recruitment trip to Sweden, Valentine drew up a map based on the information he had gathered through his circulars. Towns that purportedly had large numbers of "abandoned" farms were shaded in red. With text in both English and Swedish, the map specified where cheap farmland was available, and described the natural attractions of Vermont. The map's text promised "Good farms with impeccable buildings," for which "payments are easily done."[46] Armed with the map, Nordgren departed for the county where he had grown up, Varmland.[47]

Elgo, Varmland

Varmland was one of the poorest counties in Sweden, with a topography of mountains and large lakes. Nordgren completed his journey in the rural district of Elgo, situated on the banks of the large lake Glafsfjorden, in the municipality of Arvika.[48] Elgo sat near the top of the lake, a few miles north of the closest village, Glava, and across the lake from the capital of the municipality, the town of Arvika. Returning to Elgo was a wonderful homecoming for Nordgren. He visited with friends and relatives. After a few days, he called residents of the town to assemble in its church and hear his proposition.

Living in Elgo was a 14-year-old girl named Charlotte Nyren. Her father Augustus worked as a lumberman to support her mother, Magdelina, and her three siblings. Older brother Carl, who was 17, had begun working as a lumberman alongside his father. Charlotte also had two younger siblings, Oliver, who was six, and four-year-old Anna. One dark evening in January 1890, Charlotte and her family went to their church for a meeting with a man whom she had never met. They gathered with other members of the church she had known her whole life. Carl Westine was there. Another lumberman, he was a large, strong man in his early twenties who was friends with Charlotte's brother Carl. Westine had his eye on a local woman named Anna Svenson, and wondered how to win her hand, considering the difficulties of making a living in Varmland. Anna's sister Hilma was similarly being courted by Axel Neilson, a 23-year-old farmer who went about his work in an ambitious and determined way. Axel had an older brother, John, who was already married; he and his wife Louise had three children, Charles, Anna, and Bula. John was considerably more easygoing than his brother. Another couple with young children was in attendance:

Edwin and Emma Anderson, who had a daughter Hilma, who was three, and son Carl, who had recently turned one. A third family with young children in attendance was that of Adolph and Charlotte Swenson, whose daughter Hilda was one year old and daughter Mary was an infant. These and others settled in the church and listened as the man spelled out the reason for his return.

Nordgren began to speak. Quickly it became clear to Charlotte that he was encouraging his audience to move to America. Charlotte was of course familiar with the concept of emigrating there. Sweden as a whole sent the third-most immigrants to the United States of any European country in that era. As an especially poor province plagued by aristocratic land monopolies and political and economic disruptions, Varmland sent a disproportionately large percentage of its population to the United States.[49] Nordgren was one of these emigrants and had found success in America as a land agent. His home of Nebraska was a much more likely destination than Vermont for Swedish immigrants. For Charlotte, Midwestern places like Minnesota and Iowa were familiar names. For example, in 1890, 20-year-old Anna Sophia Nilsson left for Iowa to join fellow Elgo native Olof Olson, whom she married in 1891.[50]

The plan as laid out by the visitor was unusual. One can guess Nordgren told them that one American state, Vermont, was willing to pay for their passage, contingent on them settling there. Nordgren assured them that he had been there, traveling Vermont in the company of the state's land commissioner, and had seen abundant farms superior to what they had here. He showed them a map of the state that had a large amount of its area colored red, indicating, as the Swedish text on the map said, the "location of uncultivated farms and cultivated land. Both can be purchased for about the same price." As the map was handed around the meeting, attendees read that, "Good farms with impeccable buildings and with fields of maple sugar trees can be purchased for $3 to $5 per acre. Other farms with even better buildings and close to the railroad or a village can be bought for $5 to $10 per acre. None of the places are far away from a good fair and all of them are good as dairy farms. Payments are easily done. Farm workers are very much asked for and are paid very well." It concluded with a passage that particularly appealed to lumbermen Carl Westine and August Nyren: "In many locations they can, if they so wish, find work during the winters as lumberjacks." In addition to passage, Nordgren promised they would be given 25 dollars and a cow upon settling on a farm, and would be given a great deal of further assistance to establish themselves, including a translator. From what Charlotte could tell from the tones of approval she heard, many of the adults in the church thought the offer sounded attractive.

Nordgren later said that he experienced a great deal of resistance to his quest in Sweden from Western land agents with whom he was competing, and from government officials and the Swedish press. For the consumption of Vermont newspapers, he claimed Swedish opposition could be attributed to the fear on the part of the government that he was getting the nation's "best blood."[51] Bizarrely, Nordgren had private-sector competition in his quest to bring Swedes to Vermont: Nicholas Mannall, a businessman from Springfield, Massachusetts, who was acting as an agent for a Boston land speculator, was at the same time on a tour of Sweden and Norway, searching for people willing to be transplanted to a Scandinavian colony he proposed for the town of Norton, on Vermont's Canadian border. Mannall stated his aim was to bring at least 250 Scandinavian families to Norton.[52] The families in Elgo may or may not have known of Mannall's mission, but back in the United States the apparent rivalry in which Vermont's state government was engaged magnified the attention Valentine's program received.

Back at home, the Nyren family weighed Nordgren's offer. They would be going to a place about which they essentially knew nothing. Additionally, the decision needed to be made quickly. Any who wished to accompany Nordgren to Vermont had to make up their minds within a matter of a few months; their ship would depart Liverpool for Philadelphia on April 9, and to get there they would have to make their way to Oslo, and then on to Liverpool with enough time to catch it. Other families with whom they were close were deciding to go. The chief attraction, as one of the settlers in Wilmington would tell a newspaper reporter in the summer of 1890, was "the ownership of land," which was "impossible in their native land"—the estates being large and owned by landlords of noble birth.[53] Many of those who signed on were those with young children. Edwin Anderson was 36, his wife 24. Carl Westine was going to go, as were Adolph Swenson, 28, his wife

31

Charlotte, 27, and two small daughters. John Neilson's family was going, as well. In total, as reported by Valentine in his 1890 report to the Vermont legislature, 55 members of the Elgo congregation decided to go to America with Nordgren.

Not everyone had been convinced by Nordgren's pitch. Axel Neilson, John's brother, decided to remain in Elgo for the time being. But for John Neilson and others the offer of free passage, plus help upon arrival, seemed too good to pass up. Charlotte's father decided that he and oldest son Carl would go first; the remaining four members of the Nyren family would be sent for months later. It must have been hard on Charlotte to contemplate leaving. Memories of Elgo would fade quickly for her younger siblings, but it was the only place Charlotte had ever known, and she would be leaving her friends behind. The decision was her parents' to make, however. Emigration to a place named Vermont it would be.

Preparing for the Swedes

Back in Vermont while waiting for the Swedes to arrive in the winter of 1889-90, Valentine kept busy expanding his list of available farms. In January he released his map to the general public. The domestic version included a list of towns throughout the state where "unoccupied" farms were available, and the names of persons in each town to whom inquiries could be made.[54] The map drew yet another round of intense discussion both within and outside the state. Legitimizing the fears of many Vermonters that Valentine's immigration campaign was casting Vermont in a bad light, the St. Louis *Republic* called it a map of Vermont's "desolate regions," and wondered why Swedes would stay on such farms any more than those who had abandoned them. In Vermont, the press reaction was again mixed. The Burlington *Free Press* was among those lavishing praise on the map, calling it "a very happy idea," while the *Argus and Patriot* asserted that the map "shows the folly and nonsense of the 'deserted farm' bugaboo."[55]

Whether there was legitimacy to the fears of many Vermonters that Valentine's depiction of rural Vermont as full of "abandoned" farms was giving outsiders the impression that it was a desolate place, Valentine was indisputably bringing attention to the affordability of land in Vermont. The Providence, Rhode Island, *Journal* wrote in early January that Valentine was "sending out maps like a Western land agent." The *Journal* added that so far there had been little actual agricultural immigration into the state, except for "the cultivation of the summer boarder."[56] As far as Valentine was concerned, that was just as well. Whether or not it had been his intention all along, over the previous year he had been building a system to facilitate the sale of Vermont land to summer tourists. Having already undertaken what amounted to the first comprehensive survey of farms for sale across the state, Valentine distributed yet another circular in late January that provided a list of "gentlemen" in a number of Vermont towns to whom communication could be sent about buying land.[57] Combined with the outside attention the Swedes project had received, this information, Valentine believed, was stimulating the sale of Vermont farms. Most of these, apparently, were to people in search of vacation homes.

Whatever success Valentine anticipated that the Swedish scheme would realize, that winter saw it continue to encounter a great deal of criticism and mockery in Vermont. Farmers gave vent to their displeasure at meetings of the Vermont State Board of Agriculture, held in various locations in January and February 1890. The board had long been a political lightning rod, used in turn by Vermont urbanites to attempt to modernize farmers, and by farming interests as a forum to express their grievances.[58] The members of the board in 1890 were themselves divided on the issue: M. W. Davis, a dairy farmer from Westminster, was adamantly opposed to the project, while William Chapin of Middlesex, a farmer and real estate agent, ardently supported it.[59] Frequent board speaker T. H. Hoskins of Newport, an expert in apple cultivation, hopefully told one meeting that he foresaw the arrival of from 500 to 1,000 immigrants a year from Scandinavia, after which the prices for farms "will be wonderfully increased."[60] During the discussion period of meeting after meeting, however, farmers voiced passionate objections to the plan. During an address of welcome to a January meeting of the board in West Concord, a Reverend Seitz allowed that Vermont might have abandoned farms, "but they are of more value to grow up to wood again than to populate with Swedes," and as a result he had "very little faith in the Swedish immigration scheme." M. W. Davis followed Seitz by saying that "we ask no Swedes to come here; rather have the native stock." At a meeting of the board in late January in South Royalton, 21-year-old farmer Fred Morse declared that, as far as land was concerned, the state should "let the native Vermonter have it." A speaker at a February board meeting in Brandon succinctly called the plan "a humbug."[61]

Valentine's defenders, however, could point to something that seemed at the time to be an unexpected, ancillary benefit of the colonization project. In February the New York *Tribune* published an article that was quite typical of many printed by out-of-state newspapers in the winter of 1890. It first noted that Vermont had in past years tried "a number of schemes to supply the farms with farmers, but none of them proved satisfactory." But now, the *Tribune* wrote, Vermont had decided, "I will advertise," and the result of advertisements was that "several thousand" letters had been received by Valentine from every section of the United States, resulting in the sale of many farms. The article made no mention at all of Swedes, nor of the limitations placed by the state legislature on Valentine's ability to advertise.[62]

In Vermont, Swedes remained very much on the public mind. To keep busy, Valentine issued yet another circular in March that requested town listers to send him information related to manufacturing.[63] Mainly, though, Valentine shuttled between Weston, Wilmington, and Vershire finalizing plans for the Swedes' arrival. In each town a citizens' committee was established that promised to provide each Swedish family with the promised 25 dollars and a cow. Valentine reported receiving word from Nordgren in Sweden that he had secured 30 families, comprising around 150 people.[64] But press coverage of the program exhibited confusion about exactly how many Swedes were on their way: Various reports put the total at 75 persons, 150 persons, 15 families, and 30 families.[65]

Vermonters were keenly aware that, as the New York *Herald-Tribune* wrote in March, the Swedish experiment was being "observed with deep and general interest throughout the country."[66] Apparently, the original curiosity with which the scheme was treated had worn off; by the spring of 1890, out-of-state newspapers were increasingly critical of it. Many newspapers dwelled on estimates of the amount of farm acreage, exclusive of timber land, that was currently unused, variously reported at between 200,000 and 500,000 acres.[67] The Topeka *Capital* of Kansas wrote derisively in February that Valentine was merely "a manufacturer of woolen goods, without any knowledge of farming," whose work had done no more than to "have further strengthened the public impression that these lands are worthless."[68] The Providence *Journal* of Rhode Island was among those newspapers wondering why, if Yankee farmers had abandoned the farms, Swedes would do any better on them.[69] Other newspapers, however, still predicted success for the program. Summarizing how deeply rooted in ethnocentrism the whole scheme was, the New York *Herald-Tribune* wrote that "as a class the Swedes are frugal, industrious and patient, and in Vermont colonists ought to flourish."[70] For Valentine's purposes, however, it did not much matter whether the press coverage was positive. All publicity was good in the interest of selling farms as second homes, and the cheaper land was reported to be, the better.

The Arrival of the Swedes

In March 1890 Charlotte Nyren said goodbye to her father and older brother, knowing she would soon be joining them. They and the others made their way overland on rough roads to Oslo, their meager possessions pulled along in carts. From there they traveled to Liverpool, where they boarded the ship *British Princess* for Philadelphia. The *British Princess* arrived in Philadelphia on April 22. The members of Nordgren's party were grateful to have him with them; his knowledge of English smoothed their way past immigration officials. Once through immigration, Nordgren led them to the imposing Broad Street Station, where they boarded a train to New York City.

It is difficult to ascertain exactly which Swedish passengers on that ship were Nordgren's recruits. Valentine later put the total number of April immigrants at "representatives of 27 families" comprising 55 people. It is possible that other colonists traveled separately, but it is certain that at least four families destined for the planned "Weston colony" arrived with Nordgren: the two Nyrens, four Andersons, five Neilsons, and Carl Westine. Westine and August Nyren listed their occupations on the Philadelphia immigration form as sawmill hands, while Edwin

Anderson and John Neilson described themselves as farmers.[71] Also on board was the family of Adolph Swenson, recorded as an ironworker.

Valentine met Nordgren and his recruits in New York City, and then chaperoned the group to Vermont. Upon arrival the Swedish families were divided into three groups. Most Vermont newspapers reported that seven families went to Wilmington, 12 to Weston, and the remaining eight went to Vershire, but even about this there was confusion.[72] Wilmington's local paper reported that only four families were settled in town.[73] Valentine reportedly supplied each colony with a temporary Swedish translator. The Swedes' arrival incited great interest in Wilmington and Weston. In Wilmington, business leaders fussed over them, temporarily boarding them in their own homes. As for the "Weston colony," some men from the town drove wagons through the mountains to Danby, where they met the Swedes at the depot. When they arrived back in Weston, a crowd of curious onlookers gathered to meet them.[74] It is unknown how the immigrants felt about their division into the three colonies, relatively far from each other, and upon how the division was decided. Perhaps they had been made aware of it by Nordgren when still in Sweden; perhaps it came as a surprise to them. Perhaps they were able to choose where and with whom they went, or maybe Valentine divided them up himself. In a move that confused coverage of the scheme, the members of the "Weston colony" were not settled in Weston, but instead went straight into a boarding house in Landgrove.

After two weeks had passed, Wilmington's leaders felt comfortable declaring "Mr. Valentine's colonization scheme" a "grand success so far."[75] Valentine, often accompanied by Hosea Mann, continued to check up on his Swedish colonies in the months after their arrival. In mid-May he toured the Wilmington and Weston colonies accompanied by Nordgren and declared the colonists to be "delighted with Vermont." Nordgren claimed portentously that "no immigrants were ever better received or better treated on arriving in America than these Swedish families," and gave assurances that more Swedes were set to join them.[76] In June, Wilmington's local newspaper reported that the Swedes were "doing finely," proving the program so far was "undoubtedly a success in every way."[77] National coverage of the Swedes' arrival, meanwhile, was often characterized by misinformation and exaggeration; the San Francisco *Bulletin*, for example, put the number of Swedes brought to Vermont by Valentine at 350, while the Chicago *Herald* called it "several hundred."[78]

Concerned that Vermonters would see the program as too expensive, Valentine insisted that the Swedes had paid their own way to Vermont. Based on the massive cost overruns of the commission, however, it was generally assumed that the state had paid their travel costs. Either way, by many reports the Swedes in all three colonies were essentially destitute. When criticized later for bringing to Vermont impoverished immigrants, Nordgren insisted that it was necessary that they be poor; if he had brought colonists with resources, he argued in a statement seemingly designed to antagonize skeptical Vermonters, "then perhaps the next thing we should find them in Nebraska."[79] Valentine declared that the Swedes had been given up to five years to pay off the farms on which they were supposedly settled.[80] Their desperate circumstances, however, required them to immediately search for employment. In Wilmington, a group of businessmen led by Mann provided their colonists with a variety of jobs. The Swedes in Landgrove entered into employment in the Griffith & McIntyre charcoal operation located in Mount Tabor and Peru.[81]

Vershire's Swedes did not receive equivalent support and immediately found themselves in desperate circumstances. Between May and July these colonists dispersed. One individual moved to Weston, while a family moved to Brattleboro. The remaining seven Swedes were lured to Nicholas Mannall's new colony in Norton. Mannall had arrived back in the United States in April, still greatly enthusiastic about his project but now only projecting in the short term 12 of his own Swedish families. Though Mannall promised that at least 40 families would be settled in Norton by June, he had an immediate need for settlers to make the colony he named "New Scandinavia" viable.[82] By May Mannall's colony was widely reported to be utterly primitive and foundering, with the Scandinavians attracted there only remaining because they could not afford to leave.[83] Rather desperately, Valentine sought to explain the loss of the Vershire colony as evidence of the Swedes' quality and the scheme's success, saying that by leaving Vershire the colonists showed good sense in going to a place where the prospects of their success were much more encouraging. They had come to Vershire without money, Valentine said, and were "destined to starve" before their farms became productive enough to support them. Now in Norton they had "every chance to get a living" while they waited for their farms in Vershire to become productive. Anyway, the other two colonies, Valentine reassured, were certain to survive because their Swedes had "proved themselves to be useful and industrious citizens."[84]

Throughout the summer the project's supporters did their best to reinforce the idea that it was a big success. Governor Dillingham accompanied Valentine on a visit to the remaining two colonies in July and described the Swedes in both places to be "contented" and "flourishing."[85] Valentine particularly took pains to win supporters by emphasizing that the Weston settlers had brought with them a Lutheran minister, sure evidence that they intended to stay and were upstanding people.[86] Writing in a Boston newspaper, Hosea Mann described the Wilmington colony as a great success and described the Swedes, in terms designed to win sympathy with a Yankee audience, as "frugal, honest and industrious."[87] Valentine repeatedly insisted that the colonists had assured him that they would be joined by many of their "friends" from Sweden soon.[88] Much of Vermont's press was compliant in repeating these descriptions of success. The St. Albans *Messenger*, for example, ran an article in July headlined "The Swedes are Happy."[89]

Try as Valentine might to explain it away, the almost immediate failure of the Vershire colony gave ammunition to foes of the program both inside and outside the state. A farmer in Fairfax wondered why, in light of the colony's dispersal, the "deserted farms" had not been turned over to poor native farm hands who could not afford farms of their own.[90] Newspapers in such places as Wichita, Baltimore, and Portland, Oregon, reported the scheme to be, as the Kansas City *Star* called it, an "utter failure."[91] Other reports were much more positive, as if describing a completely different program. The *Daily Advertiser* of Boston reported the colonies to be "flourishing," while Boston's *Daily Journal* called the Swedish colonies "prosperous."[92] Responding to a Richmond, Virginia, *Times* report in July that the project had already failed, the Cincinnati *Commercial-Gazette* allowed that there had been some "missgoes," but "upon the whole the Vermonters are greatly encouraged over their adventure."[93]

What was most important, however, was simply that so much discussion of the Swedish scheme was taking place at all. Both supporters and detractors treated the actual Swedes like a monolithic abstraction, on the one hand all frugal, industrious, and peaceable, on the other hand just another set of impoverished immigrants, though especially infuriating as their immigration had been paid for with public money. Whether the program and all its accompanying talk of "abandoned farms" hurt Vermont's reputation, the concrete result of publicity was the large number of inquiries about the availability of land that Valentine continued to receive from outside the state. The Boston *Journal* noted that the scheme had benefited the state by "attracting public notice to the fact that good farms could be had in Vermont," and as a consequence some of the "deserted Vermont farms" were being "repeopled" by residents of other states. Vermont's problem was not poor soil, the *Journal* concluded, but instead a lack of "sufficient pains to advertise its manifold natural advantages."[94] In a Boston newspaper, Hosea Mann reported in July that the Swedes themselves were beside the point: The result of Wilmington's colony had been a boom in Wilmington real estate sales, with many farms in the last year sold to people from other states, and many more inquiries received. Valentine estimated that more than 100 farms had been sold around the state because of the publicity he had brought to Vermont. "The repopulating of Vermont," wrote Mann, "is auspiciously begun," and it was not with Swedes. It was with American buyers of second homes.[95]

The Swedish immigration program was certainly not solely responsible for this development. For years Vermonters had become ever more aware that, as a forestry expert told New Hampshire's legislature in January 1890, "More and more people have to come here as other places are being destroyed. They want to go where they can see green things."[96] The sale of Vermont farms as summer homes to middle-class families, and not just to wealthy businessmen like William Seward Webb and Frederick Billings, was already underway. In the spring of 1890, Burlington's municipal government paid for the publication of the pamphlet "Attractions In and About Burlington," which described the city as "a point of much interest to tourists" that was "a delightful place for a tarry of a few days."[97] Rather than a distraction from the promotion of summer tourism, the Swedish scheme complemented it. The Boston *Evening Transcript*, for example, in reporting on Valentine and Dillingham's visit to the Swedish colonies, not only wrote that the prosperity of the colonies was "assured," but added that another way of redeeming "these deserted farms" was "by their purchase by city people for summer homes." The *Transcript* continued, "A permanent summer home, with scores of acres of woodland and pasture, all to be had for a thousand dollars at the most, often merely for repairs and taxes—there is an inducement for the city man, who is not to be counted as rich and who has dreamed in vain of owning a country home."[98] A prosperous dairy farmer optimistically told the 1890 annual meeting of the Board of Agriculture that Vermont was "near the turning point in farm values" because "in the near future our beautiful hills and valleys, with their health-giving breezes, will be occupied by the increasing number of rich men, who will improve our farms for summer homes."[99]

The End of the Program

Charlotte Nyren might very well have been unaware of the debate within Vermont over the program that had brought her father and brother to the state, or of the attention the program had received nationwide. She was surely unaware that the immediate consequence of the program was to stimulate the sale of Vermont farms as summer homes. All she knew was that by mid-summer her father had sent for her, her mother, and her two younger siblings. In the days before they left she said goodbye to local friends forever. The four of them followed the same path as August and Carl had months earlier: overland to Oslo, then to Liverpool, and finally to Philadelphia aboard the *British Princess*. Many years later, Lottie Nyren recalled her main memory of the trip was being told by someone on board that if anyone became sick enough to threaten the health of other passengers, their bodies were thrown overboard. Lottie became very concerned that this would happen to her younger sister Anna when she fell ill. They arrived in Philadelphia on August 5, 1890. The immigration agent in Philadelphia recorded the Nyrens' nationality incorrectly as Norwegian. In the box noting the family's destination, either the agent misunderstood Magdelina Nyren's accent, or Magdelina herself was confused about the name of her new home: The agent recorded their destination as "Fairmount," and not "Vermont," where her father and brother in the "Weston colony" in Landgrove awaited them.[100]

The first weeks in Landgrove were disorienting for Charlotte. She spoke no English, and it was hard to ascertain why locals were making a fuss over her and the other Swedes. Sundays were the best days: Other members of Nordgren's recruits, including those in Wilmington forty miles to the south, gathered in Landgrove for church services. It was on such a Sunday that Alonzo Valentine visited them again in mid-September. He chose Sunday as the day for the visit, a newspaper reported, "in order to see the colony together." The reporter wrote, "the colonists were found gathered at the minister's house, a cleanly, decently dressed, bright-looking group of 40 or 50 people." He noted that none of them spoke English save one young woman who acted as interpreter. Reporting on the same visit, a Ludlow, Vermont, paper wrote that it would be "impossible to draw together in any average back district" a better group of laboring people, "who are so unwelcomed by certain classes of loud mouthed shriekers over the degradation of our American population by the importation of these people." The article went on to say that it was the Swedes' intention to take up farming, but "in the meanwhile the men are attempting to get a little start by working in lumber mills. One lad, sixteen years of age, with a bright and clean look, counts the lumber in one mill with great rapidity and accuracy, and his foreman considers him a valuable acquisition."[101] It is almost certain this was Carl Nyren.

By the time of his September visit, Valentine's concerns were increasingly political. His focus was on submitting a persuasive report to the legislature that would convince lawmakers to fund the continuation of an office that, as Vermont author Frederick Wells wrote in a Boston newspaper in 1904, "had become a virtual real estate agency."[102] As the legislative session approached, Valentine's work continued to receive mixed press coverage. The Boston *Daily Journal* wrote in September that the Weston and Wilmington colonies were a "continuous success," full of "well and happy" Swedes who had sent for their friends. Around the same time newspapers such as the Brenham, Texas, *Weekly Banner* reprinted a widely distributed report that "the attempt to colonize the deserted farms of Vermont with Swedes has resulted in complete failure."[103] The reality, at least for the Swedes in Landgrove, was somewhere in between. But as long as outsiders were discussing Vermont's "deserted" farms, Valentine might well have felt that the Swedes' actual condition was beside the point.

The legislative session in which Valentine and his supporters sought continuation of the immigration scheme was extraordinarily contentious. Farmers and their allies in state government were energized by the establishment in Vermont over the summer of the Farmers' League, an advocacy organization that had previously been established in other Northeastern states. The State Patrons of Husbandry was also in a particularly activist phase, and its leadership was firmly opposed to Valentine's work.[104] Members of the business elite, on the other hand, came to Montpelier determined to achieve some of their long-term goals to modernize the state. In the end, the 1890 legislative session passed the first laws that put the cost of highways and schools on the state; both laws passed only after a great deal of acrimonious debate. The question of extending municipal suffrage to women also stimulated contentious deliberation. The bill that provoked the most rancor during the session sought to separate the Vermont State Agricultural College from the University of Vermont, an ardent goal of farming interests for more than a decade. The result of these and other issues was a legislative session that the Burlington *Free Press* called "notorious" for its bitter politics.[105]

In this atmosphere, Valentine and his supporters sought to see his work continue. At the beginning of September, Valentine submitted his report to the legislature. It began with a summary of the commission's goals, and then recounted Valentine's first efforts to gather information on the state, gave a brief sketch of the historical conditions and events that had resulted in the "abandoned" farm crisis, and described the Swedish experiment, from its inception to the arrival of the Swedes the next year. Sprinkled throughout the passage, however, were intimations by Valentine that his goals were larger than merely the Swedish experiment. He described his work as having the bigger goal of capturing the general attention of "those seeking cheap, good farms," and using the position "to impart information which will bring seller and purchaser into business relations."[106] Valentine concluded his discussion of the experiment by calling the Weston and Wilmington colonies a great success, dismissing the significance of the abandonment of Vershire, and calling for the program to continue with the establishment of a permanent commissioner of immigration. Valentine's conclusion made two requests. First, that a program must continue that would bring Scandinavians to Vermont's farms, as they were so much more desirable than the "vicious and undesirable classes" who constituted the majority of the state's immigrants. Second, it was no less important for the commission's work to continue because of the many farms that had been sold to Americans as a direct result of his labors. The greatest contribution of his work, wrote Valentine, was that "the press of our large cities and far-away States has echoed the sentiments of the press of Vermont, and the result has been that Vermont's enterprises, her desirable farms and natural advantages, are known through the land."[107]

Pleased with the report, the state senate ordered 1,000 copies printed. At the same time, a bill to create a permanent Commission of Immigration and Industrial Interests was introduced in the senate. In his farewell address to the legislature, Governor Dillingham enthusiastically urged continuation of the commission's work, sentiments echoed by his successor, Carroll S. Page. The next week, however, a bill was introduced into the house to abolish Valentine's office. The senate, a majority of which favored continuation of the commission, quickly appointed a special joint committee to study the issue.[108]

As the future of the experiment hung in the balance, Valentine came under a great deal of criticism for a variety of reasons in the house, a body dominated by representatives of small towns.[109] The main complaint was the cost of his work: Valentine put the cost of bringing his 68 Swedes to Vermont at $3,150, including a $1,250 payment to Nordgren for his work. The whole cost of Valentine's effort was not listed in the report, however, which weakened it considerably in the minds of many in the legislature and portions of the state press. Those adding Valentine's clerical, travel, and other expenses generally calculated the total expense of the office at around $6,000, though estimates went as high as $15,000.[110] According to the *Argus and Patriot*, the general feeling of "the people" was that the results of Valentine's work "were not at all commensurate to the cost," and that, reading the report, even the most astute would wonder if he had "accomplished anything worthy of mention."[111] The attempt to repopulate Vermont by the importation of Swedes, concluded the *Argus*, "was a mistake and should never have been attempted." As critics had been arguing since the previous year, opponents of the commission continued to insist that Vermont had no "abandoned" farms in the first place, but rather a combination of farms for sale and land better suited to other purposes.

In dismissing the Swedish project, however, the *Argus* had to admit that many farms had been sold to native Vermonters returning from the West, and to other outsiders, as a result of the publicity Valentine brought to the state. Valentine emphasized this same point repeatedly to the press. As the bill to end his work sat in committee, he issued another circular requesting listers in each town to submit information on all sales of farms that had taken place because of his work. That circular did him no good. On November 22, the special committee on the bill to abolish the commission reported negatively on it, hoping to perpetuate Valentine's work, but the house had made up its mind. On the final day of the session, the house voted not to renew the commission. Valentine's work was over. The Bennington *Banner* ruefully noted that, because of the publicity generated by the program, "in one town *ten* farms have been sold, in another *twenty*, in another 20,000 acres, and several in almost all the towns colored on the Commissioner's map." And yet, inexplicably to the *Banner* despite these sales, the program had been ended, and there was "no one to blame but the farmers themselves, who, for some unaccountable reason were almost to a man opposed to the bureau."[112] As residents of rural Vermont would find out in the coming decades, they had good reason to oppose Valentine's work. Abolishing Valentine's commission, however, did not prevent it from affecting the state for many decades to come.

Valentine did not give up. In the months after the commission was abolished he was still showing newspapers examples of the letters of inquiry he had received about Vermont farms.[113] In January 1891 the Brattleboro *Vermont Phoenix* noted a letter from a Missouri resident who had decided against buying a farm in Vermont because of "his disgust at the act of the legislature in repealing the measures for promoting the growth of the state in wealth and population, so successfully inaugurated under Commissioner Valentine."[114] But many Vermonters were pleased by the scheme's apparent failure, agreeing with the Burlington *Clipper* that the whole program had been a "foolish expenditure."[115] Little was said of the Swedes themselves. Increasingly forgotten though they might be, Valentine's Swedes in the "Weston colony" were settling into their surroundings. In December 1890, the Andersons gave birth to their third child, and first to be born in Vermont, a boy they named Charles. By then the local novelty of Valentine's recruits had largely worn off. Carl Westine, an especially large and strong man, was earning the respect of the other lumbermen at the McIntyre Mill, a mixture of men of Yankee, Irish, and French-Canadian descent. August Nyren, by profession a lumberjack like Westine, also settled into his job, as did his son Carl. Edwin Anderson and John Neilson, farmers by trade, worked with them for the time being but looked forward to the day they could acquire farms. Eight months after they arrived, they had chosen to settle where they had been placed.

Major Valentine's Swedish immigration program was over, and was quickly on its way to being mostly forgotten. What remained were the list of farms for sale that he had compiled, the network of contacts he had built in towns across the state, and the publicity generated by his scheme. What also remained was Valentine's "Swedish colony" in Landgrove, living in a boarding house and preparing for a winter of lumbering on Peru Mountain.

CHAPTER 3

The Tourism Boom

The Tiffts and the Swedes Hold a Wedding

The weather was sunny and mild on the morning of Friday, May 5, 1893, as a crowd made its way to a church in Peru.[1] Normal church services remained a special event for Major Valentine's Landgrove Swedes. For a group of families who had been members of the same church in rural Sweden, and who had come together to a distant and isolated place, gathering for services provided togetherness. The Westines, Nyrens, and both Neilson families would assemble, as would the family of Edwin and Emma Anderson, now numbering four children with the birth of son Harry the year before, taking the short walk from their farm over the town line in Weston.

This day was particularly special, however. Charlotte Nyren, now 17 years old, was marrying Edward Tifft, a local man who listed himself on his marriage certificate as a "laborer," and who was older than her by a decade. Eddie was the son of Henry Tifft and had grown up in Peru. He had become acquainted with Charlotte's father and brother while working in lumber camps in Peru and Mount Tabor over the previous couple of years. At the time of their wedding, Charlotte still struggled with English; her marriage certificate listed her last name as "Loraine," while a newspaper announcement listed her first name as "Orletta."[2] But that was no obstacle for Eddie. Charlotte, or "Lottie" as she was known, was tall and strikingly attractive. For a bachelor laborer in his late twenties, considerably shorter than his bride with little in the way of accomplishments, Lottie was a catch.

Presiding over the wedding was Landgrove's Warren W. Wiley. Born in Landgrove in 1833, he was a prominent farmer locally, and at the time was serving in the state legislature and as the town's clerk, treasurer, overseer of the poor, and justice of the peace.[3] This seems like a rather large number of responsibilities for one man, but Landgrove was a small town, and getting smaller. After reaching its peak of 385 residents in 1830, a continuous slide had left only 220 there in 1890. The Swedes who settled there in 1890 were still relatively new, but in such a small town it had not taken long for them to become well known. A wedding to a local man, part of an extensive local family, further cemented their immersion in their surroundings.

Much had happened to Landgrove's Swedes in the three years since their arrival. Carl Westine had married Anna Svenson in Weston; it is unclear if she was also part of Nordgren's party that had arrived in April, but she did emigrate in 1890.[4] The Westines' first child, a daughter named Jennie, was born in Landgrove in 1891.[5] When the Westines arrived at the wedding they brought Jennie and their son William, born less than two months earlier. Another one of Valentine's families, that of Adolph Swenson, may have lived in Landgrove in 1893, but they certainly lived in Vermont and were very close to the other families. In 1891 their daughter Eva was born in Vermont, adding her to the two daughters born in Sweden.[6] John and Louise Neilson added a fourth child, a son Harry, in 1892 at a time that the family was temporarily living in the town of Jamaica, about 12 miles south of Landgrove.[7] Perhaps the biggest event had been the 1892 arrival in Landgrove of Axel Neilson, brother of John Neilson. On April 30, 1893, one week before Charlotte and Eddie's wedding, Axel married Hilma Svenson, the sister of Anna Westine.

Axel and Hilma's wedding had been a festive occasion, uniting in marriage the brother of one Landgrove Swede with the sister of another. The marriage of Charlotte Nyren to Eddie Tifft was on a different scale. The number of attendees swelled with members of the numerous Tifft family and their friends. Eddie Tifft had six siblings, and his three aunts and two uncles had produced many more cousins. The Tiffts's extensive intermarriage with other families in the area around neighboring Dorset—the Reeds, Crandalls, Hazeltons, and others—drew even more locals to the wedding. Eddie and Charlotte's wedding was one sign, if perhaps a small one, that Major Valentine's Swedes were becoming part of the community.

How Major Valentine's Swedes had fared in those early years after their arrival had been a topic of minor public interest. There were reports in the summer of their arrival that they had felt aggrieved at their treatment, finding the support provided them less than they were led to anticipate. In 1907, recalling their early years in Vermont, the Burlington *Free Press* recollected that, "Some of the Swedes expressed discouragement because friends expected to join them were not able to do so owing to failure of arrangements, and they were also dissatisfied because they did not receive the full advantages of...an interpreter as expected." In the isolation of Landgrove this inability to communicate must have been onerous. A 1921 newspaper article claimed that Valentine lent the Swedes money "with which to buy tools and machinery and build homes," but coming 30 years later the claim cannot be assumed to be true.[8] What is without doubt is that, with the abandonment of the recruitment scheme in 1890, Alonzo Valentine and the program's other supporters lost interest in the Swedish recruits. The confusion on the part of many that the failure of the Vershire colony was true of all three colonies did much to cause the public mind to assume no trace of Valentine's scheme remained.

There were rather more newspaper accounts in 1891 of the experience of the Swedes who went to Norton, which included some from the Vershire colony. The Boston *Globe* reported in April that the Swedes in Norton were "suffering" and making an "earnest plea for aid" so they could leave, while the St. Albans *Messenger* described Norton's Swedes as "in destitute circumstances."[9] A month later the *Messenger* reported that while "very little has been said about the Swedes in Vermont since the meeting of the legislature" the previous autumn, "some mischievous fellow" had been attempting recently to revive "the free advertising scheme" by getting a letter into a newspaper purportedly written by a Swedish settler at Norton's Mills. The letter claimed that the Swedes in Norton were having "an exceedingly hard time of it in lumbering. Their destitution was pictured in somber colors."[10] Governor Carroll Page felt compelled to personally investigate conditions in Norton after concern was expressed by the Swedish vice consul in Boston. The *Messenger* then dismissed this picture, writing that Page's investigation revealed that the Swedes were working and getting along quite well. "The newspapers should now let them alone," added the *Messenger* with finality, "The Swedish immigration business has had its day." And Ver-monters of all kinds could agree, the less said about it the better.

Major Valentine, the Board of Agriculture, and the Rise of Tourism

Alonzo Valentine continued to justify his program in the year follow-ing its abandonment. In March 1891 he told the Brattleboro *Phoenix* that he was "in constant receipt" of letters from around the country inquiring about land. One he showed the reporter was from a Pennsyl-vania man who sought "a home of our own where we can enjoy the pure country air and the freedom which we were used to in our boyhood."[11] Writing thirteen years later, a journalist who had little sympathy for the recruitment scheme reported that between 1890 and 1891 Valentine received and answered around 5,000 letters.[12] Segments of the press did not entirely dismiss the program as a failure. In an August 1891 article generally sympathetic to Valentine's program, the St. Albans *Messenger* wrote that, "In the main Mr. Valentine did well, as well as could be expected of any one attempting to organize something out of chaos, limited as he was in help." Echoing the frequent ridicule received by the scheme, however, the *Messenger* added, "the Valentine map was a ter-rible reflection upon the state and conveyed a much worse impression than the facts would warrant." One quarter of all Vermont was not, the *Messenger* averred, composed of "abandoned farms."[13] A number of newspapers reported in 1891 that, ironically, the effect of Valentine's work was to alert farmers in Québec of farms for sale in Vermont. Val-entine's work thus had the effect not of combatting the immigration of "undesirable" Catholics, but of increasing it. The Montpelier *Argus and Patriot* declared this consequence of Valentine's map evidence of "the way in which the money of the State was uselessly squandered by the late Commission of Agriculture."[14] In the context of a state in which anti-Catholic bias was an element of public policy, Valentine could be accused of few greater sins.[15]

For many rural Vermonters, the bottom line about the program was that it did not matter if Valentine's targets were Protestant Swedes rather than Catholics from Québec or Ireland. Addressing a meeting of the Board of Agriculture in January 1891, board member M. W. Davis, from the beginning a staunch opponent of the scheme, declared that, "When they talk of populating the State with Swedes, I must say I have no sympathy with it, and never had. I am a true Vermonter, and I am proud of being a Vermonter. I never could sanction the idea of filling up our homes with foreigners."[16] The Bennington *Banner*, ever supportive of its local pillar, defended Valentine and bemoaned in 1891 the "slurs which it is the fashion in some quarters to cast on the work done by the commissioner."[17] Mostly, however, Vermonters lost interest in the Swedish experiment, and Valentine's program was drifting off as little more than a bad memory. The Burlington *Clipper* wrote in the summer of 1891 of its relief that the "abandoned farm nonsense is gradually going out of fashion."[18] Similarly, the *Argus and Patriot* was pleased to sarcastically note that, "we hear less talk now-a-days as to the so-called 'abandoned farms' of Vermont than we did at a time when legislatures were creating and later destroying the commission that was to bring about a 'grand transformation.'"[19] The *Argus*'s mockery was misplaced. The recruitment program would do much to bring about a transformation of Vermont that would shape its future for generations to come. M. W. Davis spoke of not desiring people from other countries, but if he had been worried about outsiders changing Vermont, he should have been more concerned about a domestic threat. Valentine's program played an instrumental role in making possible the boom in tourism that Vermont experienced in the 1890s.

The boom did not come out of thin air. The impulse of middle-class Americans to escape the city had been growing hand-in-hand with the instinct to reform urban ills. As Vermont's business elite had long tended to wish the state was *more* urban, the appeal of its backwardness could be difficult for them to comprehend, but that sentiment was setting in. An 1890 volume titled *The Industrial Advantages of the State of Vermont* intended to encourage manufacturing noted that, "Thousands of tourists visit Vermont during the heated term, and derive the greatest benefits from the influence of its pure mountain air and atmosphere, loaded with life-giving ozone." The author went on to give hope that this would lead entrepreneurial visitors to relocate to Vermont, begin new enterprises, and thereby make Vermont more prosperous, progressive, and modern.[20] It was, of course, the very lack of manufacturing that attracted most of those tourists.

Tourism was not new to Vermont, by any means, but the early 1890s began a new era in the industry's history. Wilmington was one of the early towns to understand the implications of the new era. Even as its leaders welcomed Valentine's Swedes, they turned decisively to tourism as an important part of the town's future. A town heretofore reputed to be "fifty years behind the times," Wilmington was about to be a stop on a new short rail line, the Hoosac Tunnel and Wilmington Railroad. In the years immediately after 1890 a number of Wilmington houses, including farmhouses, were sold as summer homes, and in 1890 a group of investors began an enterprise to build tourist hotels in the town, including on the banks of a modest lake named Ray's Pond. Dissatisfied by that mundane name, the investors saw to it that the lake's name was changed to Lake Raponda.[21] It was not the last time that the needs of tourism would alter and reinvent Vermont's landscape.

In the early 1890s a new, hopeful spirit was palpable among Vermont boosters of progress. Governor Carroll Page's inaugural address in 1891 pointed out that New Hampshire was solving its own "abandoned" farm problem by attracting summer residents, and stated his hope that "Vermont may well follow her example."[22] The spirit even reached Peru, whose population had gone down from 556 in 1880 to 445 in 1890. Peru's leading citizen, M. J. Hapgood, a native of the town, Harvard graduate, and operator of its general store, was so discouraged by the number of young people leaving that he had begun the practice of making a deposit in a Bennington bank upon the birth of every child in Peru, to be redeemed if that person remained in Peru as an adult.[23] But at an 1891 reunion celebration he organized, Hapgood enthusiastically told attendees that Peru had a bright future because "no other place in these parts offers equal attractions for the tired and dejected denizens of our cities who seek rest, recreation and quiet."[24]

In the context of this recognition of the potential of tourism to vitalize the state, Vermonters paying attention could have begun to perceive by 1891 significant, if perhaps unintentional, consequences to Valentine's work. Media coverage of Valentine's program in its one year of existence had brought the availability of cheap Vermont farms to a national audience. Valentine's office became the focus of inquiries by those interested in purchasing farms as summer homes. He had built a network of contacts in towns across the state to whom such inquiries could be forwarded. And Valentine had compiled the first comprehensive list of Vermont farms for sale. The Bennington *Banner* was moved in the summer of 1891 to describe Valentine's labors as "very much like a sacrifice hit" in baseball: "Had not this agitation roused the inert press of this state to advertising its resources as they should be," the *Banner* wrote, the many land sales that had occurred in the last year would not have taken place.[25] The St. Albans *Messenger* credited Valentine with "bringing forward a practical discussion of the many superior advantages of the state and its unimproved opportunities."[26] Noting that Valentine had "been derided and even abused for advertising" Vermont's available farms, the Brattleboro *Phoenix* pointed to the fact that New Hampshire and Massachusetts were pursuing programs to compile and publicize lists of farms for sale modeled on Valentine's work.[27] For such observers, the main product of Valentine's work was his compilation of a list of farms for sale, and the extent to which he had been able to make outsiders aware of them. The Swedish element of the program, meanwhile, receded to insignificance.

There had been opposition, though not universal, among members of the Board of Agriculture to Valentine's Swedish program during its existence. But with the program over, the board became the primary vehicle of continuing his work of promoting the sale of summer homes. In March 1891, it voted to assume the work of advertising the state, "carrying on," wrote the Brattleboro *Phoenix*, "the work so well begun by Commissioner Valentine."[28] The St. Albans *Messenger* reported later in 1891 that the work of the commission had been turned over to the Board of Agriculture: "The policy of advertising is continued but in a different manner."[29] The board published Valentine's list of farms for sale as a pamphlet in 1891 titled *The Resources and Attractions of Vermont: With a List of Desirable Homes for Sale*.[30] Added to the list was prose that generally described Vermont as a place of "peculiar charm and beauty." The Springfield *Republican* described the pamphlet as "setting forth in poetry and prose the attractions of the state as a place to live in, and gives over the names of owners, descriptions and locations of some of the desirable farms offered for sale." The *Republican* continued, "Unfortunately, however, the farms advertised do not generally appear to be of the abandoned class, and it looks very much as if the owners were seizing this opportunity to market property that the state board is not or should not be concerned about at present."[31] If, as Valentine's many critics had argued the previous year, there were no "abandoned" farms in the first place, the board can hardly be faulted for not confining itself to such sales. As incongruous as it might have been, the Board of Agriculture had become the primary institution for the promotion of summer tourism.

From the beginning, the Board of Agriculture sold Vermont not just as a place with cheap farms for sale, but as a place of resplendent pastoral beauty, a landscape unaffected by the problems and disruptions brought about by urbanization. In the board's rendering Vermont was largely a place of villages with a "single church spire and country store," and "ponds and lakes nestled among the hills and mountains."[32] The board was selling Vermont as a place that had remained what industrialized places elsewhere had once been. So successful was its list of farms for sale that the pamphlet was reprinted the next year, along with another titled, "A List of Desirable Vermont Farms at Low Prices." The board reported in 1892 that in the previous year, 1,764 farms had been sold across 220 Vermont towns, of which 252 were "of the class known as unoccupied farms."[33]

In that same year Victor Spear, a Dartmouth College graduate and successful sheep farmer, was appointed statistical secretary for the Board of Agriculture.[34] Under Spear's leadership, the agency threw itself even more deeply into promoting tourism. In an 1893 pamphlet titled *Vermont: A Glimpse of its Scenery and Industries*, Spear exclaimed that Vermont possessed "advantages and attractions which commend it to either the business man, the seeker of a home, or the tourist." Spear especially directed his appeal to Vermont natives who had left the state: "The streams have neither changed their courses nor lost their beauty," he wrote, "the mountains retain the same rugged and interesting outlines, hills have lost none of their former freshness, nor valleys their peculiar charm. The water is as sparkling, the air still laden with health and the winters as cold and the summers as delightful as ever, and will all seem to give a welcome greeting to those who have once known them."[35] Echoing what was becoming the dominant narrative of tourism promotion, Spear depicted Vermont's relative backwardness as its prime attraction.

At a board meeting that same year, Spear gave a talk titled "Farm Management" in which he promoted tourism as the solution to farmers' problems. He told his audience, "there is no crop more profitable than this crop from the city, and it is one that comes directly to the farmer, and he should encourage and promote this visiting from our city cousins."[36] In 1894, the Board of Agriculture delegated to Spear responsibility for compiling a report on summer travel. Because not every town returned the questionnaires Spear sent to them, he could not report on the whole state, and chose not to estimate. But based on the information he received, Spear was doubtful that "any agricultural product, except the dairy product, is bringing as much money to the State at the present time as our summer visitors, and even our dairy product would find there a close rival in point of profit."[37] Vermont's best path forward, he concluded, was through its marketing as a rural paradise. As the 1890s progressed, the board's "List of Desirable Vermont Farms at Low Prices" evolved, moving decisively away from the pretense of marketing to farmers. The pamphlet was renamed "The List of Desirable Farms and Summer Homes in Vermont" in 1895, and "Vermont: Its Fertile Fields and Summer Homes" in 1897. By then, the boom in summer tourism was fully underway.[38]

Tourism's Dilemma

The growth of tourism engendered a new optimism among Vermont's business leaders. The state's backwardness was becoming the key to its future growth and development. Many boosters saw tourism as a means to the industrial development they had long desired. An 1891 book titled *The Industries and Wealth of the Principal Points in Vermont*, for example, exclaimed about a town it described as resplendently beautiful, that "Thanks to the push, progressiveness and enterprise of its business leaders, the world has awakened to the unexcelled inducements and advantages which Swanton offers, and it unmistakably has a great future before it." The landscape, both physical and human, would lead visitors to relocate to Vermont, the author wrote, begin new enterprises, and make Vermont more prosperous, progressive, and ultimately more modern. In that volume, as in others, there was little recognition that it was the very lack of development that attracted tourists. The principle of diminishing returns had largely not sunk in; for boosters, natural beauty and industrial development were entirely complementary.[39]

Despite the paradoxical nature of selling Vermont's backwardness to push the state forward, enthusiasm built as the decade went along that

Vermont could successfully negotiate using tradition to accomplish progress, without compromising what was being sold. That ethic was a founding principle of *The Vermonter* magazine, which began publication in 1895. From the beginning, *The Vermonter* was a vehicle to both sell Vermont beauty and promote Vermont progress. That ethic likewise underpinned the Vermont Development Association (VDA), also founded in 1895. The VDA was comprised of many of the state's most successful businessmen and politicians who enthusiastically sensed a reversal of Vermont's fortunes, and intended to use the organization as a vehicle to capitalize on it. Developing the state was their goal, and summer tourism was the primary vehicle to accomplish it. The Burlington *Free Press* called the VDA one more reason to believe that "Vermont will soon realize some of the wonderful possibilities which nature has placed in store for her." "This organization," wrote the *Free Press*, "ought to be the beginning of a new era for the Green Mountain State. If Vermont's attractions could be properly placed before the public, the rapid development of the State would be assured."[40] Such boosters of progress saw in tourism possibilities to reverse the course of a state still far too much in decline. Indeed, during the 1890s 163 of Vermont's 249 towns lost population.[41] If tourism could play a central role in stopping the bleeding and bringing the state into a new era of prosperity and growth, then tourism would be promoted enthusiastically. It was too early in the tourism boom for its promoters to be concerned about limitations on growth. For now, Vermont's leaders could revel in newfound confidence that the state had a bright future ahead of it.

Tourism Edges In On the Swedes

For most of the 1890s, the boom in tourism did not touch Peru or Landgrove in any significant way. The towns were too remote from railway access and too primitive. In the years after Lottie and Eddie Tifft's marriage in 1893, Valentine's Swedes had quietly continued on with their lives. The family of Adolph Swenson relocated to Orange, Massachusetts, in either 1893 or 1894, but its members maintained contact with their friends in Landgrove. The Andersons worked their Weston farm while adding daughters Esther, Ellen, and Agnes to their other four children between 1894 and 1899. Meanwhile, the Nyrens, Westines, and the two Neilson families lived on or just off the main road in Landgrove.[42] Carl Westine, August Nyren, and his son Carl continued to make their living primarily in lumbering; Carl Westine became a foreman at the McIntyre Mill.[43] August Nyren purchased 50 acres of land in 1894. His closest neighbors were the family of John Neilson, who were still renting a homestead. Axel and Hilma Neilson acquired a 60-acre lot, 100 percent on mortgage, in 1895 on the north side of Uphill Road, just off of the Landgrove Road.[44] There they produced a second son, John Dolph, in 1896. The family of Carl and Anna Westine grew as well: A daughter Nola was born in 1895, and another daughter Della two years later.[45] Valentine's projected Swedish colony was apparently flourishing, if in the obscurity of one of Vermont's smallest and poorest towns.

While Landgrove remained in relative isolation, however, nearby towns were beginning to be dramatically affected by tourism. One of the towns most significantly reshaped by the tourist boom was Manchester, close by to the southeast of Peru but very differently situated. Whereas Peru was heavily wooded, mountainous, sparsely populated, and hard to reach, Manchester lay along a river, and the Rutland Railroad came right through the center of the main village, where there was a depot. This made the town easily accessible, and the Equinox Hotel, which opened in 1853, prospered and expanded in the 1890s. In 1899 the Ekwanok Golf Club opened in Manchester, confirming the town's status as a tourist destination.[46] Next-door Dorset followed Manchester's promotion of tourism, as much out of necessity as desire. The marble industry in Dorset had gone into a severe decline after the Panic of 1893, and by 1897 almost all the quarries and mills in town were closed.[47] By then Dorset's leading citizens had seen the advantage of pursuing summer tourists as the town's salvation. The Dorset Field Club was founded in 1886 to provide golf and other recreational activities to both locals and tourists. A clubhouse for the golf course was built in 1896. A few years later the town commissioned the publication of a pamphlet titled *Dorset, Vermont, as a Summer Home*.[48] Promoters of Manchester and Dorset marketed the towns as relatively fancy destinations for the wealthy, out of reach of most in the middle class. Apparently some locals grew concerned about this wave of tourists; Dorset town historian Tyler Resch writes that an air of resentment circulated among those in

Dorset who wanted "to keep things just the way they [were]."[49] One can certainly imagine the Tiffts, Reeds, and other families in their strata feeling that way. By their very presence however—the inns they patronized, the houses they bought, the golf course where they played, the money they spent—tourists were changing the town. By 1900, Dorset had nine boarding houses and two hotels, and those tourists who could afford to do so increasingly bought or built homes.[50]

Pressure from tourism edged closer to Landgrove from the east, as well. In 1895, the St. Albans *Messenger* reported that in one formerly "deserted" section of the town of Chester, which sits next to Weston, a number of professors from Harvard and Bowdoin recently had purchased farms as summer homes. "To be sure," the *Messenger* wrote, "the owners of the places spend only three or four months a year there, but their money is adding value to the town." The *Messenger* added that the summer residents were "a welcome change from the colony of Swedes which was established just over the line in Weston."[51] Of course, most of the local Swedes had landed in Landgrove and not Weston—at that time only the Andersons lived in Weston—but the point was taken: Five years before, Vermont had briefly pursued an absurd program that had failed, but tourism was coming to the state's rescue. A promotional issue of the *Vermont Tribune* of Ludlow in 1899 described Chester as "larger, busier, more attractive, more prosperous, more hopeful than ever before." Having "secured more public improvements in the last five years than during the preceding century," Chester was "awakening from its hibernation of a century; Young America is coming to the front, taking the bits in its teeth and setting a pace that startles the old time." "The golden age is now," the *Tribune* gushed, "prosperity beckons from the threshold of the new century."[52] The apparent path to this new golden age, in Chester as elsewhere in Vermont, was through promoting the state's idyllic backwardness.

Valentine's recruitment program was fading from memory, rarely mentioned in newspapers or by politicians. The Burlington *Free Press* wrote sympathetically in 1897 that Valentine had been "undoubtedly on the right track" with his scheme before his project had "succumbed in the face of hostile public sentiment."[53] If one had sought tangible evidence of the track Valentine had been on, a walk down the Landgrove Road, and the conversations in Swedish one would have heard, would have provided one glimpse of it. But a round of golf in Dorset with visitors from New York City was a more significant consequence of his exertions.

A Walk Through Landgrove in 1900

When Henry and Harriet Tifft left their Peru farm in late 1900 to visit their son, daughter-in-law, and two children in Landgrove, their carriage had to jog west along the rough path that today is named Hapgood Pond Road. Entering Landgrove, they drove on half a mile, with fields on both sides, and across a bridge over Utley Brook, until they hit a T at the Landgrove Road. There they turned to the left. As they progressed northward they passed the house of John and Louise Neilson on the left. John cherished aspirations of owning his own farm but in 1900 still worked as a day laborer, as did his 17-year-old son, Charlie. Sixteen-year-old daughter Anna worked as a servant in a boarding house at a Mount Tabor lumber camp, where Carl Nyren also boarded during the lumbering season.[54] Three younger Neilson siblings ranged in age from two to fourteen.[55]

After another quarter-mile, Henry and Harriet arrived at Eddie and Charlotte's small farmhouse on the right. They lived next door to Carl and Anna Westine, whose four children ranged from nine-year-old Jennie down to two-year-old Della. Anna was in the late stages of another pregnancy.[56] Entering the house, Henry and Harriet were greeted by their son and daughter-in-law. Charlotte, speaking halting English with a heavy Swedish accent, was just getting their infant daughter Addie down for a nap. Eddie had spent the summer picking up odd jobs on local farms, and was looking forward to the steady work provided by lumber mills in the winter.[57] There was nothing unusual about Eddie's peripatetic work life. In Landgrove, as for rural Vermonters throughout the state, there was little in the way of a dividing line between those who owned or worked on farms and those who worked for wages. Doing both was an essential part of their survival strategy.[58]

A little farther north and to the left up Little Michigan Road was the house of August Nyren. His vocation was listed in the 1900 census as a farmer, though he still considered himself primarily a lumberman.

August's sons Carl and Oliver were listed as day laborers. There is no indication that daughter Anna, 15, was in school. On the other side of the Landgrove Road, Axel Neilson, then in his early thirties and a better farmer than his brother John, was successfully working a farm with his wife and three children. In 1901, Axel built a house on Uphill Road to go with the 60-acre farm he acquired. Two years later he came into possession of a larger farmstead on Little Michigan Road, and sold the Uphill Road house to Carl Westine, his brother-in-law. The family of Edwin and Emma Anderson, whose farm was just up the road in Weston, were also a presence in Landgrove. The family barely avoided tragedy in December 1900: Emma worked at a steam-powered mill in Landgrove, and one day another worker replenished the engine with cold water straight from the stream. The ensuing explosion killed three workers and knocked Emma unconscious, but she luckily survived.[59]

Thus, if one was to pass through Landgrove in 1900, the visitor might have been struck by the large amount of Swedish being spoken. This portion of Major Valentine's Swedes had indeed formed a colony, as he had predicted would happen. Their children played together, they attended church together, and their lives were intertwined in numerous other ways. But their immersion in the local community was well underway. The ways they participated in the local economy replicated that of the Yankees around them. The traditional world of diversified farming on a small scale, supplemented by seasonal employment, especially in extractive industries, was a typical pattern across the state. It was a world of limited education, hard work, and intensely parochial interests, but one that many rural Vermonters found attractive.

The Maturation of Tourism to 1904

Isolated as they were, the outside world was increasingly encroaching on the lives of Landgrove's Swedes and their neighbors in many ways. Among them was tourism. By the turn of the century tourism was big business in Vermont. It affected the state unevenly, dramatically impacting some locations while barely touching others. In places with easy access to major lakes and rivers, locals accustomed to the use of natural resources without outside interference were often increasingly aggrieved by the sacrifices they were required to make to accommodate outsiders. Some traditional patterns of life needed to be altered or abandoned, and new traditions that served tourism's interests needed to commence. The 1902 report of the commissioner of fish and game reported, for example, that, "lake shore property is becoming more valuable every year, and the seine fishermen who now want to use nets would eventually be much better off if they would advocate the protection of the fish and cater to the sportsmen who are willing to pay liberally for good fishing and for summer homes along the shores of the lake where good fishing prevails."[60] To the commissioner's exasperation, many fishermen preferred to continue to carry on as they had previously. In 1901 state government instituted Old Home Weeks, an effort to bring emigrants back to their native towns as a way to stimulate the local economy, and to encourage townspeople to make a greater effort to achieve progress. Though Old Home Weeks took root in the years to come in the state's largest towns, most smaller ones were indifferent. There was plenty of sentiment in small towns that things were fine how they were.

The growing tension over tourism's threat to tradition manifested itself in politics. For example, state law had prohibited the manufacture and sale of alcohol for half a century, and temperance had become a social custom in small towns. In large part to accommodate tourists, however, a movement originating the big towns built to introduce "local option," wherein towns could choose if they wanted to be wet or dry. Adopted after much rancor in 1903, local option was popular in big towns, unpopular in small ones, and created tension between them. The availability of alcohol was merely one of the gripes of small-town residents, though: Tension around education, roads, taxation, and a host of other issues made the early twentieth century a politically divisive period.[61] For their part, state leaders representing the business class largely brushed off such dissatisfaction and resistance, pressing ahead with their belief that Vermont had entered a new era of openness and prosperity. The phrase commonly attached to this spirit of optimism was the "New Vermont," or the "Greater Vermont." There was irony to the touting of Vermont as "new," since much of the fuel for that optimism came from the selling of Vermont as old and unchanged. Nevertheless, boosters of the "New Vermont" saw great promise in the future, with a more industrial, progressive economy hopefully to come. Meanwhile, the selling of Vermont as old and unadulterated accelerated.

Tourism crept closer to the Swedes in Landgrove. The nearest rail line had been the West River Railroad, which had reached South Londonderry, its northern terminus, in 1880. This line had never been profitable, locally called "six miles of trouble."[62] A new railroad line arrived in Dorset in 1903, though not all the way to the town's main village, but instead to a quarry in the southern part of town, to supply marble for the construction of the New York Public Library. While not yet reaching Landgrove, the line made the town that much more accessible to the outside world.[63] The railroad line inspired Marshall Hapgood to open a hotel, Bromley House, in Peru in 1903. The hotel was conducted, as a biographer of Hapgood put it, "solely for summer resort." Hapgood insisted that a "unique feature" of Bromley House was that there were no roadside advertisements within the boundaries of Peru to disturb the natural beauty of the place.[64] Hapgood's refusal to allow advertising to besmirch the landscape's integrity speaks to the psychic appeal of Vermont scenery to visitors. In a nation that had become decisively urban and industrial, with all the attendant problems that drove the Progressive impulse, Hapgood was banking on Vermont's pastoral character possessing an appeal as a place in which a rural landscape and traditional values persisted. Vermont could be sold as having remained what America had once been. The rise of Vermont tourism spoke to the ambivalence many Americans felt about progress and modernity. As such, tourism committed promoters of progress to contrary goals, not only to pursuing growth but necessarily also to acknowledge limitations on development. In those limitations, and the management of growth they required, lay danger to the way of life known by people like Landgrove's Swedes and their neighbors.

Ends and Beginnings in the Early Twentieth Century

Nevertheless, in the first years of the twentieth century life for the Swedes in Landgrove and Peru went on without yet having been particularly affected by tourism. The Anderson family moved in 1902 from Weston to Londonderry, where daughter Hazel was born a year later.[65]

Eddie and Charlotte Tifft temporarily moved to New Hampshire; a son Carl was born there in 1904.[66] There were still four families in Landgrove—the Westines, Nyrens, and two Neilson families—but as they reached adulthood many of the children were moving on.[67] Anna Nyren, for example, moved to Hanover, New Hampshire, to work as a servant early in the century. In 1904 Anna married Peter Fountain, the son of immigrants from Québec, who worked in a Hanover paper mill.[68] Also marrying in 1904 was the oldest Anderson child, Hilma, who at the age of sixteen was betrothed to Dorset native Alonzo Butler. His mother, Agnes Beebe Butler, was from an old Dorset family; his father Charles was listed on the census as a "common laborer."

Alonzo Valentine might have found some irony in Anna Nyren marrying a working-class man of French Canadian heritage, as his Swedes were meant to replace such people. But Valentine's work was at its end: He died in July 1904. One obituary called him "a thorough Vermonter" whose "services in the promotion of the state's material interests have been widely recognized." Reflecting back on his career, some remembered his tenure as agriculture commissioner warmly. His hometown Bennington *Banner* recalled the Swedish program fondly, writing that, "As state immigration commissioner Major Valentine had a prominent part in a systematic attempt to repeople the abandoned farms of Vermont, a work which the state legislature foolishly allowed to lapse even though the work done bore abundant fruits."[69] A month later the Burlington *Free Press*, which had also been supportive of Valentine's efforts fourteen years earlier, published an article titled "Not Wholly a Failure," reporting that "the Swedes brought here by the Vermont immigration commissioner did not stay where they were put, that is on Vermont's abandoned farms, but they and others remained in the state largely." The *Free Press* concluded that "it was a mistake on the part of the State not to continue the immigration commission, modified and improved as experience suggested," but not because of the actual work done in the area of Scandinavian immigration. Instead the newspaper was "inclined to think that the experiment was a success—perhaps not in the way it was intended but in attracting attention to Vermont."[70]

A quite different opinion was voiced in November 1904 in a report on Vermont agriculture published in a Boston newspaper by Frederick Wells, a recent graduate of the University of Vermont's Agricultural

College. Wells dismissed the idea that there had ever been "abandoned" farms in Vermont and cited a number of Vermont agricultural experts who criticized Valentine's program. Victor Spear of the Board of Agriculture, for example, was quoted as describing "the theory" behind the program as "wrong." Wells found it hard to grasp why Valentine repeatedly referred to farms as "abandoned" when they were, in fact, for sale. To Wells, the final word on the program was that "the colonies soon died out, not having accomplished their end, and are now little heard of."[71] Wells was not alone in his condemnation; in 1904 the Burlington *News* called the Swedish experiment "an absolute, unmitigated failure."[72] From the perspective of more than a decade, it was easy to see why the program could be considered a fiasco. Unless they accounted for the growth of summer home sales, most Vermonters would see no trace remaining of it. Promoters of progress would feel it did nothing to stimulate economic development, while rural folk would have wondered how someone could so deeply misread the dynamics of rural life. There was plenty of merit to farmers' argument that their local economies were evolving naturally, in a way that bred homogeneity and stability. Change could be desirable to them, but only if locals had some measure of control over its pace and magnitude, and not if it was imposed from outside. Perhaps the greatest miscalculation of all was the belief that Swedes would more quickly become parts of the communities in which they settled than could immigrants from Ireland or Québec. For rural folk, ethnicity, or the gradations of whiteness which for many Americans organized society, was not the point; familiarity, interdependence, shared experiences, and family ties were. In blending into their community over time, Valentine's Swedes were taking a very traditional path to becoming a certain kind of Vermonter.

One more event occurred in 1904 that illustrates the legacy of Valentine's program, and it would have the greatest impact on the future of Landgrove. One spring morning after services at the Westminster Methodist Church in Elizabeth, New Jersey, a 40-year-old bank clerk named David Grant happened to have a conversation with a visiting minister who was a native of Peru, Vermont. According to what Samuel Ogden, at the time the young son of an Elizabeth insurance salesman, wrote about it over 70 years later, the conversation turned to the minister's hometown. The minister described "with sadness the dryrot which seemed to have attacked" Peru. Ogden later speculated that the minister might also have described Peru's "untrammeled and unspoiled beauty," and told Grant about how its "abandoned farms...could now be had for a song." The minister's description of Peru enchanted David Grant. Early that summer Grant set off in search of Peru, and upon finding it rented for the summer a farm that, Ogden wrote, "had been abandoned." Soon after the Grants bought an old Peru farmhouse as a permanent summer home. In 1909, 12-year-old Sam Ogden accompanied the Grants, including his best friend Duncan, to Peru for a summer vacation for the first time.[73] "And from this beginning," wrote Ogden decades later, "great things were to develop."[74]

CHAPTER 4

Creating an Unspoiled Landscape

Landgrove in the Era of the "Greater Vermont"

I N August 1907, The Burlington *Free Press* was moved to recall
the Swedes scheme, now 17 years in the past and feeling like an even
more distant memory. Summarizing the program's legacy, the newspaper
reported that most of Valentine's Swedes had left the state, though
"some of the original families may be scattered within our borders." It
concluded, "the experiment as such has been completely lost to view."[1]
One may have gotten a very different impression of how lost to view the
program was by an event that had taken place less than three months
earlier. In late May 1907, the family of Adolph Swenson traveled north
from Orange, Massachusetts. Spring was late in coming that year. There
was still snow on the farthest tops of mountains; the Bennington *Banner*
reported two days later that a heavy frost had killed early garden plants.[2]
The valley floors were blooming with spring wildflowers, however,
adding beauty to what was a joyous trip. Adolph, his wife Charlotte, and
two young daughters, Hilda and Mary, had been among Valentine's
Swedes in 1890.[3] Another daughter had been born to them in Vermont.
They had left Vermont sometime between 1891 and 1896, settling in the
heavily Swedish town of Orange, where two more daughters were added
to the family. Now they traveled back north to Landgrove for a very
special event. Mary, who was 18 and known as "May," was marrying
Charlie Neilson, the son of John and Louise.

The Swensons arrival at John Neilson's Landgrove farmhouse was
cause for great celebration. John was very proud to have acquired the

modest property, a 100-acre farm locally called the old "Bolster place," the year before. Carl and Anna Westine made the short walk from their house on Uphill Road with their five children to welcome the Swensons. The Westines were accompanied by Julius Westine, the son of Carl's brother. Julius had emigrated from Sweden in 1903 and was working as a carpenter, dividing his time between Landgrove and the lumbering operations up in the mountains of Peru. A young man with a sweet temperament (in contrast to his Uncle Carl, who was given to fits of rage when drinking), Julius was enamored with his cousin Jennie. The four other Westine children, William (14), Nola (11), Della (9), and Freda (6) trailed behind. The family of John's brother Axel likewise lived within walking distance. The joyful reunion was enlarged by the arrival of the Nyren and Anderson families, the Nyrens from Pawlet and the Andersons from Londonderry.[4]

Charlie Neilson and May Swenson's wedding more than a decade after the Swensons had moved to Massachusetts attests to the close connections that some of Valentine's Swedes had maintained. Another 1907 marriage that many of them attended illustrated how much they had become enmeshed with the local community. Earlier that year, the twice-widowed, 48-year-old Agnes Beebe Butler Reed, Hilma Anderson Butler's mother-in-law, married John Tifft, age 27, a farm laborer who was the cousin of Charlotte Nyren's husband, Eddie Tifft.[5] After the death of her first husband Agnes had briefly been married to Richard Reed, from the same Reed family with which the Tiffts were heavily intermarried.[6] After their marriage Agnes and John Tifft lived in Danby, where they raised grandson Cecil Twyne. In the 1920s, Cecil Twyne would marry Hazel, the youngest Anderson daughter, while Harry Anderson married Cora Wilkins, the daughter of Agnes's sister Julia Beebe Wilkins. In the Dorset/Peru/Landgrove area, the web of familial relations reached dizzying complexity, and provided the foundation for the strong sense of community in which the Swedes became immersed.

The move away from Landgrove by the Nyrens had somewhat diminished the "colony" of Swedes that Alonzo Valentine had once envisioned. They had sold their Landgrove farm in 1906 and moved to Pawlet, about 25 miles away, where patriarch August had found work in a sawmill. Son Oliver, a bright, musically inclined man who had no interest in making his living on a mountain, had just landed a job work-ing as a clerk in a general store.[7] The move had not ended their ties to their friends in Landgrove, however. When in 1906 Carl and Oliver Nyren became naturalized citizens in the county courthouse in Rut-land, Charlie Neilson had been their witness. And the oldest Nyren daughter, Lottie, her husband Eddie, and their three children remained in the Landgrove area, Eddie bouncing between jobs in a vain effort to establish a solid economic foothold. The Andersons, meanwhile, owned a farm in the adjoining town of Londonderry, so maintaining close contact with Landgrove's Swedes was no problem. The only Anderson married child, Hilma, also lived in Londonderry, where her husband Alonzo worked "odd jobs" to get by.[8] At the time of the 1907 wedding they had given birth to a son, and Hilma was pregnant again. The oth-er seven Anderson children, ranging in age from four to 19, remained at home. Some of the Landgrove children had moved on. To reach her brother Charlie's wedding, Anna Neilson had to travel from the Ver-mont town of New Haven, many miles to the north, where she lived with her lumberman husband, whom she married in 1906. Despite dis-persal among Landgrove's Swedes, however, after almost two decades of intermarriage and interdependence the tentacles of their familial and social relations stretched out from Landgrove to surrounding towns. Landgrove's Swedes took on their share of local responsibilities. Carl Westine, for example, had the job of transporting students from the town's northern district to the school, which was located in an inconve-nient spot away from most of Landgrove's population.[9]

Whatever the strength of its communal life, Landgrove appeared to be in deep trouble. The population, 225 in 1900, was shrinking. Land-grove was a hard place to make a go of life. There was less work up in the mountains with the closure in 1905 of the McIntyre Mill, a part of the general decline of the lumbering industry in the region. Good dairy farms were hard to come by, and many young men like Eddie Tifft and Charlie Neilson could only make ends meet by taking on odd jobs and seasonal work. Things had gotten so bad that in 1906, Landgrove's rep-resentative in the Vermont state legislature submitted a bill titled "An Act to Aid the Town of Landgrove in the Payment of Its Indebted-ness." Remarkably, considering the traditionally parsimonious nature of the legislature, Landgrove was granted a thousand dollars, saving it from financial ruin.[10] Many large forces brought it to that state, some long term and some new. One cause was the decline of the lumber industry, not just as a result of natural economic forces, but also because, after decades of increasing public agitation, the state of Vermont had begun managing its forestlands. Gone were the days of environmentally destructive, large-scale clear cutting that had left a majority of the state deforested.[11] In its place had arisen Vermont's "forestry movement," a belief in public management and conservation that culminated in the founding in 1904' of the Forestry Association of Vermont. Vermont was with the national current on the issue (the federal Forest Service was founded in 1905), and a number of wealthy Vermonters, such as railroad executive Frederick H. Billings, had engaged in private conservation activities. One among a number of motivations for expanding forest conservation work in Vermont was concern that the compromised natural scenery caused by destructive lumbering endangered tourism; one newspaper in 1909 celebrated the "dawn of a new day" for the environment in which "a judicious mixture of common sense, horse sense and forestry sense will preserve our forests and beautiful scenery."[12] Landgrove may also have simply suffered from incompetent management by townspeople of its financial affairs. Whatever the factors that brought it to a state of needing state relief to survive, Landgrove was a deeply troubled town.

Yet there was a lot to recommend life in Landgrove, as well. A writer to the Springfield (MA) *Republican* in 1909 described the appeal of the area in an article on next-door Peru. He began by describing the extensive effort it took to get to Peru Village, involving a train ride and then a sequence of two stagecoaches that went steeply uphill. There the author described a majestic landscape that was sublimely beautiful, a place of green hills and imposing mountains interspersed with small farms. Rather than wholly natural, it was a landscape that had been created by those who lived there and worked the land. It was not the physical landscape that most impressed the author, however, but the human landscape. The reporter called Peru Village "the perfect specimen of the old New England. When one sees this hamlet, he realizes what New England means to elder Yankees—what Vermont still largely is in these sequestered neighborhoods—a region of quiet and orderly life, and though not so populous or prosperous as in the days of the fathers, yet thrifty and cheery and unspoiled and in some respects better than it ever was."[13] As another one of these "sequestered neighborhoods," Landgrove also offered a strong community, beautiful scenery, and, for those who desired it, shelter from the fast pace of the outside world.

The outside world was coming. The impact of tourism was inexorably creeping closer to Landgrove. Two years before the Swenson-Neilson wedding the region to the west of Landgrove had been particularly elevated in its profile as a tourist destination by the construction in Manchester of Hildene, the summer home for Robert Todd Lincoln. Now, as Charlie and May prepared to wed, the residents of Landgrove looked on in wonder as cartload after cartload of building material and furnishings were brought through town from the south, up from the train station in Londonderry. The materials were headed through town to its northwestern edge, where construction had begun the previous summer on a lavish mountain vacation house. Construction had halted for the winter, but by spring 1907 was back in full operation, rushing to meet a deadline. The house was being built at the direction of New York City resident Stephen Carlton Clark. Clark was the grandson of Edward Clark, the founder of the Singer Sewing Machine Company and owner of the Singer Building, then the tallest in the world. Stephen Clark wanted the mountaintop house in Landgrove finished in time for his honeymoon two years later. When completed it was a grand house with extensive porches, a large main room, and five bedrooms. According to an account by Axel Neilson's son Alve, who was later the house's caretaker, it also had a wine cellar, a "magnificent" fireplace surrounded by colored glass bookcases, and red leather upholstery. The overall view of the inside, Alve remembered, was "absolutely beautiful, with exquisite architectural proportions so that nothing could be changed to improve it."[14] In the summer of 1909 Clark married Albany socialite Susan Vanderpoel Hun, and with great hopes took her to the lodge for their honeymoon, but to Clark's dismay she decisively disliked the experience. The couple never returned, and in the years that followed, Landgrove's Log Castle sat mostly unused.[15] Over in Peru, Marshall Hapgood's Bromley House hotel was doing good summer business by the year of Charlie and May's wedding. Among those who worked at Bromley House in these years was Jennie Westine, Carl and Anna's oldest daughter.[16]

Meanwhile, young Samuel Ogden of Elizabeth, New Jersey, continued to spend portions of each summers at the Grant's house in Peru. To get there, first a train took him from Elizabeth to a ferry across the Hudson River, and then he would board a steamboat to Troy, New York. From there he took a "hinky-dinky" train with only two passenger cars to Manchester, Vermont. The final stage of the journey from Manchester to Peru was only 11 miles but took three hours on the stagecoach that ran to Chester. For the part of the journey that climbed steep mountains the passengers disembarked and walked so as not to put unnecessary strain on the horses. After a journey of around 27 total hours, the Grant family, with young Sam Ogden in tow, would arrive at their vacation house. Ogden and his friend Duncan spent many hours there exploring the mountains and streams that surrounded the home. Ogden speculated later that, in the course of those adventures, he must have entered Landgrove, swum in its ponds, and visited its chief village, called Clarksville. It might have looked charmingly primitive to Ogden, who was acquiring a deep love for rural life and high regard for farmers. He would later also attribute his respect for farmers to the many long visits he made to his uncle's farm in northeastern Pennsylvania. It was there, he wrote in the 1940s, that "from infancy I experienced the ways of country life." His time at the farm meant cherished experiences, such as "lying under the Snow apple tree in the evening and listening to the mournful cry of the screech owl in the woods across the river." It also meant admiring the independence and broad skills of his uncle, who he considered wise and learned despite little formal education. Ogden came to regard rural life as fulfilling in ways he thought the specialization and monotony of urban life could not be.[17]

Thus the people of Landgrove might have appeared in Ogden's young eyes a noble and independent people. To many Vermonters, however, the town would have been emblematic of the problems facing rural areas. There were other towns like it in Vermont, and many proposed solutions to their problems. In an age when people spoke of a new, "Greater Vermont," chief among the potential sources of salvation for Landgrove was the promotion of tourism. But for now, the Clark Lodge aside, Landgrove remained largely isolated, divorced to an appreciable extent from the pressures of the outside world. It would not last.

Progressive Legislation in the Age of the "Greater Vermont"

Landgrove's relative isolation increasingly differentiated it in these years from much of the rest of the state. Summer tourism was most assuredly big business for Vermont. Evidence of the enthusiasm with which state leaders greeted this perceived trend away from a stagnant past was clear in the summer of 1907. In the same season that Charlie Neilson and May Swenson were married, and in which Stephen Clark built his honeymoon home, Vermont staged an exhibit at the Jamestown Tercentennial Exposition in Virginia. The exposition was a world's fair celebrating the 300th anniversary of the settlement of Jamestown. The state paid to have a house built for its exhibits, as did a number of other states. The Vermont exhibit portrayed a newly revitalized state on its way to a bright and prosperous future, balanced by encouragements to visit because of the its natural beauty and hospitality to tourists. The message of the exhibit was that, in Vermont, the past and the future comfortably complemented each other.

To accompany the exhibit, the Vermont Commission to the Jamestown Tercentennial Exposition published a promotional handbook, *Vermont: The Green Mountain State, Past, Present, Prospective.* It related how the state had cast off its dreary late nineteenth-century languor. "Finally," the handbook exulted, "the Vermont farmer can live closer to the village life and be in more reciprocal social relations with the busier world outside because of the nearness of his farm and constantly extending transportation facilities." It went on to say that farmers' children were now "nearer to more advanced schools than the old time rural districts once afforded," and families in general could "enjoy the recreations and amusements that the village and city life next door at all times offer." Free mail delivery brought newspapers to farmers' doorsteps, and telephones allowed them "momentary communication" with friends, stores, and doctors. "The Vermont farmer," the handbook concluded approvingly, "is no longer a pastoral recluse, a rural type in voluntary exile from the social, business, and political life of the township to which he belongs."[18]

Farmers' supposed emergence from isolation was just one of the reasons for Vermont's leaders to celebrate the state's progress in recent years. In the first decade of the twentieth century the state experienced a period of progressive reform that contemporaries considered unparalleled in the state's history, especially during the governorship of Fletcher Proctor from 1906 to 1908. Declaring that the state had "a higher duty than to live cheaply," Proctor pursued an unusually ambitious political agenda.[19] Proctor was fully a man of his era on a national scale: An historian of Vermont Progressivism wrote in 1941 that the years surrounding Proctor's term "might well be called 'the flowering era of reform.'"[20] In 1905 the state passed a child labor law that a newspaper wrote in 1911 was regarded as "a well-nigh model statute by various persons in the country at large," concluding with what can charitably be called exaggeration that, "this vexed question of sociology [child labor] does not trouble this state today."[21] The state also adopted a law compelling the weekly payment of wages by employers, and an employer's liability law. A law reforming education that passed in 1906 allowed towns to voluntarily join together to form larger supervisory districts, and to employ a full-time professional superintendent, half of whose salary was paid by the state.[22] According to the Bennington *Banner*, the state was also "in the forefront of the most progressive states with regard to the regulation of the public health" because it had adopted an "excellent" pure food law. Proponents of bureaucratization, standardization, and efficiency were clearly in the ascendancy. Accompanying this spate of reforms, the spirit of industrial development and economic progress encapsulated in the popular phrase "Greater Vermont" continued to build. In addition to its many progressive reforms, the *Banner* added in 1911, "the real truth is that Vermont is an industrial state and that progress and development along industrial lines here have not only been enormous, proportionately, in the past twenty years, but are growing at a rate that some day will make some sister New England states sit up and take notice."[23] Vermont would become modern, even if state agencies sold Vermont as oppositional to modern America.

Amidst this spirit of reform, progress, and development, state leaders were rethinking the proper approach to agriculture and the natural environment. The Board of Agriculture, in existence since 1870 with a few minor alterations, had long been an important part of how those topics were addressed. Almost by happenstance the board had also became the chief vehicle for the public promotion of tourism. In 1908, Governor Proctor recommended that the board be abolished with the goal of obtaining greater effectiveness and efficiency. As Austin F. Hawes, Vermont's first state forester, wrote, the board "had existed for a great many years and had done a good deal of valuable missionary work, although by many it was considered somewhat of a joke." To rectify the situation, the legislature abolished the board and replaced it with a single Commissioner of Agriculture, something the first commissioner called a "revolution in our Agricultural Laws."[24] Alongside the new commissioner position, the 1908 legislature created a new Board of Agriculture and Forestry, entrusted among other things with appointing a state forester.[25] Within a year the agriculture commissioner reported that "a bare beginning" of forest conservation had been made.[26]

Promoting Tourism in the Era of the "Greater Vermont"

If a chief advantage of abolishing the Board of Agriculture was better management of forests, that step left a hole in need of filling: the board's nearly two-decade role as the primary vehicle for the promotion of tourism. In 1907, the last year of its existence, the board published the pamphlet *Beautiful Vermont: Unsurpassed as a Residence or Playground; for the Summer Resident; the Summer Visitor; the Tourist; the Capitalist and the Workingman.*[27] Like the board publications that had preceded it, *Beautiful Vermont* presented a dual narrative of the state as both a pastoral escape from the modern world and a place ripe for economic development. Rejecting the description "abandoned," as had been the tendency of the board's members since Valentine had popularized the term, the pamphlet insisted that, "There are no 'abandoned farms' in Vermont," even if some of them appeared that way; "There is, however, considerable desirable property for sale at a reasonable rate." The pamphlet emphasized that, "To those who are tired of the worry and waste of the town, [Vermont farms] still offer a good living under comfortable conditions."[28]

That same year a coalition of hotel proprietors foresaw a new way to make Vermont accessible to outsiders. Automobiles were still a rare luxury item but were common enough to offer a potential supply of patrons to New England hotels. Working in cooperation with the Automobile Club of America, the hoteliers conceived the "Ideal Tour," which traveled over a series of roads in a circuit through the region. Among the supporters of the Ideal Tour was the proprietor of the Equinox Hotel in Manchester, Vermont. The next year the initial run by members of the Automobile Club was made over the Ideal Tour's route, a patchwork of local roads of greatly varying quality. The tour's backers then began advertising it in newspapers, complete with maps specifying the establishments at which tourists could stop. Calling it "The Mecca of the Motorist," advertisements promised "sapphire skies overhead, this great interstate highway under wheel, and at every turn a magnificent vista of ever-changing scenery."[29] The quality of many of the roads belied this rosy description. From Manchester heading east the only option was for the Ideal Tour to go past Bromley House over Peru Pass, following roughly the line of present-day Route 11, passing south of Landgrove and on through Londonderry. The road through Peru Pass was, as later described by Samuel Ogden, a narrow dirt toll road frequently impassable because of mud; as part of the Ideal Tour it was generously described as "difficult" by a Chicago newspaper in 1910.[30] It would obviously need improvement.

The problem of poor roads at the dawn of the automobile era was not confined to Peru Pass. This was pressed home in a 1909 interview with Almon Judd, a Connecticut hotel proprietor and leading force behind the Ideal Tour, titled "Good Roads Mean Summer Tourists." Judd impressed upon the reporter that auto tourists offered Vermont great possibilities, but that the deplorable condition of its roads needed to be rectified. He stated that good roads would do more than any other one thing to promote "the provision of the right kind of hotels in Vermont." Judd described his testimony on the handling of summer tourists as simply in line with the evidence of other reliable authorities, saying that "if any doubt remained concerning Vermont's need of trunk lines of good roads it must have been thoroughly dissipated. Good roads are the best investment the State of Vermont can possibly make."[31]

With the auto traffic through the Peru/Landgrove area increasing yearly, what most locals made of it is unknown. It at least had a positive impact on the life of a sawmill worker named Edward Hartwell, described as "a young man without means." The sawmill in which he worked was owned by Marshall Hapgood, who Hartwell believed had mistreated him. Their acrimony resulted in an altercation in 1911 that ended with Hapgood's nose "pushed over on the other side of his face and a couple of shanties over his eyes." Hartwell was unable to pay the fine of $51 levied on him for the violence and was imprisoned, throwing his wife and three children onto Peru's relief rolls. A week after Hartwell's conviction, an auto tourist taking the Ideal Tour ran his car onto the lawn of Hapgood's Bromley House, resulting in what was described as a "vigorous controversy" between the two. Hapgood had the tourist's car impounded and sued him for trespassing. In the process of resolving his case, the tourist heard of Hartwell's imprisonment and gleefully paid his fine as a way to spite Hapgood.[32]

In this case, at least, tourism came to the defense of locals. Whether it would benefit them in the long run was in question, but if they were skeptical, there was little they could do to stop it. The Ideal Tour's managers commenced publication of a booklet that could be acquired at hotels or from the Automobile Club of America in New York City, and Vermont's legislature supplied funds to improve its path. By 1914, Peru Pass was described as "very much improved" by the Brooklyn (NY) *Daily Eagle*.[33] By 1920, its promoters were calling the Tour's route "a great interstate highway," and Peru Pass both "much improved in grade" through "perhaps the most primitive section of the entire tour," a place where "one feels the old New England atmosphere of granite hills and stony farms."[34] It was only in its infancy, but the coming of auto tourism promised to remove tourists from their traditional networks of railroads and hotels, opening pathways to the reservoir of Vermont's most isolated "old New England atmosphere."

The promotion of tourism, as much as it had been intended to complement the economic development of the state, had forced Vermont state leaders to acknowledge the need for limits. Tourism necessitated a recognition of the principle of diminishing returns, as can be seen in the promotion of forest conservation. For the state to fully capitalize on tourism as one of its primary economic engines, it would have to make compromises with unrestrained growth and manage its environment in ways that complemented what tourists desired, even if that came at the expense of traditional uses of the land by everyday state residents. The benefits to such people and their local economies, thought state leaders, outweighed the sacrifices they were forced to make. Everyone, tourism's boosters believed, would benefit. The Burlington *Free Press* wrote that the State Board of Agriculture's 1908 booklet *Beautiful Vermont* was "good advertising, and either directly or indirectly it is helpful to our farmers, in whose interest the publication is issued."[35] But who would now undertake that advertising was temporarily in question. Responsibility for that job was taken up by the new Secretary of State, Guy W. Bailey.

The Bureau of Publicity is Born

When elected secretary of state in 1908, Guy W. Bailey was a 34-year-old man of energy, enthusiasm, and charisma. He grew up in the village of Essex Junction near Burlington, where his father owned a granite monument business. After graduating from the University of Vermont, Bailey became a lawyer. He was elected to the Vermont House of Representatives in 1904 and again in 1906 and then acceded to the secretary of state's office.[36] The traditional responsibilities of the office were things like writing insurance commission reports, keeping track of the issuance of liquor licenses, publishing records of public acts, and representing the state at ceremonial events. But seeing the vacuum in state promotion of tourism, Bailey offered to take it over. At his urging the 1910 state legislature created the Bureau of Publicity (BOP), with its own budget and located in the secretary of state's office.[37] The first state institution of its kind in the United States, the BOP was initially granted a $5,000 budget.[38] According to the legislation establishing it, the bureau was created with two missions of equal importance: promoting industrial development and promoting tourism.[39] From the beginning the BOP was most immediately associated in the public mind with the latter task. "The attractions of the Green Mountains need to be brought more fully to the attention of the public," the Springfield (MA) *Union* wrote early in the bureau's existence, and promoting tourism "doubtless will receive attention from the newly established publicity bureau." The *Union* predicted that the bureau's work "will place Vermont in the forefront of the progressive and prosperous states."[40] In the BOP's mission were commingled the paradoxical dual narratives of the state, in which natural beauty and tradition were assets to be exploited to the end of modernizing the state. Vermont's newspapers largely greeted the Bureau of Publicity with great enthusiasm. The Montpelier *Vermont Watchman* summarized their optimistic attitude by writing, "The turn in the road has come for Vermont—look ahead a little and you can see it."[41]

Bailey's work began in earnest in 1911. From the beginning, he carefully tailored the Bureau of Publicity's advertising to appeal to a select, wealthy audience. Vermont, he believed, wanted only the right kind of tourists, and Vermont's image and landscape would be organized to accommodate their desires and expectations. H. H. Chadwick, the director of the BOP in the 1930s, wrote that the agency's elitist approach "may be subject to criticism but it is felt that what Vermont has to offer appeals to discriminating people and that our hotels, tourist and farm homes are looking for that type of trade."[42] The bureau's first publication was *Vermont: Designed by the Creator for the Playground of the Continent*, written by Bailey himself. He began the pamphlet stating that it was for those "who feel, with the coming warm June days, a recurrence of the primitive longing to recline on the green bosom of Earth, shaded and sheltered by rustling, leafy boughs, soothed by the murmur of soft breezes and lulled by the rippling tinkle of silver streams." He went on to express the "hope that you may essay a visit, expand with the strength of the breezes that blow from the hills, repose in the quiet of the valleys and rejuvenate in the peace that abides in the shadow of the mountains." Bailey's Vermont was a place of unparalleled scenic beauty, perfectly suited as an escape from the modern world. Among the attractions the pamphlet listed was Peru, a place of leisure and tradition with "the only remaining toll road in the State, and the famous hotel with a fireplace on the veranda." The latter is a reference to Bromley House, which is described as having "delightful climate and scenery" and usually hosting 675 guests, "principally from New York, Montclair, and Elizabeth."[43]

Bailey also collaborated with the Commissioner of Agriculture, Orlando Martin, to pull together a pamphlet titled *Homeseekers' Guide to Vermont Farms*.[44] Bailey wrote in it that "One of the important side lines of Vermont agriculture is the taking of summer boarders and this is a business that is destined to increase year by year. No State in the

Union surpasses Vermont in variety and beauty of scenery. Many a farm high up on the mountain slopes, which produces but scanty crops of grain, reaps bountiful scenic harvests and these harvests never impoverish the soil." Following that introduction, the pamphlet contained a list of Vermont farms available either for commercial agriculture or as summer homes. The bureau also published brief pamphlets of the state's automobile laws and fish and game laws. All were free upon request. Bailey sent embossed cards to hotels and automobile clubs to states as far west as Ohio and as far south as Maryland bearing the words "Tour Vermont First. Plan a Vacation in the Green Mountain State. Good Roads. Grand Scenery."

Bailey's exertions on behalf of tourism earned him general praise. By May 1911, the Bennington *Banner* reported that despite the BOP's brief existence, "letters in large numbers are pouring in upon Secretary of State Guy W. Bailey in every mail. The response is both remarkable and gratifying…the indications are that the publicity work begun in a modest way, with a small appropriation, will prove an unqualified success."[45] Bailey reprinted the previous year's pamphlets and issued a new directory of hotels and inns, *Where to Stop When in Vermont*. Success for the bureau seemed to come quickly. In May 1912 the Burlington *Free Press* reported enthusiastically that the Bureau of Publicity had received at least 2,800 inquiries from potential tourists so far that year, "as a result of the profitable advertising campaign conducted." The *Free Press* concluded, "There is not room for doubt that Vermont is beginning to come into its own as a tourist resort and region of recreation."[46] The *Vermont Watchman* wrote similarly that, "As a direct result of the distribution of 'Vermont Summer Resorts' tourists are coming to Vermont in larger numbers than ever before. They will find a state beautiful beyond their expectations and they will spread the story of Vermont's scenic attractions." That year's state Republican platform declared, "No small investment by the state has yielded better returns than the appropriation made to establish the Publicity Bureau."[47] The Bennington *Banner* congratulated Bailey on his success in "working for a Greater Vermont," praising him as a perfect example of how "an efficient public servant can make a small sum go a long way." The *Banner* went on to quote a BOP publication that claimed, "Vermont has fish and game laws especially devised to accommodate the visitor, and money is expended freely to keep the waters of the state plentifully supplied with trout, bass, pike and other fish."[48] Guy Bailey was doing his best to let the world know that Vermont was open for the pleasure of outsiders.

Bailey was not alone in that mission. Vermont's leaders were charging forward with a vision of the dual narratives of tradition and progress as complementary to each other. This vision was the motivating force behind the founding in February 1912 of the Greater Vermont Association (GVA). The GVA got its name from the phrase popular among the advocates of progress since early in the previous decade; essentially interchangeable with the also-popular "New Vermont," it had originated to describe a new air of optimism, much of which was owed to the tourism boom. The association was pledged to serve as a federation of local and state organizations to the end of "the social and intellectual uplift of the State, as well as the development of Vermont's natural resources," and also "as a means of enabling visitors to become favorably impressed by the manifold beauties and resources of the Green Mountain State."[49] The Burlington *Free Press* greeted it by saying that it would be "a central organization which shall stand for the whole State, representing this forward sweep in the various towns, and which shall mean a 'Greater Vermont.'" That development of resources and preservation of beauties might be in conflict with each other was not part of the association's narrative. According to its constitution, the GVA's mission was "to foster Vermont's agricultural, industrial and commercial interests," and its members recognized that outsiders to the state must play an essential role in working toward that goal.[50] At the meeting at which it was founded, Guy Bailey gave a speech describing the work of the Bureau of Publicity.[51] The GVA began lobbying out-of-state magazines and newspapers to profile Vermont, and in 1913 it published the pamphlet, *The Salient Features of Vermont as a Vacation State.*[52]

James P. Taylor was the key figure behind the GVA's founding. A New York native, Taylor had been hired as a teacher at a private Vermont high school in 1908. An outdoor enthusiast, Taylor organized a hiking club at the school. Expanding his vision, the next year he founded the Green Mountain Club (GMC) at a meeting in Burlington. It was Taylor's vision to "make the Vermont mountains play a larger part in the life of the people."[53] To that end he wanted to develop a hiking trail that would span the whole state. The Bureau of Publicity praised the Green Mountain Club, writing in its 1911 pamphlet *Playground of the Continent* that, led by "some prominent people in the State," the club planned to "make the various peaks more accessible." Peru's most prominent citizen, Marshall Hapgood, was a vice president of the Green Mountain Club, and Guy Bailey was chair of its publicity committee. In 1912 work began on the Long Trail, its route taking it through Peru. The GMC made quick progress: Taylor reported the Long Trail half completed by the end of 1914. That year an estimated 15,000 people hiked on the trail.[54] By that time Taylor had resigned his teaching position to become secretary of the Greater Vermont Association.

Meanwhile, so successful did the legislature consider the Bureau of Publicity's work that it doubled its appropriation in 1913 to $10,000.[55] This generous allotment followed an appearance by Bailey before the legislature during which he read requests for his publications from across the country, and from letters from some of those who had purchased farms as a direct result of his advertising.[56] Armed with that extra money, Bailey hired Walter H. Crockett, a well-regarded historian, to occupy the new position of director of the bureau.[57] Crockett's first contribution, an update of *Vermont Summer Resorts*, described Vermont in such glowing terms that its prose surpassed even Bailey's previous paeans to the state. Crockett wrote,

> To you, whether weary in mind and body you seek repose, or whether in the flush of health you seek recreation, whosoever you may be and wheresoever you may abide, but more especially to you who dwell in the brick and marble canyons of great cities, and are weary of the never-ending crash and clangor of man-made noises and the ceaseless refrain of hurrying feet, this is presented, in the sincere hope that in the balsam laden breezes that murmur over her hilltops, or in the silvery whisper of her lakes and streams, or in the peace that abides in the shadow of her mountains, you may find your heart's desire.[58]

The following year Bailey commenced publication of a list of Vermont summer resorts. Bailey and Crockett expanded their efforts to publicize Vermont in 1913, placing advertisements in East Coast newspapers for the first time.[59] They also published a new brochure, *Vermont:*

The Land of Green Mountains.[60] The Boston *Transcript* called the pamphlet "an admirable presentation of Vermont's unappreciated capacities for meeting the desires of a large class of vacationists…one would have to go far to find a piece of advertising literature at once so dignified, so charming, and so full of informational value." Reprinting the *Transcript's* article, the Barre *Times* concluded, "It does seem that Vermont is on the right track toward the New Vermont which has been largely on paper."[61]

If Vermont was headed toward renewal, the increasing popularity of the automobile had more and more to do with it. The Bureau of Publicity's road map pamphlet was among its most requested. A businessman from Brookline, Massachusetts, wrote to the Publicity Bureau that he had made four trips to St. Albans and wanted to "congratulate you and your State on the fine roads you are building and know it is only a question of time when Vermont will rank high up among the States that are the tourists' delight for motor travel."[62] Description of Vermont roads as already good and improving was something state leaders loved to hear, but they knew there was much work to be done on them.

In 1913 the Bureau of Publicity also began to take more seriously the task given it to stimulate the economy beyond increasing tourism. In late 1913 it published *Vermont Farms: Some Facts and Figures Concerning the Agricultural Resources and Opportunities of the Green Mountain State*, a pamphlet designed to create greater interest in the purchase of Vermont farms for agriculture. It claimed, "the state of Vermont offers opportunities for profitable farming equal to all and superior to most of the states of the Union."[63] The following year the bureau published the first edition of a volume called *Industrial Vermont*. This lengthy book detailed the possibilities for industrial development in each Vermont town. In an echo of Alonzo Valentine 25 years before, Bailey compiled it by sending forms he called "blanks" to "five or six" people in each town. Bailey added in the introduction to this pamphlet that if readers desired, they could also receive copies of other Publicity Bureau publications, including *Vermont, the Land of Green Mountains*, the purpose of which was to "set forth the scenic attractions of the state." The publication displayed no sense at all that there was any conflict between the bureau's work promoting Vermont as an idyllic retreat from the modern world for tourists, and its work promoting the state as a place with natural resources to be exploited. Indeed, scenic beauty and industrial development were portrayed as complementary, with no perceived inconsistency or conflict between them.[64]

Family Tragedies and Economic Hardships

The Bureau of Publicity was selling a beautiful, flawless, pristine state. That was very much how young Samuel Ogden of Elizabeth, New Jersey, saw Peru. He later remembered with special fondness a Christmas vacation in 1910 at the Grants' place just east of the village.[65] Two years later he was photographed holding one wing of an experimental glider built by Charles Grant, the family's older son.[66] Peru's reputation as a tourist town continued to grow. Despite the challenge of reaching it from the train stations in Danby, Dorset, or Manchester, farms continued to be purchased as summer homes, and Bromley House was doing very good business.

For Major Valentine's Swedes, life had not been ideal. In 1909 tragedy struck the Anderson family: Father Edwin died of trichinosis, leaving his widow Emma and her seven children at home to make a go at working their mortgaged farm in Londonderry. Oldest sons Carl and Charles worked in a nearby lumber mill. Eighteen-year-old son Harry worked as a farm laborer, while 16-year-old Esther worked for a local family as a servant.[67] Daughter Hilma and her husband Alonzo Butler were also living in Londonderry, with Alonzo supporting their two young sons doing what the census recorded as "odd jobs."[68] Tragedy also struck the Westines in 1910: A son, Francis Carl, died at the age of two days after being born prematurely. It was not a new experience; Carl and Anna had lost an infant in 1900.

It was not just misfortune and tragedy that made the Swedes' lives hard. The evolution of the local economy around them was gradually making life more difficult. The peak number of Vermont farms had been registered in the 1880 census, at around 35,500. By 1910 that number was down to around 32,700, which if not a dramatic decrease indicated the trend at work.[69] Likewise, the timber industry was in decline, due not just to the forest management movement but also to longer-term processes having to do with shifting markets and the depleted stock of Vermont timber. Forest conservation certainly mattered, however, and the Landgrove Swedes' region is an instructive example. In 1910 Marshall Hapgood, owner of not only the Bromley House but also a large lumber mill, donated the summit of Bromley Mountain and a large surrounding area to the state. Hapgood, who reveled in his nickname "the rugged reformer," stipulated that no trees would ever again be cut on the mountain's summit.[70] These and other long-term trends caused Landgrove's population to decline yet further. The population of the town in 1910 was 160 compared to 225 ten years earlier, a loss of nearly 30 percent. To an extent Landgrove's economy was interwoven with that of surrounding towns, and Dorset's marble industry had never regained the stature it held in the 1890s.[71] There was among state leaders and newspapers much talk about a "New Vermont," with its promise of more industrial development and increased tourism revenue. But to the extent that the old Vermont of small-scale farming and unfettered resource extraction had sustained the regular families in the Landgrove area, the "New Vermont" did not promise much.

This evolution is reflected in the degree to which Valentine's Swedes were engaged in unsteady work. Three years after his 1907 marriage to May Swenson, and with two small boys, Charlie Neilson was working as a farm laborer in Putney. Charlie's brother also worked as a farm laborer, in Weston. Lottie Nyren's husband, Eddie Tifft, was doing no better, except that at the age of 48 he was 20 years older than Charlie Neilson. Eddie, Lottie, and their four children rented a small house in Weston, where Eddie worked as a farm laborer. Three years later, when their final child, a son named Richard, was born, Eddie's prospects were no brighter.[72] Eddie might have been wise to follow Lottie's brothers in moving away from the traditional occupations of farming and lumbering: Oliver gained an insurance license around this time, while Carl found work as a machinist at a refrigerator repair shop in Arlington. Meanwhile, when the oldest Westine child, Jennie, married, it was not without some irony. Were he still alive, Alonzo Valentine might have found it disconcerting that some of his Swedes, such as Anna Nyren, married people of French Canadian heritage. Jennie's choice of a husband presented a different renunciation of the task Valentine had assigned his recruits. Back in 1890 a Wilmington attorney, writing to a newspaper in support of the Valentine's scheme and complaining that out-migration had taken away "those with the most energetic push," frowned that among those left behind "cousin has married cousin until the race has about run out."[73] These were the people Swedes were to replace. Twenty years later, Jennie married her cousin Julius Westine, who worked as a carpenter in Londonderry.[74] At the time of the ceremony Jennie was three months pregnant.

Despite the challenges, it was still possible to make a living farming in Landgrove. Axel Neilson was doing well on his farm just over the town line in Peru. Like Carl Westine, Axel was well on his way to becoming, according to a town historian later, a "useful citizen of the community."[75] His brother John was not as successful, but by 1910 he owned his own farm in Landgrove, and there was much compensation for a challenging line of work in the rich community life that surrounded him. His son Charlie lived in Athol, Massachusetts, and his daughter Anna lived in Reading, Vermont, where her husband worked in the lumber industry, but he still had two sons at home.[76] His brother lived a short walk away, and the Westine family lived even closer. The Andersons were not far away in Londonderry, nor were the Nyrens in Pawlet. Through his son Charlie's marriage to May, John Neilson was able to stay close to the Swensons in Massachusetts. These were families he had known back in Glava, Varmland, and John could take pleasure in seeing their children grow.

In April 1914 Charlie Neilson visited Landgrove from Massachusetts with good news: May was pregnant again with a child to add to their two sons, and Charlie and May were planning on moving back to Landgrove. The weather was unusually warm for late April, and with the snow melting the early wildflowers were coming out in the valleys.[77] Around ten o'clock on the night of April 19, Charlie, his brother Harry, and uncle Axel set out from John's house to Axel's, from where Charlie could get an earlier start the next day to catch a train back to Athol. To get there they needed to cross over a bridge, known locally as the "Michigan Bridge," that spanned the West River in Peru. The rapid spring thaw caused the river to be very high and the current swift. The bridge had no railing, and in the darkness the three men became separated. Axel and Harry made their way to Axel's house, and it was only there that they realized Charlie was not with them. Charlie had, in fact, lost his footing on the bridge (one newspaper reported he "walked off the side"), been swept away by the river, and drowned. His body was found the next day in a nearby field.[78] Seven months later May gave birth to a daughter, Mildred Arlene Neilson. In December a United States marshal in Rutland filed suit against the town of Peru on behalf of the administrator of Charlie's estate, his father-in-law Adolph Swenson. Requesting $15,000, the suit alleged that the bridge was "not sufficiently protected for the safe use of persons." The claim was ultimately unsuccessful. In a newspaper article on the suit, Peru was described as a "well known Vermont summer and winter resort."[79]

To Guy Bailey's Bureau of Publicity, Vermont was *Designed by the Creator for the Playground of the Continent.* But it was not a playground for many working-class Vermonters. The burst of progressive reform fervor that had characterized the state after 1900 had not solved all of its problems; the Michigan Bridge in Peru was hardly the only unsafe aspect of the state. For many Vermont was a hard place to live. It was the poorest state in New England, characterized by remote communities linked by poor transportation. Boosters of tourism conjured an idyllic narrative of the state's scenery, but it was a working landscape as well, not only for agriculture but also for industry, and the mills and factories spread throughout the state were prone to the same problems as elsewhere. Indeed, in 1915 Carl Nyren was injured so badly while working at the refrigerator shop that he lost sight in one eye.[80] But these problems were gaining greater attention. A coalition of civic interest groups, including the recently formed Vermont branch of the National Child Labor Committee, conducted investigations that found that many workers, and especially women, worked in dark, unhealthful factories and mills for up to 14 hours a day. The state legislature responded to these reports by raising the age threshold for children employed in railroads, mills, factories, and quarries to 14. The law was largely ignored, however, and child labor, along with unsafe work conditions and long hours, remained a problem.[81] Efforts were also made to improve the education system by further centralizing authority over schools in state agencies, and standardizing the length of school terms and the course of study.[82] Yet, like the conditions of child labor, the education Vermont children earned varied widely and could be very poor. Most towns' system of welfare, the "poor farms" to which indigent citizens were consigned, was another source of exasperation. When one reformer conducted a study of welfare in 1916, titled *Poor Relief in Vermont,* he condemned poor farms as capricious, cruel, and

antiquated, writing that he "hoped to see more of the tendency to cen-
tralize the agencies for relief and care of the dependent classes," as was
the trend in other aspects of the state. In these and other areas of life,
the general direction of reformers and politicians was to use increasingly modern methods, and increasingly larger institutions, to rectify
the problems that plagued Vermont.[83]

"Unspoiled Vermont"

Problems like inadequate education, the persistence of child labor, and
unsafe working conditions across a range of industries, and the modern, centralized institutions constructed to address them, did not fit the
narrative constructed for Vermont by boosters of tourism. Indeed, a 1915
Bureau of Publicity pamphlet promoting automobile tourism outdid its
predecessors in touting Vermont as idyllic. *The Green Mountain Tour:
Vermont, The Unspoiled Land* was co-written by Mortimer Proctor of
the wealthy Rutland marble family. It began, "Vermont, the Unspoiled
Land, is a region of hills, valleys, forests, lakes, rivers, meadowlands,
mountains, sturdy men and noble women. Within the borders of this
Commonwealth one finds Nature unspoiled. Nature revealing won-
drous beauty, and offering a charming, friendly pleasure ground which
invites most heartily the wanderer and explorer." The pamphlet's message to out-of-state tourists was, "If you come to Vermont from another
state, we welcome you most cordially into the heart of Old New England, into Vermont, the Unspoiled Land." Unspoiled Vermont obviously was not, but if the phrase resonated with visitors, then that was
how the bureau would portray Vermont. It continued its advertising
efforts in the years that followed, issuing new pamphlets with florid
names that sent much of the same message as Proctor's: that Vermont
was "unspoiled" by modern problems, and maintained a traditional way
of life that stood in sharp contrast to more modern places. First came
The Lake Region of Eastern Vermont and *The Lake Region of Western Vermont*. Another 1918 release was *The Lure of Vermont's Silent Places*, which
rhapsodized that, "where deer browse lazily in verdant upland pastures;
where the she-bear rears her cub in the depths of virgin forests; where
countless brooks and rivers hide the shy and wily trout; where all Nature seems a-calling; there, there you'll find the Silent Places of Ver-

mont." Vermont was special because "No large cities have sprung up with their attendant evils and advantages. Life in Vermont is true country life more so than in any other Eastern state. There are no grimy cities where hearthstones are cold and tables bare, where poverty brings misery and crime rages rampant." Appealing not just to many Americans' affinity for rural life but also their ethnic prejudices, the pamphlet claimed that "Today Vermont is one of the few remaining places where the ideals of our forefathers have a chance to be nurtured and brought to a full realization." The mission of the Bureau of Publicity had never been to play a direct role in rectifying problems like poverty, unsafe work conditions, and child labor. Its responsibility was to give its out-of-state audience the impression such things did not exist in Vermont.[84]

Despite tourism's expanding centrality to Vermont's economy, in the 1910s there was quite a bit of resentment toward the industry. Many Vermonters were distressed that, as one newspaper wrote, "Vermont has fish and game laws especially devised to accommodate the visitor."[85] The slogan "Vermont for Vermonters" gained popularity among those who thought the state was overrun with, and overly supplicant to, outsiders.[86] One letter to the editor of a newspaper in 1913 denounced the Bureau of Publicity's slogans and offered "Vermont for Vermonters" as a replacement, asking in frustration, "why should Vermont become a 'playground for the rest of the country,' a place for 'tired city dwellers' to congregate, a haven of refuge for worn-out millionaires to spend their last days?" The letter wondered if it was worth it if the cost of the effort to alleviate "the sufferings of the city dwellers" was that the state was "moved to sacrifice its own interests." Even if it was, the writer called it "charity largely misdirected," since "those who most need it are not able to take advantage of it. Those who do reap the benefit are the owners of motor cars and yachts." Another newspaper noted in 1913 the "desire among some otherwise good citizens to have our scanty population build a wall around the limits of Vermont...to preserve 'Vermont for Vermonters.'"[87] But those with misgivings about the wisdom of emphasizing tourism had a negligible effect on state policy.

In 1915 the publisher of the magazine *The Vermonter* wrote that the work of institutions like the Greater Vermont Association and the Bureau of Publicity had led to "New forces...being propelled across our state—into industrial, agricultural, and social life," creating a "Utopian dream of Vermont—'Perfect as a garden and as beautiful as a park.'"[88]

If it could be utopian in its beauty, it also needed to be a place that provided jobs for its citizens. But by the time *The Lure of Vermont's Silent Places* was published, such a reconciliation of beauty and industrial development left public discourse in Vermont of two minds, which can be seen in how Valentine's Swedish recruitment scheme was recalled. On one hand was a narrative that Vermont's backwardness had become a great asset. In a 1915 article titled "Vermont Offers Cheap Summer Homes," a reporter for the Burlington *Free Press* wrote that "once upon a time the abandoned farm was hailed as a disgrace," but in fact the belief they existed "seems to have served a splendid purpose to attract summer residents on the plea that a summer home could be purchased cheap." The article then recalled the "hullaballoo" surrounding Valentine's scheme. The fact that "that project did not succeed entirely" in regenerating rural Vermont was fortunate, "for many neglected spots in the Green Mountain State are now occupied by the summer homes of prosperous citizens of other States who are bringing their wealth to Vermont."[89] On the other hand, a desire for economic growth caused the Bennington *Banner* to look back at Valentine's scheme when recommending that the state provide a "farm sale agent in connection with the publicity department" to attract farmers to available properties. "Twenty years ago" Valentine had made "a good start in this line" by recruiting "a number of Swedish and Norwegian families" who had proven themselves to be "among the best citizens of Vermont." Regrettably, the program was "choked to death without being given a fair trial," which the *Banner* saw as "one of the most unfortunate things that ever happened in Vermont." Writing that "the chance to develop the agricultural resources of the state were never so good as now," the *Banner* called for a new effort similar to Valentine's, though focused on American farmers and not Scandinavians.[90]

Certainly, many of Vermont's leaders were intensely conscious of the need to develop and exploit the state's natural resources. In the vision they conjured, development would not contradict Vermont being "perfect as a park." Among the advantages would be the amelioration of the great problem Vermonters had long faced of how to keep their children from emigrating. Walter Crockett directly addressed this issue in the Bureau of Publicity's 1916 edition of *Vermont: Its Resources and Opportunities*. He wrote that the volume's goal was to "present for the consideration of the pupils in Vermont schools, facts concerning the agricultural, industrial and other resources of Vermont already developed." Crockett offered the volume to young Vermonters who "desire to know what opportunities the state can offer its ambitious sons and daughters before they seek opportunities elsewhere."[91] It is a fair question to ask, however, if providing those opportunities was being made more difficult when Vermont, much because of the work of the Bureau of Publicity, was putting so much effort into satisfying the desires of affluent tourists.

The Kerosene Fire

Children leaving Vermont had been a prime issue of concern for Vermonters going back a century, but Carl Westine was doing well in that regard. He may not have qualified as one of "the best citizens of Vermont," but he was one of Landgrove's. All five of his children lived either at home or close by. Further cementing the family's close ties to the local community, daughter Della married Lyle Bolster, from a long-standing Landgrove family, in May 1916, six months after the birth of their son, Floyd. Lyle had been lured away by employment in Massachusetts for a few weeks earlier that spring, but he was back and intended to stay. The child's birth certificate listed Lyle as a farmer, and a farmer he wanted to remain.[92] The wedding was a highlight of a good period of life for Carl Westine. He was the foreman at a local sawmill owned by Marshall Hapgood, and played a useful role in the public affairs of Landgrove.[93] Axel Neilson could tell a similar story of success. His farm was thriving, and in 1915 his son Alve married Mary Ethel Beers; like the Bolsters, the Beers were a long-time local family. Charlotte Nyren Tifft found life much more difficult. By 1917 she had taken a job as a cook in the boarding house of a Sandgate lumber camp in which her husband Eddie worked. Her marriage was crumbling; Eddie was both unfaithful and oppressively jealous. Her oldest children, Charles, Addie, and Carl, were approaching marrying age. Charles, born in 1894, was working as a lumberman. The other Nyrens remained connected to the Swedish families in Landgrove; Harry Neilson, for example, was employed for a while around 1916 in Pawlet, and must have had contact with a family around whom he had been raised.[94] But life for Lottie Tifft in the remote lumber camp was not only hard, it was extremely isolating. It hardly fit the image of the "Unspoiled Vermont."

Lottie Tifft had her own troubles, and might have given little thought to the European war that was now in its third year, or the re-election campaign of President Woodrow Wilson, who was vowing in the summer of 1916 to keep America out of that war. Large, long-term social and economic forces were working against the kind of isolation Lottie experienced. Progressive reforms had led to greater standard-ization and oversight by state government. Automobiles were increas-ingly reshaping everyday life. And the exertions of Guy Bailey's Bu-reau of Publicity, in concert with the Greater Vermont Association, the Green Mountain Club, and other agencies and individuals, were spreading the message that Vermont was open for the use of outsiders. Promoters of tourism even saw the war in Europe as an opportunity. James Taylor, speaking to a meeting of the Vermont Maple Sugar Makers' Association in 1915 in his capacity as secretary of the Greater Vermont Association, said that a "special effort" should be made to attract people "in the large centers who long for the rest and quiet and beauty of the country" because "they cannot go abroad on account of the conditions existing there."[95] Apparently, slaughter on the fields of Europe presented opportunity.

After their wedding, Lyle and Della Bolster settled in South Lon-donderry, where Della's sisters Jennie and Nola lived. Lyle worked as a store clerk while looking to take up a farm.[96] Woodrow Wilson won reelection as president, and soon after invited the warring European nations to a peace conference. Della Bolster, her husband, son, and sis-ter Nola spent Thanksgiving of 1916 at her parents' house in Landgrove. Lyle Bolster was hired in December to drive the stagecoach that trav-eled from Londonderry to Manchester. Della and family again visited her parents a few days before Christmas.[97] As 1917 began the prospects that America might enter the war increased, as German submarines sank American merchant vessels. At the beginning of March, Wilson released the Zimmerman Telegram, and the sinking of three American ships on March 18 pushed the United States to the brink of war.[98]

Those global events seemed far off in the area surrounding Land-grove. In the middle of the month Lyle, Della, and their 15-month-old infant Floyd moved to a rented farm in Jamaica. On March 24, Della was preparing a meal in the kitchen while Floyd played on the floor. A spark from the kitchen stove flew into a can of kerosene sitting near the baby, igniting it. The flames immediately caught Floyd's clothes on fire. Della grabbed the baby and tried to rush out of the house, but the first door she tried was locked, costing her precious seconds. When she made it outside she rolled herself and the baby in snow, and her cries attracted neighbors, who rushed over and extinguished the flames. A doctor was summoned as quickly as possible, but the child died that night. Della was alive, but with the exception of one leg she was burned "practically all over," and was not expected to survive.[99] A newspaper reported three days later that Della's condition had improved a bit, but only in that she was more comfortable. There was, reported a newspaper, "small hope of recovery." Her mother Anna at her side, Della died on April 4. That same day, Congress began deliberation of the resolution to declare war against Germany, and two workers at the Fairbanks Scales factory in St. Johnsbury, Vermont, had a fistfight over American entry into the war in what the Brattleboro *Reformer* called the "First War Clash in [a] Vermont Shop." On April 6, the day of Della's funeral, the United States Senate voted 82 to 6 in favor of the declaration of war. The Londonderry *Sifter* reported two days later that Della's mother had returned to Landgrove, where her daughter "will be remembered as Della Westine and will be greatly missed by her many friends here." The *Sifter* also reported in the same issue that Harold Neilson, son of John Nielson, had gone to Bellows Falls to enlist in the army.[100]

CHAPTER 5

The Last Years of the Old Landgrove

Landgrove at the Outset of the "New Era"

AMERICA IN THE YEARS immediately following World War I was characterized by reaction and social conflict, as illustrated by the Red Scare and the rise of the second Ku Klux Klan. Some pointed to America's increasingly urban nature as a source of the nation's problems. Rural America, they believed, was the *real* America, the virtuous reservoir of proper American values.[1] In March 1921 the Burlington *Free Press* reported on a proposed federal program to divert immigrants to rural places as a means to assimilate them. The point of the program would be, reported the *Free Press*, to "do away with the 'Red' danger," based on the principle that a farm was "the best sort of an Americanization school." The *Free Press* thought the plan well-intentioned, if unusual, since movement from city to country at the time was generally confined to those "in fashionable life," the wealthy who wanted a country home. In recent years, however, had come the telephone, the daily delivery of morning newspapers, automobiles, and "community uplift movements," the result of which was to put farming areas "in touch with the whole world, and rural communities began to come into their own." Rural places had benefited no less than cities from progress. It was a line of thinking consistent with the narrative espoused by Vermont's Bureau of Publicity, in which the state balanced modernity with the remnants of an older, better America. That *Free Press* article went on to recall Alonzo Valentine's Swedish experiment. The reporter, who recalled being informed about the program by

95

Valentine directly, thought it had been a promising opportunity that state government had squandered. Valentine had established "colonies of Swedes in Vermont, not with the idea of making a profit from the sale of land but building up Vermont as a commonwealth and developing her natural resources." The author concluded, "We would like to know what has been the final influence of those Swedish colonists on Vermont."[2]

Of course, the recruitment program's major influence on the state had been its role in stimulating tourism. The influence of the Swedes on Landgrove, meanwhile, had been that they had gone about their lives quietly. When the United States entered World War I, many of the children of Valentine's Swedes served their country. Willie Westine, Carl's only son, was still mourning his sister Della when on June 4, 1917, he registered for the draft.[3] He was called up for training later that year, but did not go off to the war immediately; the next summer saw him still in Landgrove, where he spent some of his time working as a carpenter and performing road work for the town.[4] In June 1918 he married a woman from the nearby the town of Chester.[5] Called up for active service soon after, he was given leave from the Army in September for the birth of his first child, a daughter named Reta Della.[6] Willie's sister Freda also married in 1918, to a Londonderry man employed in construction by her cousin, and brother-in-law, Julius. The Anderson family was barely hanging on to their farm in Londonderry when 30-year-old Carl, employed in a sawmill, registered for the draft. He applied for relief on account of his mother's dependence on him, but his draft card noted "mother cares for self." The sons of Axel and John Neilson also played their part in the war. Axel's son Alve, at the time a tenant farmer in Massachusetts with a pregnant wife, was drafted in 1917 and served nearly two years in France.[7] Alve's cousin Harry Neilson also applied for a draft exemption on account of the dependence of his mother and father, but that only delayed his service for a year; called up for service in July 1918, he served until the following January.[8] His brother Harold had a dramatic military experience: Enlisting in 1917, he was assigned to the 1st Vermont Infantry and found himself overseas by October 1917. He was slightly wounded in action in June 1918. For a time he was reported missing in action, and there was relief among his acquaintances when his parents received a letter from him.[9] When Charlotte Nyren

Tifft's oldest son Charles registered for the draft in 1917 his profession was listed as a teamster; in the place where his employer was to be listed was written, "no one just now." Though he perhaps could have used the work, Charles was never called into service.

Meanwhile, in 1917 Guy Bailey resigned as secretary of state to become controller of the University of Vermont. There was some discussion in newspapers that Walter Crockett should be appointed to replace Bailey, but he was passed over for the job and remained in charge of the Bureau of Publicity. Throughout the war the bureau continued to publish and distribute promotional pamphlets.[10] In 1917 Crockett went on an automobile tour of the state, after which he published a letter in a Vermont newspaper advocating that the roads along Lake Champlain be widened, improved, and linked together. This, Crockett wrote, "would be one of the greatest attractions that any state could offer to tourists."[11] In 1918 the BOP issued new editions of the two companion volumes, *The Lakes of Eastern Vermont* and *The Lakes of Western Vermont*.[12] In his usual florid prose, Crockett wrote that there was "no region in this or any other country possessing a beauty more alluring, or expressing the grace of the fashion of Nature's charm more eloquently than Vermont."

Some of those who visited Vermont to avail themselves of Crockett's alluring beauty also served in the war. Samuel Ogden, at the time an undergraduate at Swarthmore College, enlisted in the Army in August 1917. He was sent overseas and saw combat on the front lines. By the end of the war he had achieved the rank of first lieutenant and was awarded the Croix de Guerre for bravery.[13] Ogden survived the trenches, but his dear friend Duncan Grant, whose family had introduced Ogden to Peru, was not as lucky. Duncan had acquired his brother Charlie's fascination with aviation and became a pilot. In 1918 he died in an airplane accident at an English airfield and was buried in a Peru cemetery. Following the end of the war Ogden studied briefly at the Université de Grenoble before returning home to finish impatiently his Swarthmore education ahead of schedule.[14] The war had a profound impact on Ogden. While an undergraduate at Swarthmore he had felt, as he later put it, "very much at loose ends." "I dreamed dreams," he recalled, "but somehow I lacked faith, and there was no confidence within me that the stuff of romantical dreams could be transmuted by me into the sober patterns of reality, and all of life seemed unspeakably dull." He reminisced that he had felt that "things were off track, and that more spiritual and more humane considerations were being left behind" by the trajectory of modern society. The experience of the war impressed upon him greatly that "the things which had truly mattered in the life of human beings were not the fast buck nor submission to the materialistic rat race." He returned after graduation to New Jersey, "unable to easily accept the options which confronted me."[15] Accept them he nevertheless did, taking the position in his father's insurance firm prepared for him.

The war brought changes large and small to Vermont. It briefly improved the agricultural economy, as prices for crops like dairy products, wheat, corn, and potatoes increased.[16] The war also stimulated some segments of Vermont manufacturing. The machine-tool industry, for example, centered to the east of Landgrove along the Connecticut River and already expanding because of its ties to automobile manufacturing, benefited greatly. Other important sectors of Vermont manufacturing did not fare as well. Stone and quarrying companies not only saw a decline in demand for their products, but also experienced a loss of workers to military service and to better-paying jobs elsewhere.[17] Closer to Landgrove, the Peru Turnpike, built around 1810 and the last of Vermont's private toll roads, was taken over by the state through eminent domain. For many years motorists had complained of the road's deplorable condition; early motorists had been forced to carry planks to place across ruts. The state committed funds to the road's improvement, and in yet another incremental way, Landgrove was opened further to the outside world.[18]

The economic boom brought on by the war ended with it. As the demand for agricultural products slackened, so did prices. Manufacturing generally went into decline, as well, as America headed into a severe economic contraction that lasted until 1921. For a while, Willie Westine was able to ride out the postwar downturn with continued military service, but that did not protect him from tragedy. While he was stationed at a Massachusetts army base in January 1919 his infant daughter Reta took sick with pneumonia. Willie was given leave, but she died before he could arrive home in Weston. The ranks of the five Landgrove patriarchs dwindled to three in 1920 when John Neilson died. In that year's census, his wife Louise was listed as owner of their farm, and the only one of her three living children still at home was son Harry. Soon after her husband's death, Louise leased the farm to Harry for ten years, hoping it would continue to provide her a home. Axel Neilson had done considerably better financially than his brother John, and in 1920 he sold his farm over the town line in Peru to his oldest son Alve and purchased a larger farm, known as the "corner house," along the Landgrove Road.[19] Axel was a respected man locally who, among other things, had served as a grand juror in Bennington County, and when they moved into their new home a Brattleboro newspaper reported that "everyone is glad to welcome them."[20] His second son, John Dolph, moved with his father and mother. John Dolph was a heavyset, cheerful man, rather childlike in disposition, and popular around town for it. Other descendants of the original Swedes remained nearby. Lottie Tifft's son Carl lived in Peru, boarding with a family for whom he worked as farm laborer. For her own part, in 1920 Lottie was still the cook at the Sandgate lumber camp of entrepreneur Richard Miles, living in a boarding house with 27 male workers, including her husband Eddie. Perhaps indicative of her failing marriage, the census listed her separately from her husband. Their son Richard, who was seven, also lived in the camp. A mountaintop lumber camp was apparently too rough a place for a girl, however: Daughter Mildred Tifft, who was 11, lived with her uncle Oliver and grandparents in Pawlet, so that she would have easier access to schooling.[21]

Of the five families, the Andersons had the least presence in the area by the end of the war. Hilma Anderson Butler lived in nearby Danby with husband Alonzo, and Harry and wife Cora Wilkins lived a few miles away in Jamaica. Harry's marriage was an indication of how integrated into the surrounding community the Swedes had become after 30 years: The Wilkinses were a numerous family that went back in Dorset over a hundred years, and Cora was the daughter of Julia Beebe Wilkins, the sister of Hilma's mother-in-law, Agnes.[22] Sometime in 1919 the rest of the Anderson family—mother Emma, four daughters, and son Carl and his wife Celia—finally gave up on the Londonderry farm and moved to Greenfield, Massachusetts, where the daughters and Celia found work as polishers in a tool shop while Carl was a bottler at a creamery.

Thus, if the *Free Press* had wanted to know what had become of Valentine's Landgrove Swedes, the answer was that they had blended in. The cohort of the second generation, the children of the five original couples, had reached maturity. Most lived in Vermont. Some had moved to industrial towns in other regions of the state; Anna Nyren, for example, lived in White River Junction. Others had stayed in the Landgrove area, intermarrying with local families and mostly employed in traditional rural jobs. The population of almost all of these towns—Landgrove, Peru, Dorset, and others—declined between 1910 and 1920, but for those who stayed any limitations or sacrifices required to live in the area were superseded by its attractions. Not least of these was that it was a genuinely beautiful place. That landscape was partly natural, but significantly—in its farms, its buildings, its mostly denuded hillsides—it was the creation of people like them. As the 1920s proceeded, the pressure from those outside the state who were attracted to that landscape, and who perhaps did not appreciate the extent to which it was shaped by locals, grew.

The Selling of Vermont After World War I

One wonders if, 30 years on from their arrival, Major Valentine's Swedes and their descendants gave much thought to the program that had brought them to Vermont. State newspapers on the whole had long lost interest in its memory, with a few rare exceptions. In 1921 the St. Albans *Messenger* recalled the program as having provoked "a tremendous controversy" that "raged over a publicity statement regarding abandoned farms." Dismissing the existence of abandoned farms, the *Messenger* believed that the publicity surrounding the recruitment program had led out-of-state newspapers "to speak of our commonwealth as a state of abandoned farms, and no end of damage was done as a result."[23] The Bureau of Publicity might have disagreed about the consequences of Valentine's scheme. By its account tourism was reaching unprecedented heights in the early postwar years. Director Walter Crockett and his assistant Florence Cummings were very busy.[24] The bureau still considered some of its responsibility to be promoting industry. In 1919, for example, Crockett made it known that he had forwarded to a St. Johnsbury commercial club a letter from a New York piano company looking to locate a factory in the state.[25] A few years earlier a St. Johnsbury newspaper had written that the BOP's chief job was "doing the splendid work to exploit the resources of the state," with the goal of making Vermont "as important an industrial commonwealth as any of its sister states of southern New England."[26] But decisively the bureau's focus remained the promotion of tourism. In 1919 it published the initial edition of *Vermont Cottages and Residential Properties for Rent or for Sale.*[27] To improve the publication, it placed advertisements in many Vermont newspapers requesting hotel and inn owners to contact it for free inclusion in future issues. The bureau's employees were kept busy responding to inquiries about vacations and the purchase of second homes. A newspaper in the northern part of the state wrote in January that the agency "plans to concentrate its efforts to a considerable extent in the coming year in a development of the summer homes idea," specifying especially that "there is a large number of persons, particularly in the teaching profession, who have long summer vacations. Many business men desire to establish summer homes for their families where they may spend their week-end in addition to a vacation of a few weeks." The wonderful thing about this was that, "In many mountain towns the population has decreased steadily for more than half a century. There is an opportunity to build up these waste places by attracting summer residents." The newspaper was confident that "a combination of attractive scenery and low prices will bring purchasers," and saw no drawbacks to that.[28] Second-home buyers could simply take up property left to languish by migrants. Rural depopulation, a crisis in the Gilded Age, now had its advantages.

The Bureau of Publicity was nothing else if not prolific in the volume of its publications. In 1920 a librarian in St. Johnsbury tried to gather promotional literature of the other states in the region, and found that "Vermont led them all in state publicity work and in the publication of attractive booklets describing our lakes and mountains."[29] The bureau also stepped up its campaign to advertise in out-of-state newspapers. A typical advertisement appeared in the New York *Tribune* in May headlined, "You can afford a Summer Home in Vermont." It claimed that "Vermont stands preeminent as a land of summer home opportunities" where "you and your family can rest and recuperate." Calling Vermont "the Switzerland of America," the ad assured readers that "Wonderful landscape views are everywhere available, and picturesque little farmhouses can be purchased and remodeled at very moderate expense."[30]

Crockett was eager to let Vermonters know about the fruits of the BOP's labors. An October 1920 newspaper article titled "Results Follow Work of Publicity Bureau" consisted largely of letters to the bureau from tourists. The letters are, not surprisingly, fulsome with praise both for the bureau's publications and Vermont's appeal as a vacation destination. Two things stand out in the letters. The first is the increasing impact on the state of automobiles. A banker from Maine wrote, "I have been in Vermont with an automobile and am coming again. I wish you would send me another set of these booklets and I will pass them to a friend, who has a car and is planning a trip next summer." A Massachusetts automobile club reported that it had sent Bureau of Publicity publications and maps to similar clubs across the country, calling them the best work its members had seen and praising them for making Vermont look "like a place where a man can rest and have a first-class vacation."[31] It was a reflection of how common automobiles were becoming: The number of Model Ts purchased between August 1919 and July 1920 was 941,000, nearly double that of the previous year. Because of automobiles, much more of Vermont had become easily accessible.[32] But by putting more people on the road, automobiles also brought to American attention the inadequacy of the nation's roadways, which was certainly true of Vermont's roads. The BOP's advertising sought to minimize the problem. A 1921 advertisement in the New York *Times* titled "The Road to Happiness" exclaimed that, "The thrill of thrills is an excursion by motor through the Green Mountains," and reassured readers that the roads were "for the most part cushiony gravel."[33] As "cushiony" as Vermont roads might be, they greatly needed improvement.

The second standout point common to the letters was that the evolution of Vermont's rural economy was perceived by visitors as an asset. Correspondents gasped at the affordability of a Vermont vacation. A Philadelphia man told a story of encountering a small-town Vermonter who complained about the raising of his rent from $6 to $8 a month on a house with seven rooms and a large garden. The author had been delighted to find that farms could be rented for as little as $100 a year. Other tourists' letters celebrated buying farms cheaply.

Anything negative about that was not the concern of the Bureau of Publicity. The number of active Vermont farms had been dropping steadily from its high of over 35,000 in 1880, and by 1920 was down to 29,075, a loss over the course of 40 years of nearly one out of every five farms, with the consequent displacement of people.[34] In the years following the Civil War, population decline in rural Vermont towns had been perceived a crisis by people like Alonzo Valentine. But it had been instead more of a natural process: Those leaving were largely those most superfluous to the evolving local economy, which favored those who owned land and had deep, multi-generational roots in their towns. Those people who stayed had formed the core of the insularity, homogeneity, and interdependence that had characterized rural communities in that era.[35] Over the subsequent four decades the economy had been turning against such people. According to the Bureau of Publicity, this was an advantageous state of affairs. One bureau advertisement placed in a number of big-city newspapers, promising "Days of Rest and Recreation that You'll *Never* Forget!" celebrated that "Literally thousands of beautiful sites may be had at small expense—many of them with picturesque farm buildings that lend themselves readily to the requirements of summer residents."[36] If rural Vermont was increasingly unsuited as a place to work, it could be remade as a playground for outsiders.

At the end of a busy 1920 Crockett announced that, despite the national economic downturn, Vermont summer tourism had had an excellent year. According to the bureau, this was not only true as measured by the sheer number of visitors but also in their quality: A discerning and classy group, tourists contributed to and improved rural life. The BOP publicized the report of a hotel proprietor in Lunenburg that the year had been his best, and that he was "fortunate in the class of people we get. Many who could well afford to go to the more fashionable, expensive places seem content to come here, and they bring to the town talent in various lines and are a great help to the place." The bureau held Windham County up especially as a place that could "afford an excellent field for the development of the summer homes idea" because it was "the so-called 'abandoned farm' district," and called it "curious to note the number of inquiries received from people outside the State who have the idea that Vermont consists largely of just such places to be bought for little or nothing."[37]

In 1921 there was a particularly telling addition to the Bureau of Publicity's publications: *Motor Tours in Vermont*, comprised of road maps covering almost all of the state, recommendations for points of interest, and a table showing distances between locations.[38] The era of auto tourism had truly arrived.[39] The bureau asserted that one advantage of the expected increase in tourism caused by automobiles was that successful people who made Vermont a permanent residence might then found businesses in the state. The Burlington *Free Press* wrote in August 1921 that, "if the policy of advertising the State continues, the Publicity Bureau believes it will not be long before Vermont is known not only as a vacation resort but as a commonwealth in which the natural advantage of water power, timber, etc...makes it peculiarly adapted to the establishment of big industries."[40] It was a paradoxical responsibility that the BOP maintained: simultaneously to promote Vermont as a scenic paradise of "unspoiled" tradition and as a progressive, modern society welcome to change. Whether many of those lured to Vermont by the state's contrast with city life would want to found industries, and thus make Vermont more like the places they were escaping, was open to question.

But no matter what the BOP's publications and advertisements claimed about their "cushiony gravel," Vermont's roads needed massive improvement. For years the relationship between promoting tourism and the need for better roads had been obvious. In 1917 the Burlington *Clipper* had written that, "it is up to Vermont to put her own highways in the best condition. Certainly Vermont does not want to put a Chinese wall around the State and shut out visitors." Considering the thousands of dollars expended annually on publicity, "it would be well to put one's house in order before extending the invitation to visitors."[41] The drumbeat for a major investment in roads became louder after World War I; in October 1920 the Barre *Times* reported that "Vermont's roads have been the subject of endless discussion."[42] The Bureau of Publicity's increased focus on auto tourists helped heighten the sense that roads were a major problem. The Brattleboro *Reformer* wrote in May 1921 that *Motor Tours in Vermont* was a wonderful addition to state publications, but while "In the way of scenery Vermont has much to advertise...some of the roads leading through many of the best bits of it would not stand much 'pitiless publicity,'" concluding that, "When our roads will stand the advertising our scenery can, then will Vermont be a tourist's paradise."[43] Certainly improved roads would have other benefits, making it easier for loggers and farmers to ply their trades, for example. The promotion of tourism was one among a number of motivations to improve state roads, but it played an important role in bringing the problem to the fore.

As the early 1920s moved along the Bureau of Publicity heavily advertised in big-city newspapers. A representative ad, "Motoring Where Every Trip is a Joy Ride," extolled the "cushiony gravel roads of Vermont" as "a joy of a new sort."[44] Apparently a lot of people believed that: At the conclusion of the 1921 summer season one newspaper wrote that "automobile camping parties are now frequent sights along Vermont roadsides."[45] And for those who hoped that tourism would be complementary to industrial growth there were successes to which they could point. For example, in late 1921 the Manchester *Journal* reported that a Massachusetts businessman had come to Vermont on a fishing trip, "saw the opening," and founded a manufacturing concern in the state. The *Journal* speculated, "this story could be duplicated over and over."[46] Would the contributions tourists made to the economy offer a replacement for the decline of jobs in agriculture and lumber for Valentine's Swedes and people like them? And was this particular example of the Massachusetts fisherman consistent with what promoters of tourism needed Vermont to be? A principle of diminishing returns was inescapably at work in trying to use Vermont's landscape and purported way of life as a means to achieve industrial progress. Choices in one or the other direction would need to be made. But the Bureau of Publicity was not in the business of resolving such dilemmas. It was in the business of promoting Vermont in whatever ways possible, and if that meant selling it as a natural paradise, then it would do so.[47]

Forces were colliding that made the idealized Vermont sold by the Bureau of Publicity more attractive to outsiders. For many Americans a psychological turning point occurred when the 1920 census was the first to show a majority of Americans lived in towns of 2,500 people or more. The early 1920s was a time of rapid technological and cultural change, to which Americans responded in a variety of ways. One was romanticizing rural America. This discomfort with change was something on which Vermont could capitalize. In 1922, the author Wallace Nutting published *Vermont Beautiful*, a book that idealized both the landscape and the Yankees who lived on it.[48] The Bureau of Publicity purchased a large number of copies of *Vermont Beautiful* and strategically placed them in metropolitan hotels and the headquarters of automobile clubs.[49] Working in cooperation with the Vermont Hotel Association, the bureau opened a permanent office to disseminate its publicity in New York City in May 1922.[50] The goal, wrote the Bennington *Banner*, was "to make Vermont the premier summer playground of the east and bring millions of dollars into the state."[51] The legislature increased the BOP's appropriation from $10,000 to $30,000 for 1923.[52] This was done despite some legislators objecting to the focus of its work, and criticizing the bureau for issuing its last new booklet promoting Vermont's industrial potential in 1914.[53] The bureau used the funds to expand its vacation advertisements in out-of-state newspapers. Its new slogan was that Vermont was "Vacation Land." A representative ad in the Brooklyn *Daily Eagle* promised "Motor roads on cushiony gravel that wind through an ever-changing panorama of scenic loveliness."[54]

The increased funding by the state illustrates the extent of the support the Bureau of Publicity, and by extension tourism, had in the state, even among the rural legislators who controlled the General Assembly. There were voices of dissent, however. Among the most articulate was Zephine Humphrey. A popular regional writer, in 1923 she published a somber assessment of the impact of tourism, at least on her town of Dorset, which sits on the other side of Peru from Landgrove. A native of Philadelphia, Humphrey had moved to Dorset after her marriage to an artist.[55] In her article "The New Crop," published in the magazine *The Outlook*, Humphrey alleged that at the beginning of the century there had been "summer people" who stayed in hotels and "made no impression to speak of on community life." Then, she continued, "they began buying up 'abandoned farms' and living on them for two or three months." This had been fine until the supply of "abandoned" farms ran out, at which point such people had begun to buy operating farms, or portions of farms that had been subdivided. When that happened, Humphrey believed, "it introduced the Serpent into Paradise." She saw a multitude of disadvantages to the new order of things. The visual landscape had changed for the worse, as working fields were replaced by sculpted pleasure grounds. The fact that the houses of summer people were rarely occupied gave them a sinister, dark feel, and gave the town a sense of abandonment in the winter. Most of all, summer home owners were disinterested in the social life around them, in the well-being of their neighbors. "I wonder how many farmer's wives would run to the back door of a summer cottage to borrow a cupful of sugar?" Humphrey asked poignantly. Her article caused a bit of a stir; a correspondent to a newspaper later that year felt compelled to defend Humphrey, writing that she and her husband had "sincerely tried to become Vermonters," comparing the Humphreys favorably to summer folk who "called my home a desolate place right to my face." The letter's author concluded that she liked "the way Zephine snaps her finger at [summer people]," but added pregnantly, "She can afford to."[56]

Some members of long-term Dorset families found ways to fit into the town's changing human landscape. Humphrey wrote admiringly in *The Outlook* in 1922 of John Lillie, a local artist whose grandmother was Hannah Tifft, sister of Rufus Tifft. A number of landscape painters had boarded at his house years earlier and had grown to admire him. As a carpenter, mason, and plumber he had been in demand ever since, and the quality of his work was renowned through the neighborhood. Lillie had discovered his own painting talent in the process. But mainly, wrote Humphrey, "summer homes increased, and John Lillie had all he could do planning and building and remodeling."[57] Other descendants of local families, however, found it progressively harder to remain in Dorset. There were still a few Tiffts, descendants of the three brothers Henry, Moses, and James. James's son Willard was listed in the 1920 census as engaged in "odd jobs," as was Moses's son Monte. But a telling story is that of Myron Tifft, a son of Moses, who in 1910 was a Dorset farm laborer. Between 1910 and 1920 he moved to Landgrove, where he and his wife Lutheria acquired a farm free of debt with an address, according to the census, on a "back road." Also moving to Landgrove was Ahial Crandall, a nephew of Moses and James Tifft's wives. He had been born in Peru, married in Landgrove in 1911, lived for a time in Minnesota, where he was a farm laborer, and had moved back, settling in Landgrove. For those who wanted to live, and hopefully own land, in a rural setting, Landgrove was an attractive alternative to the more industrial towns nearby like Rutland.

Refugees from tourist towns were not enough to stem the continued decline of Landgrove's population in the 1920s, however. The town had been too heavily dependent on agriculture and lumbering, both of which were shedding jobs rapidly in this era while manufacturing jobs elsewhere increased.[58] Nor did the arrival of these people help Landgrove's reputation. A half century later Samuel Ogden wrote that when he first arrived in town in 1929, "some sort of sinister miasma hung over all of Landgrove. As far as the people we knew were concerned, Landgrove sported an unsavory reputation."[59] But places like Landgrove, where land prices were cheap, taxes were low, government was close to the people, and the number of summer homes was negligible, were attractive to those who were scraping by, and for whom the evolution of the economy had not been favorable.[60] It was what they could afford.

As an increasingly significant part of Vermont's economy, perhaps tourism and summer homes had the potential to be the salvation of such people rather than driving them away. It might bring the jobs they needed, in light of the decline of traditional sectors of the rural economy. If so, tourism was given a massive boost a few weeks after Humphrey's article appeared in *The Outlook*. While visiting his father in his native town of Plymouth, Vice President Calvin Coolidge learned that President Warren Harding had died. Two weeks later, under a headline "Tourists Rush to Plymouth," the Burlington *Free Press* reported that, "Everybody wants to see the President's home, and the little crossroads hamlet has seen more automobiles in the last two weeks than have appeared in the place in years altogether." Much of this traffic, it reported, came from the east over Peru Mountain.[61] Coolidge's image as a common man with estimable rural values complemented the way the Bureau of Publicity and others marketed Vermont.[62] The simple surroundings in which Coolidge had taken the oath of office, the *Free Press* concluded on August 8, 1923, "[have] plainly appealed strongly to the popular imagination."[63] It would continue to do so for the rest of the decade.

Valentine's Swedes in the "New Era"

As the 1920s progressed, agricultural production increased overall, but trends in agriculture increasingly favored better-situated and better-funded farms, and the total number of farms continued to drop.[64] That does not imply such people only benefited from the lessening of their isolation. In rare cases, the question of what to do about the decline in farms provoked the memories of Alonzo Valentine's recruitment program. In 1922 a Vermont newspaper reported that there were "Norwegians asking about Vermont farms," in large part because "the term 'abandoned farm' has come to be applied too often to Vermont agriculture, until many people have the idea that Vermont is simply a State of abandoned farms." Reminiscing incorrectly that Valentine had gone to Europe himself, the article described the scheme as producing "a few immigrants" who proved "inclined to seek the larger centers where more of their countrymen could be found in the industries." The result was that "little was really accomplished in the way of permanent benefit for Vermont agriculture." Walter Crockett visited Norway's consul in Boston about recruiting farmers but had little faith that Norwegians could do much to invigorate Vermont agriculture. A better solution, Crockett told the reporter, was "to interest summer people in these uplands of Vermont, so that some of this land may be utilized for summer homes."[65]

As the 1920s wore on, debate over the future of rural areas continued, and Valentine's scheme remained an infrequent reference point. When the United States commissioner of immigration appeared in the state in 1925 to discuss the problems of rural America, the Burlington *Free Press* gave its coverage the headline, "What Shall Our Rural Vermont Do To Be Saved?" The commissioner decried Vermont's loss of farms, claiming the state had 600,000 acres of idle farmland. His solution was, remarkably, to bring "skilled farmers" from northern Europe to reoccupy "abandoned" farms. Thirty-five years after Valentine's program, engineering Vermont's human landscape to accentuate certain kinds of whiteness remained on the table. In covering this speech, the *Free Press* recounted Valentine's program, dramatically over-estimating the number of immigrants Valentine attracted, calling them "representative of the best class of Swedish immigrants," and lamenting that "they did not take to Vermont." When Valentine's position was abolished, the *Free Press* charged, "a large amount of excellent work done went for naught." The *Free Press* concluded that Valentine's program was ahead of its time, and suggested it should be tried again, adding that "if our State worked as hard to keep our people as we have worked to attract the attention of tourists, we would flourish galore." Walter

Crockett, who attended the presentation, described himself as open to the recruitment idea, but warned Vermonters not to be overly enthusiastic about it. According to Crockett this time, Valentine's Swedes had discovered some of their countrymen working in Barre quarries and "In short time those who came to till the soil were found working in the Barre shops."[66]

A year later Valentine's program came up again as part of a discussion of the laudable work of the Bureau of Publicity to sell farms to residents of other states. The bureau's "judicious advertising," the *Free Press* reported, "helps all classes of our people. It brings summer visitors and boarders, tourists, prospective home makers, those seeking a new place in which to do business in favorable conditions, and campers." All of this was in "marked contrast with the experiment which Vermont made in the eighties in the direction of attracting Swedish immigrants to populate Vermont's abandoned farms." The narrative this time was that "Colonists came, but they could not compete with the shrewd Yankees, especially in trade, and they soon became emigrants from Vermont." But there was better hope for a similar program in 1926 than in 1890: because of "the number of farms that can be had at a very reasonable rate in Vermont, we have wondered if it would not be worthwhile to renew or to parallel the Valentine movement of the eighties. Conditions are more favorable now."[67] That conditions are truly more favorable is doubtful. When Valentine's Swedes had arrived in 1890, they had settled into an economy familiar to them: In Sweden Carl Westine and August Nyren had been lumbermen, while Edwin Anderson and John and Axel Neilson were farmers. Such jobs had been the foundation of the rural economy, but with each passing year that was less true.

Nevertheless, some of Major Valentine's Swedes still persisted exactly where they were placed. The Neilsons and Westines were the only families with a strong presence in the Landgrove area by the mid-1920s. Alve Neilson supplemented his income by serving as caretaker of the old Clark Lodge, which Marshall Hapgood acquired in the early 1920s. While Harry Neilson struggled to make a go of his late father's farm, his siblings had scattered. His sister Anna was having problems with her marriage to her husband, a laborer in a paper mill in the village of Bellows Falls; the marriage ended in divorce late in the decade. In July

1925, brother Harold, also a paper mill worker in Bellows Falls, was married in Landgrove to the daughter of an Irish immigrant. By the mid-1920s only two of the seven houses in Landgrove's sole village of Clarksville were regularly occupied, by a pair of brothers named Colburn who operated what passed for a little country store in one of the dwellings. The village at this time was later described by a newspaper as "weather-beaten, leaking, being consumed by the slow burning of decay." Taxes on all but two of the village's buildings had been in arrears for a number of years.[68]

Meanwhile, it was an eventful couple of years for Lottie Nyren. Her marriage to Eddie Tifft reached its end in 1924. Since marrying in 1893 they had struggled, bouncing between odd jobs, rented farms, and lumber camps. Family recollections are that Eddie did not have the will to support his children and committed adultery. One descendant described Eddie as "awfully jealous" of Lottie "because she was out trying to make a living."[69] Lottie's suit for divorce was based on Eddie's "neglect and refusal to support." Son Richard was still dependent on her, but her other children were moving on. Charles, who had two children by the middle of the decade, worked as a teamster in Rutland. In 1925 Lottie's 18-year-old daughter Mildred married machinist John Henry Young, and they too settled in Rutland, moving in with Lottie's brother Oliver. Oliver had begun a career as an agent for Prudential Insurance. He relieved stress from work with frequent visits across the state to the Wilder home of his sister Anna, with whom he was very close.[70] In 1926, at the age of 50, Lottie Nyren married George Derosia, whose parents were natives of Québec. Derosia had been born in Peru in 1880, where his father worked as a teamster. In the course of his working life he had lost four fingers off of his left hand. Already twice divorced, he had two daughters by his second wife, Grace, whom he had married when he was 24 and she was 15. Derosia had spent his adult life working a series of jobs in Danby, Mount Tabor, and Peru, and they met at the Sandgate lumber camp at which Lottie was a cook.[71] Alonzo Valentine had hoped his Swedish recruits would displace migrants of French Canadian ancestry. Instead, they not only settled among them and worked with them, but in this and other cases he provided them with spouses.

How supportive Lottie and George were of efforts to modernize and organize Vermont cannot be known. They may have had little opinion at all. As Vermont's economy was undergoing a process that removed jobs they traditionally would have held, they might have hoped such efforts would provide suitable replacements. It was certainly unclear at that point whether that would happen when many of those efforts to modernize Vermont were dependent on marketing it as quite the opposite. If the Swedes had not displaced French Canadians and others whom Alonzo Valentine had seen as undesirable, other forces threatened to do so. During the 1920s the total number of farms fell from around 29,000 in 1920 to a bit more than 25,000 in 1930. Between 1900 and 1930, one quarter of all Vermont farms ceased operation, and the amount of improved land declined by 34 percent. Over those ten years, the proportion of people in Vermont working on farms declined from 36.6 percent to 27 percent.[72] Many sectors of Vermont's industrial economy were also waning: Seven of the state's ten major industries declined in output during the 1920s.[73] Jobs in the timber industry were shrinking, partially due to overuse; Vermont was at least 80 percent deforested by the mid-1920s.[74] In response to deforestation and other factors, there were increasing moves to preserve and manage the state's forests. But if the replacement for that traditional economy was a landscape on which recreation was prioritized, would that benefit people like Lottie's son Richard, who was raised largely in lumber camps and had had access only to a rudimentary education?

Vermont went further in the direction of forest management because of a natural disaster. In November 1927, much of Vermont experienced a catastrophic flood that had important consequences for the state's future. The flood had a devastating impact on Vermont's transportation networks, both road and rail. Among other damage, it destroyed the carriage road leading out of Landgrove to the east.[75] It also had a profound effect on forest management: It was clear to many that the barren condition of the hillsides exacerbated the flood's damage. The necessity of taking a new approach to forests had immediate consequences for those living in and near Landgrove. Peru's Marshall Hapgood, the area's largest landowner, had long wanted his forest holdings to become part of a national forest.[76] He had died in 1926, and now the time was right for his wish to be realized; according to one historian, the flood caused "a few voices [calling for better forest management] to become a general clamor." In 1928 the federal government acceded to the desire of state leaders and authorized the creation of a national forest in the south-central part of the state with a proposed area of 370,000 acres. The initial tract of land that got the forest started was 1,812 acres in Peru donated by Hapgood's estate.[77]

Modernizing Vermont in the "New Era"

H. H. Chadwick, director of the Bureau of Publicity in later years, wrote about the 1920s, "As cars were improved and prices lowered, the masses began to move along the highways." As a consequence, there was "a rapid rise in touring and the vacation business boomed. Tourist home signs multiplied and there was rapid growth in the number of overnight cabins, rural tea rooms, roadside filling stations and offerings of vegetables, maple products, and other wares."[78] By the middle of the decade the increase in auto tourists helped compel Vermonters to do more about their roads. One response was the formation of local "Good Road Clubs," but those proved insufficient. A variety of state organizations, and especially the state Chamber of Commerce, advocated greater action, which led in 1925 to the founding of the statewide Vermont Good Roads Club.[79] The emergence of an "awakened public sentiment for the best highways in the world," as newspaper owner Arthur Stone wrote, was a start, but actually fixing Vermont's road woes was an enormous task, and just one among a number of problems facing the state.[80]

As recounted earlier, Vermont had experienced a period of movement toward modernization earlier in the twentieth century, particularly in two bursts—the first around 1908, the second in 1915, which ushered in the primary election. The primary led to Springfield businessman James Hartness being elected governor in 1920 as an insurgent candidate against the establishment. An engineer by training, Hartness wanted to make government, and Vermont generally, more efficient and rational. The General Assembly, dominated by small towns because of its one-town, one-vote apportionment, largely stymied his efforts because of their expense and perceived threats to local control. He was succeeded by Redfield Proctor Jr. in 1922, who also sought to modernize state government, but again not much got done. Progress in modernizing Vermont mostly fell to private agencies, or public-private cooperation. The Greater Vermont Association became the Vermont State Chamber of Commerce in 1922. James P. Taylor, founder of the GVA, was retained as the chamber's secretary. The Chamber of Commerce waged many campaigns during his tenure to improve the state economically and aesthetically. Among other things, it took on water pollution and stream purification, improvement of highways, and management of forests.

The feeling among Vermont's leaders that still greater effort was needed to modernize and organize the state led in 1925 to the founding of the Vermont Cooperative Council (VCC).[81] The VCC materialized that summer at a conference convened by Governor Franklin Billings. It was comprised of representatives from 15 statewide organizations, such as the Chamber of Commerce, the Hotel Men's Association, the Forestry Association, and the Bureau of Publicity.[82] The council's founders pledged the organization to include and serve all those dedicated to boosting Vermont "truthfully and loyally at every reasonable opportunity and occasion," because "only through 'selling' Vermont to themselves can they 'sell' Vermont to the nation and the world."[83] As was the case with the Bureau of Publicity, some people objected to the council's priorities. After it began a drive to raise $25,000, one businessman complained in a newspaper that it was too narrowly focused on tourism. "The problem before the council is not wholly one of attracting tourists and other visitors," he argued, "but of building up the State itself by its industries."[84] The VCC was unmoved and continued on its path.

The Vermont Cooperative Council was very much in the spirit of its times, similar in composition and mission to organizations elsewhere like the Bureau of Municipal Research. A partnership between private and public agencies, it sought to study and remedy perceived problems and weaknesses. Within months of its founding, a similar body dedicated to coordinating development efforts across New England, named the New England Council, was founded.[85] Vermont contributed representatives to that body while continuing to charge the Cooperative Council with the task of fixing Vermont's shortcomings. Most of its work focused was on the condition of rural areas; a 1926 VCC committee declared that "the question, 'What's the Matter With Vermont?' must deal primarily with Rural Vermont." The council's answer was invariably that more publicity to those outside the state was needed. In 1926, praising the Cooperative Council's effort to address the quality of Vermont's roads, a newspaper asked, "What are good Vermont roads without publicity? What is Vermont publicity without good roads?"[86] If rural people were to be redeemed, the solutions must come from outside their communities.

For three years tourism, and not industrial progress, remained the VCC's primary focus. In 1928 the VCC was abolished, as political leaders felt that its functions were made redundant by the New England Council. Though it had recently languished, a newspaper gave the VCC credit for being "particularly active in promoting programs for wider publicity and better highways for the State."[87] The approach of the VCC—addressing large-scale problems with large-scale solutions—was increasingly the logic of the era. In 1926 a magazine titled the *Vermont Review* was founded that in its brief existence advocated what it called an "All-Vermont Program" that would lead to the "Greater Vermont" that supposedly had been on the horizon for over two decades. Accomplishing that goal required not just organization, but organization on a statewide scale. As the *Vermont Review* put it, such a program for progress required that "the whole of Vermont must be dealt with as a single unit, the body social, and not in isolated parts."[88] If rural residents' tradition of local control must be sacrificed, it was in their best interest.

Prominent among the many areas of life for which this "single unit" approach was necessary was forest management. That was a central issue not just for state agencies and organizations, but also for federal ones. The 1924 Clarke-McNary Act expanded the kind of land the Forest Service could acquire for national forests. The next year Vermont's General Assembly passed the Enabling Act, which granted the state's approval for the Forest Service to purchase land anywhere in Vermont for a national forest. The prospect of a managed forest appealed to supporters of tourism and forest-products executives alike, as it had since Vermont's legislature had passed the law allowing the state to purchase land for state forests in 1909. Sufficient money had never been available to make the preservation and management of large public forests possible, however.[89] Now Vermont was turning to the federal government to make it happen. Making rural Vermont appear natural and idyllic, it seemed, required a lot of work.

Sam Ogden in the 1920s

One of those in the 1920s who idealized rural life was Samuel Robinson Ogden Jr., real estate and insurance agent in Elizabeth, New Jersey. He did not need the Bureau of Publicity to alert him to Vermont's appeal: Ogden continued to spend parts of some summers in Peru with the Grant family.[90] He married Mary Campbell, a Kentucky native, in 1921.[91] Ogden spent the 1920s increasingly dissatisfied with his life. He was contemptuous of materialism, and of the shallow and rote social relationships required to sell insurance.[92] Nearing 30, Ogden had no great accomplishments. He awoke on workdays, took the trolley to his office, returned home, and each day thought in frustration that he wanted a more meaningful, more engaged life. He found his escape from drudgery in buying dilapidated houses, renovating them himself, and selling them at a profit. To him it was real work, skillful labor performed with one's hands.

In 1926, Ogden's frustration with urban life boiled over on a camping trip with another couple in Pennsylvania. He later wrote that, after a number of days in the woods, "I came all at once to…a revelation; I felt an intense revulsion for the life we had been living in the city, and on this wet afternoon I blurted out that all of us were living stupid lives. I scorned the rut that we all were in, the absence of real joy, the futility of boredom-inspired cocktail parties. I swore that we were but pawns in the uncreative game known as 'Keeping up with the Joneses,' and I was fed up to the teeth with it. I shouted for freedom…My disgust could not find words to tell how unreal our lives had become." Challenged to do something about it, Ogden responded, without entirely believing it himself, "Someday I will."[93]

"Keeping the Advertising Dignified"

At the end of the 1923 tourist season Walter Crockett called it Vermont's best ever, claiming he had received more inquiries than his office could handle.[94] The Bureau of Publicity's state appropriation was held at $30,000 for 1924, and with Calvin Coolidge in the White House, Vermont geared up for the summer season. In April the Burlington *Free Press* congratulated the agency on its work, writing that, "The Vermont Publicity Bureau, ably started by Guy W. Bailey and continued under the skillful direction of Walter H. Crockett, has expended the small amount of its budget wisely and advantageously." Much of that money, it noted, was spent on "high-class publicity" in metropolitan newspapers. Following the 1924 summer season Crockett again told reporters Vermont had experienced "the greatest summer tourist season the State of Vermont has ever seen." Noticeably more tourists arrived in cars with camping equipment, bypassing hotels altogether; Crockett largely credited this to the improving condition Vermont's major roads.[95] While continuing to publish a variety of promotional pamphlets and road and rail maps of the state, the bureau also worked in cooperation with the office of the state forester to establish free camping sites for auto tourists, which one newspaper called "a forward-looking move."[96] Advertisements appeared in newspapers in such far-flung locales as Louisville, Chicago, St. Louis, and Detroit.[97] A typical ad in the Brooklyn *Daily Eagle* claimed that, "Hundreds of beauty spots in every variety of scenic setting may be secured at very modest,—almost nominal—cost."

With an eye to its other, less-important responsibility, the BOP also published a new pamphlet titled *Where Vermont Leads* that extolled its prowess in the areas of maple sugar, hydro power, quarrying, and dairying.[98] The bureau's essential mission remained to peddle the idea that progress and tradition could complement each other. And as always, as H. H. Chadwick would later describe, its policy was to "keep the advertising dignified" and aim it at "discriminating people."[99] In 1925 the bureau published the pamphlet *Golfing on the Green Hills of Vermont, in a Country Built for Golf*. It exclaimed, "There's a country built for golf—and that's Vermont! On the long rolling green hills the pursuer of the white pill finds his paradise."[100] The bureau's budget was cut back to $10,000 in 1926, but to its rescue came the Vermont Cooperative Council, which raised around $15,000 to supplement the state appropriation.[101] Armed with the extra money, the Bureau of Publicity made a gesture toward promoting industry, republishing the pamphlet *Where Vermont Leads*. With exaggeration the *Free Press* headlined an article on the pamphlet "New Pamphlet Booms Vermont."[102] Selling Vermont as a scenic wonderland and not a fertile field for industrial development remained the BOP's primary goal, however.[103] A typical advertisement in a Louisville newspaper described Vermont as "Coolidge Land, Vacation Land."[104] An advertisement the following year promised that "Somewhere in the friendly acres of Vermont is just the spot for the summer home of your dreams: Here are literally thousands of farms and homes with shapely buildings that lend themselves so readily to summer home development." The year 1927 also found the bureau advertising Vermont as "A Continuous Park of Natural Vacation Loveliness"[105]

The Bureau of Publicity, in partnership with other parts of state government, private agencies, and business leaders, further publicized this message in 1926 by sending around the eastern half of the United States a train named the "Vermont Special." Carrying state leaders, including the governor, it made it as far west as Chicago, gathering enough publicity along the way for its supporters to consider it a great success. In its cars were exhibits promoting both Vermont as a tourist destination and Vermont products, especially maple syrup.[106] According to one journalist, "We might think of the train simply as an advertising scheme to attract the attention of many States to the manifold beauties of our State," but in fact, "The splendid exhibits in the different cars representing Vermont scenery and products of Vermont industries are intended to help the people of other States to 'Have faith in Vermont.'"[107] Similar Vermont Special trips were undertaken each of the next three years. There was some concern that the dignitaries aboard the train would be seen by people in other states as not what they expected from Vermonters; one newspaper speculated in 1929 they would be disappointed "not to see real dirt farmers in straw hats, overalls and cowhide boots and talking a picturesque Yankee twang, in short the native Vermonter as visualized by the country at large as a result of the drama and movies." The author acknowledged the argument that such exploitation of rural Vermonters would "not be dignified," to which he responded that, "the people of the United States are not particularly interested in a dignified Vermonter."[108] Thus, even as many common Vermonters were being displaced by the evolution of the economy, they remained central to promotion of the state, at least for iconographic purposes.[109]

Studying the State, Planning the Future

The 1927 flood also helped spur the creation of, and built enthusiasm for, the Vermont Commission on Country Life (VCCL). The VCCL was constituted in May 1928 as a means to identify and remedy the evils plaguing rural Vermont. Led by a national figure in the field of rural economics and sociology, and with the governor and Guy Bailey, now president of the University of Vermont, and members of the executive committee, the commission took upon itself the task of organizing 17 separate committees, comprising around 200 volunteers. A great deal of excellent analysis of the VCCL has been written by other historians, especially on its abhorrent eugenics program.[110] Most relevant here are the committees on Land Utilization and on Summer Residents and Tourists, on both of which Walter Crockett served. If they were less sinister than the Eugenics Survey, the two committees had a similar purpose: to engineer Vermont's human landscape. As the commission's work got fully underway in 1929, Crockett decided to undertake a comprehensive study of the impact of tourism on Vermont. He had done basic research previously; in 1928 he had found that there had been two million visitors to the state, the value of which he estimated at $40 million. Given license by the VCCL to undertake a more comprehensive study, Crockett hired an assistant, Pearl Brown, to do most of the field-work. Crockett probably entered the study full of confidence for the future, despite, or indeed because of, signs of economic problems. One way to counteract the faltering industrial economy was to expand the promotion of tourism. Appearing to agree, the legislature increased the Bureau of Publicity's appropriation to $15,000 for 1928 and 1929.[111]

The idea that tourism could save the state rankled some observers. In a speech to Rutland's Rotary Club in 1929 the writer Sinclair Lewis, who had a summer house in the area, said that he liked Vermont "because it is quiet, because you have a population not driven mad by the American mania." Citing Florida and Cape Cod as examples of the consequences of excessive tourism, he exhorted Vermonters to preserve their priceless heritage: It was up to Vermonters to save "Old houses that must not be torn down, beauty that must not be defiled, roads that must not be cluttered with billboards and hot dog stands."[112] Similar concerns were expressed by Vermont native Vrest Orton, a writer who had worked in New York City before returning. In 1929 Orton declared himself a member of a "Vigilance Committee" dedicated to preventing such "un-Vermontish" things as "tourists who patronize natives" and "jerry-built roadside shacks, summer camps [and] hot dog stands." For Orton, as historian Dona Brown writes, Vermont's true future lay "in the decentralist landscape out-of-staters found so appealing: the farms of its hillsides and the self-sufficient small-scale village industries of its river valleys."[113] Orton warned that Vermont must not sacrifice its way of life to become merely "a Summer Playground for the Nation." With a sense of mischievousness Orton recommended Vermont's secession from the Union. More practical mechanisms to protect Vermont as Orton wished it to be were not obvious.

Such voices remained on the periphery. At the end of the 1920s the consensus among state political leaders was that Vermont needed to do what it could to bend to the desires of outsiders. In a three-day conference on tourism at the University of Vermont in 1929 the industry's leading promoters made clear the extent to which Vermont's landscape, and the behavior of its people, should be harnessed to match outsiders' expectations. On the first day Walter Crockett spoke on "What the Tourist Should See in Vermont." He pointed out the growing importance of the tourist business, stimulated by the ease with which people could get about the country with cars, "and by the prosperous condition of nearly everybody in the country." Crockett advised Vermonters that "The average tourist seeks a clean, well-kept, well-painted place," and therefore Vermonters should be sure to maintain "A lawn which is kept mowed [and] flowers and trees which add to the attractiveness of the exterior appearance."[114] The following day James P. Taylor, speaking on behalf of the State Chamber of Commerce, gave a talk on "How to Attract and Hold the Tourist" that advised Vermonters to change their behavior on behalf of tourists. He lamented that Vermonters "are reported to be somewhat cold and unenthusiastic about greeting strangers." Describing Vermont as having a reputation as "more or less a hermit state," he rued the "general opinion abroad that Vermonters did not wish to have visitors come into their State, particularly if they intended to remain for any length of time." Regrettably, Taylor said, "Vermonters are not noted as an elation releasing people." In closing, Taylor advocated what he called "beauty-parloring the face of the farm, such as addressing "drunken fence posts" that "should be straightened up and made to look less shiftless." "Symbolize your hospitality by adorning the face of the farm," Crockett pleaded. "Let us have miles and miles of radiant roadsides."[115]

Despite such shortcomings, both visual and human, Crockett, Taylor, and other leaders of the state were feeling enthusiastic about the future. The reasons why were summed up in a Burlington *Free Press* article titled "Vermont's Big Year" that was published in late September 1929. It exulted that "a number of things have happened in year 1929 which should go far to make Vermonters 'as happy as kings.'" It claimed 1929 would be remembered by Vermonters for wonderful things: as the year in which the Champlain Bridge was completed and dedicated; the year in which the Vermont building at the Eastern State Exposition was erected; the year in which Vermont reached practically a complete recovery from the flood, so far as its highways and ridgelines were concerned; and the year in which "an unrivaled number of visitors discovered Vermont and came flocking through the State." It concluded, "Truly, Vermont is on the road of Progress in 1929...We are ready to entertain anybody and we know we have the goods to show them...It may be said without fear of contradiction that in no decade has Vermont made such remarkable progress as during the decade which is just closing. In fact, we have built more first-class roads in the past five years than during all the previous history of the state. And good roads are a real indication of progress."[116] And progress, of course, was a good thing, including to those selling Vermont as unspoiled and traditional.

Valentine's Swedes on the Verge of the Depression

The situation might have looked a little less rosy when viewed from the perspective of Major Valentine's Swedes. There were certainly moments of joy. In 1929 Clarence Neilson, born in Landgrove in 1908, and whose father Charlie had drowned in 1914, married Mildred Underwood in Chesterfield, New Hampshire. The marriage certificate listed him as a "laborer"; the bride was 17 years old. Also in 1929, 18-year-old Verna Westine, the oldest daughter of Jennie and Julius, married William Carleton in Londonderry; Carleton worked in trucking. Their wedding was an opportunity for the reunion of at least some of Valentine's Swedes. Those still in Landgrove were in attendance. Grandparents of the bride, Carl and Anna Westine, took great pride in their expanding flock of grandchildren. Leslie Westine, the oldest son of Willie who was born in 1920, remembered spending many happy summer weeks at his grandparents' house.[117] It was not a long way to go: Willie was living in Weston with his wife Mary and five sons, working as a teamster, as the 1930 census put it, in "woods (lumber)." The bride's parents Jennie and Julius still lived in Londonderry, Julius working as a carpenter at a sawmill. Freda Westine Wilson's husband had taken a job in a lumber mill in nearby Chester, while Nola Westine Carver's husband worked in a Brattleboro lumber yard.

A host of Neilsons attended the wedding. Axel, Hilma, and their son John Dolph remained on their Landgrove dairy farm, while son Alve lived down the road in Peru with his wife and three children. Axel's nephew Harry Neilson was still running his father John's farm at the beginning of 1929, but barely hanging on. Landgrove as a whole was similarly struggling. In that year it had 37 delinquent taxpayers out of a total population of 104; its population had been 143 a decade earlier. About Landgrove as a whole, one historian of the town wrote that at the end of the 1920s, "The mills were gone, and no industry had come to take their place. In agriculture the multiple-crop farming of the mid 1800s had been replaced by dairy farming. The mail order catalog had driven the shoemaker out of business, and the horse and the blacksmith had been supplanted by the automobile."[118] The Colburn brothers continued the operation of their small country store in Clarksville. John Colburn, an artist, taxidermist, woodworker, and violin maker, was highly regarded locally for extending a liberal line of credit to his customers, so his store was popular, even if no sign indicated its presence.[119] At the other end of the village an abandoned house had been commandeered by moonshiners. Otherwise the village was empty, the victim of the long-term forces that had driven so many away from the town. As for some of those among Valentine's Swedes who had scattered, Emma Anderson, widowed 20 years earlier and now in her 70s, lived in Westminster where she worked as a housekeeper. Most of her children lived nearby in Brattleboro. Lottie Nyren Derosia was living in Mount Tabor with George, who worked as a teamster in a Danby marble quarry. Living with them was George's unmarried daughter Aleathea (age 20), and her children George (4) and Patricia (3), along with George's other daughter, Grace (14).[120]

In the autumn of 1929, Harry Neilson admitted defeat in his effort to hold on to his Landgrove farm. His mother Louise sold the 100-acre farm for $325, with another $275 for its timber rights. By then she had moved to New Jersey to live with divorced daughter Anna and her two young children. Harry had no desire to leave the Landgrove area, but he would need to scramble to come up with a way to make staying work.

Sam Ogden Arrives in Landgrove

Into this picture stepped Samuel Robinson Ogden in September 1929. He was actually preceded in Landgrove by two months by another native of New Jersey named William Badger, who bought a farm in the south part of town as a summer home.[121] Sam and Mamie Ogden arrived in what he would always consider a stupendous case of luck. Ogden's father had died in 1927, freeing him from the responsibility of maintaining the family insurance and real estate business. In 1929, Sam and Mamie embarked on a long trip that took then to Kentucky and then to New England in search of, as Ogden put it, "a new place to live, and a new way of life." Ogden wanted to escape the rat race he hated, to engage in meaningful work with his hands, to have fulfilling and genuine social relationships, and to live in a place where he could have a tangible influence on public affairs. Near the end of this long trip, the Ogdens stopped in Peru to visit their old friends, the family of David Grant, who had introduced Ogden to Peru as a young boy.

One morning David Grant announced that the larder was out of cheese, and that the only place where cheese meeting his standards could be purchased was in Landgrove. On a beautiful autumn Vermont morning Sam, Mamie, and David set out in the Ogdens' car. Entering the town from the west, they drove along a heavily wooded road, with the land rising up on the right and falling away to the left. They found a house by the road that was uninhabited but in good condition. Told he could have it for $400, Ogden immediately committed to buying it. Making a left turn farther on, they drove north to the village of Clarksville. Finally the trees gave way to a row of houses in a clearing, with a river on the right that crossed under the road just beyond the end of the village. Distant mountains rose up on the horizon to the left, behind the ramshackle houses. They entered the Colburn store to buy the cheese. Charles Colburn was attending the store, and in the course of the conversation that ensued Colburn mentioned that he and his brother owned most of land in the village, and that they and the other landowners were eager to sell their holdings. Ogden listened in disbelief as Colburn listed the prices of the properties: "Did he say that this place could be had for two hundred dollars? And that one for two hundred seventy-five? And this one for seventy above the one hundred and fifty dollar mortgage? My goodness, I said to myself, for I had been in the real estate business in Elizabeth, New Jersey, the very least we can do is to look at these places." Sam and Mamie made their way down the street, looking in the windows of structures and talking excitedly about the potential they saw. Ogden immediately decided that it was essential that he purchase all the structures in the village. "It all ended up," he later wrote, "with Uncle Davie having bought two pounds of cheese, and the Ogdens having bought a village."[122] The village he purchased could accurately be described at the time, by and large, as "abandoned." Had Alonzo Valentine been around to know of this, he might have felt a sense of vindication.

A month later, the bottom fell out of the stock market. Business was bad for Ogden in Elizabeth; a 1947 profile of him said that the Ogdens "were left with nothing but their village."[123] With that, he and Mamie fully committed themselves to their Landgrove project. In March 1930 they drove up to Vermont and attended their first town meeting, held at the lodge of the Free and Accredited Masons, and Ogden called it "an eyeopener." Ogden found two factions in the town: those with better farms in the valleys and the impoverished who lived in the hills, and the meeting was "the occasion for giving vent to all the accumulated and pent-up animosity and spleen which the winter engendered." At lunchtime, when the meeting took a break, "the combat ceased briefly" while the attendees ate cold lunches washed down by tea, and then they went back at it again. Ogden felt like he and Mamie learned a lot that day about Landgrove's inhabitants and the town's business, but recognized there was much more to learn.[124]

Ogden also had a lot to learn about the physical town, and he spent some of 1930 exploring it. Among the places to which he paid a visit was Stephen Clark's lodge, which still stood up Clark Lodge Road. Since Clark's wife had turned her back on it in disgust and he had stopped

visiting it, the lodge had been used periodically.[125] Alve Neilson's service as caretaker of the lodge ended when Marshall Hapgood died in
1926, and the lodge had fallen into serious disrepair. [126] Ogden found all
of the windows broken, and, he wrote later, "those effete symbols of a
more civilized place, the flush toilets, had been wrenched from their
foundations and smashed. In fact, there was nothing that was not
smashed, including all of the elaborate and sturdy rustic furniture."[127]
Ogden was fortunate to have seen the lodge when he did. Two years
later, because it sat on the land donated by Hapgood as the seed for the
Green Mountain National Forest, the Forest Service burned the lodge
to the ground, as it did other structures within the boundaries of the
preserve. With the burning of the Clark Lodge came the end of one era
in Landgrove's history. With the arrival of Samuel and Mamie Ogden,
a new one began.

CHAPTER 6

Planning the Future

The Ogdens Settle Into Landgrove

S AM AND MAMIE OGDEN had a lot of work to do in 1930. From the beginning, Sam had a clear vision of what he wanted, and what would be required to see that vision materialize. He thought it imperative that he acquire ownership of all the properties in the village of Clarksville. With the exception of the Colburns' store he accomplished that straightaway, spending $4,385 to buy seven houses and two barns.[1] He later described all of the houses as "broken and dejected," and the village as a whole as "sad and dispiriting." But where others might see a nearly abandoned clump of dilapidation, Ogden saw the potential, as he said later, for "a summer place which had all the advantages of a natural setting with a brook, hills and a fine landscape for people who wished to spend the summer months in the country."[2] After asking around and receiving estimates on the cost of rehabilitating the houses, Ogden decided that the local contractors wanted too much. He would do the work himself.[3]

The first order of business was to make habitable the house in which they lived, which was located a couple hundred yards away from the village. By the end of the summer that house was sufficiently repaired that Ogden was able to sell it to a local man. He then moved his wife and two children to a house in the village. The move to Landgrove from the comforts of Elizabeth was a dramatic change in living conditions. Sam Ogden was fortunate that in his partner, Mamie, he had a woman of grace, spirit, energy, and eternal patience, willing to live without electricity, a gas stove, and other urban comforts. Mamie threw herself into the Landgrove project no less than did Sam. Their foremost concern was the quality of the education their children would receive.[4] The school they found in Landgrove was a run-down building located in an inconvenient spot. This, they thought, would not do for eight-year-old Jane and five-year-old Samuel Jr. For the first few months of the school year Mamie educated them at home, but after a time Jane expressed a desire to be in school with the other children.[5] In preparation to do something about the school at the next town meeting in March, Mamie laid the groundwork by informally discussing it with townspeople. Like her husband, she needed to know who lived in this town and how best to get along with them.

According to Sam Ogden, in surrounding towns Landgrove had a poor reputation, something akin to "living on the wrong side of the tracks." As the Ogdens had discovered at the 1930 town meeting, the town was bitterly divided between the more-respectable valley land-owners and those who lived in the hills, who were poorer and in the majority. A newspaper wrote many years later that the Ogdens felt it was their responsibility to settle the feud between what Sam perceived were "the respectable citizens of the valley farms and the more lawless residents of the surrounding hills."[6] Despite the feud, Ogden delighted in his new neighbors. The way they lived their lives, he thought, was in stark contrast to the modes of urban life he had found so unsatisfying, and very much in line with his vision of a fulfilling life. "The thing that endeared Vermont to Mamie and me," he wrote later, "was the character of her citizens...These were unique human beings, each with his own special stamp, his peculiarities, his crochets and his independent individualism. These were people, not stereotypes—some more peculiar than others, but thank the Good Lord, all of them peculiar."[7]

These people, like the size of the community, the town's political institutions, and its physical setting, appealed immensely to Sam Ogden. Forthright, opinionated, passionate about art and culture, he considered himself a conservative man with libertarian impulses. For him Vermont, and especially its smallest communities like Landgrove, provided the ideal setting for individualistic living and thinking in a world growing ever more bland and conformist. It was the ideal antidote to New York City: a place where a meaningful life could be lived, provided one was willing to work for it. Conjuring memories of the summers he had spent at his uncle's farm in Pennsylvania, Sam laid out an extensive vegetable garden, to which he devoted a great deal of time, care, and planning, reading omnivorously about its proper cultivation. Having grown up in relative comfort, Ogden found himself nearly destitute in one of Vermont's most isolated and backward places, but he was much happier. Ogden was very much in line with many of the other back-to-the-landers of the 1930s, people motivated by a belief, as historian Dona Brown has written, "that the system was broken—that the country had gone too far down the path of industrialism, urbanism, and specialization."[8] There was not the slightest doubt in his mind that he had done the right thing.

Despite the qualities he admired in Landgrove's residents, the animosities between them at that first town meeting shocked Ogden. Fortunately, according to Sam, Mamie "possessed the gift of turning ancient hurts and slights into forgetfulness." This would take time, of course, but a major first step was when, at the 1931 town meeting, Mamie arranged for a hot and nourishing lunch to be available, in contrast to the cold sandwiches citizens had brought themselves the year before.[9] Mamie was elected to the school board that year and succeeded in convincing the town to transfer ownership of the Farmers and Mechanics Hall, conveniently located in the center of town, over to the town's building committee for use as a school.[10] By the time the school year began in the fall of 1931 it was ready, the money to renovate it raised through dances put on by Mamie and Sam.[11] In addition to joining the town's school board, she founded a 4-H chapter in the fall of 1931.[12] Sam had been elected a town selectman in 1930, a role he cherished and would continue to perform for decades.[13] It was exactly this type of direct, participatory democracy he had idealized and now found. The idea of government being so close to the people thrilled him.

Meanwhile, Sam was pressing ahead renovating houses at a feverish pace. His first great success occurred late in the summer of 1931 when the Ogdens were visited by friends from New Jersey. Albert Merritt "Pitch" Pitcher was a chemical engineer, the son of missionaries in China who like Sam Ogden had attended Swarthmore College. Pitcher's job forced him to move frequently, disrupting the lives of his three young children, and he was looking for a place where he could root his family during summers. The Pitchers found what they were looking for in Landgrove by purchasing a barn that Ogden had renovated. They were the first of many friends from away who would become at least part-time residents of Landgrove.[14] Soon thereafter William Faulks, an architect from Elizabeth, bought the house next door to the Ogdens.

This was the same house that had been used for a bootlegging operation before their arrival and left in utter disrepair before Sam had turned it into a lovely summer home. Little more than a year into their project, Sam and Mamie Ogden could see signs that it was bearing fruit. By 1932, with the sale of more village houses to New Jersey friends, Landgrove's village was on its way to becoming a thriving summer community.

Weathering the Depression

Among the townspeople whom Sam and Mamie encountered as they ingratiated themselves into the community were the remaining members of Alonzo Valentine's project of four decades earlier. If taken at face value, and not solely as a gimmick to attract attention to Vermont, Valentine had had a vision of a state saved and reinvigorated from decline, economic and human, and abandonment by Swedish outsiders. There are many differences between that project and the Ogdens', of course, but Sam also had a vision of a town saved from decline and abandonment by the arrival of outsiders. Unlike Valentine, Ogden had a great and genuine respect for the town's citizens and their way of life, among them Carl and Anna Westine and Axel and Hilma Neilson. Both Carl and Axel were listed in the 1930 census as farmers; at the age of 63, Carl may have fully retired from working in the woods. Down the road in the Little Michigan neighborhood of Peru, which is geographically tightly interwoven with Landgrove, lived Axel's son Alve, his wife Mary, and their two daughters. The Neilsons and Westines were part of the respectable valley set in Landgrove.

However much social peace Sam and Mamie Ogden brought to Landgrove, everyone in town, valley and hill alike, was coping with the effects of the deepening Great Depression. They were, however, better positioned to weather the Depression than many Americans. Its effects were felt throughout Vermont, of course. The value of Vermont industrial products declined by about 60 percent between 1929 and 1933. In the same period the number of industrial wage earners in the state fell from 27,421 to 15,083, and nearly 40 percent of Vermont's manufacturing plants closed.[15] The Depression was felt in the agricultural sector, as well: Milk prices dropped precipitously.[16] But the onset of the Depression in Vermont was less visible and dramatic than in many other places. In *The New Deal in Vermont*, Richard M. Judd emphasizes that, despite the hardships incurred by Vermonters, "There were no Hoovervilles or shantytowns. Jobless citizens did not form parades or terrorize bill collectors." Vermont business firms, Judd writes, tended to fail "gradually and inconspicuously."[17] Similarly, Sara Gregg observes that, "Vermont initially suffered little from low agricultural prices, food shortages, and industrial failures that plagued most of the rest of the nation during the 1930s."[18] A large part of the reason is that, as a relatively poor and rural state, Vermont simply did not have very far down to go. Rural Vermonters had little money, but they were largely able to make do, and they even made some political progress in those years: To a great extent as a result of pressure from the Vermont Farm Bureau, a state income tax was established in 1931, replacing the straight property tax that had burdened farmers disproportionately. In Landgrove the effects of the Depression were surely felt, but there remained plenty of work to do and enough food to eat. Indeed, Landgrove's residents could take pride in the fact that in 1933 the town was one of only three in Vermont with no unemployment at all.[19]

The Nyrens, Neilsons, Andersons, and Westines who had left the Landgrove area behind likewise endured in the early years of the Depression. But if Vermont as a whole, like them, generally survived without suffering in extreme deprivation, the Depression dramatically changed the state. The last half-century had seen accelerating efforts to organize, reform, and modernize Vermont. The early 1930s, however, witnessed for the first time the articulation of a comprehensive vision, and comprehensive planning, for Vermont's future.[20] This process fully began in 1931 with the publication of the findings of the Commission on Country Life. Titled *Rural Vermont: A Program for the Future*, the collection of reports by the commission's 17 committees constituted a wide-ranging examination of the state's problems and concerns. The report is deeply flawed by ethnocentrism and bigotry, but *Rural Vermont* was a serious attempt to address the state's problems through extensive planning.[21] The cross-over of interests between many of its committees allowed the VCCL to examine the interrelationship between various areas of life, and its report provided a framework through which the issues challenging rural Vermont could be better understood.[22]

Among the committees were the two on which Walter Crockett served in his capacity as director of the Bureau of Publicity. Not surprisingly, on both committees he encouraged the state to pursue the promotion of tourism and the sale of property as summer homes. The Committee on Land Utilization based its findings on a study of 13 towns, ascertaining that in them in 1919 there were 16 summer homes on farms, a number that by 1929 had increased to 63. Finding that "There are some very excellent houses on the abandoned farms of Vermont," the committee concluded that, "In some towns, there are exceptional opportunities for the development of the land resources for recreational uses," because, "while the number of summer homes in these areas is increasing, the increase is less rapid than the rate of abandonment of farmhouses." Anticipating the further centralization of government services and planning that was to come, the committee recommended that, "The responsibility for the solution of the hill town problem should be assumed by the state."[23]

Crockett was merely a member of the Committee on Land Utilization. For the Committee on Summer Residents and Tourists he was executive secretary. That committee began its report by stating, "Vermont's development as a recreational region affords the most promising opportunity for business growth in the state at the present time, and so far as can be foreseen, for a considerable period in the future." In light of the challenges facing both industry and agriculture, the report recommended "wise and consistent policies of protection of our scenic assets." The report gushed with praise for the quality of summer homeowners, who "take a real interest in the communities in which they are located," getting involved in and supporting the churches, schools, libraries and other community enterprises. The reason for this, according to the committee, was that a great many of these part-time residents were college professors, lawyers, artists, authors, and "other persons who are a distinct asset to any community," whose "influence is wholesome and helpful." Describing the existence of hundreds of abandoned farmhouses across the state that could be purchased "by city dwellers at small cost," the report was certain that the conversion of farms to summer homes "benefits both the purchasers and the community in which the purchase is made." Offering nothing but praise for tourists who, from an economic perspective, were "desirable in every way," the committee recommended that the state extend the scope of the Bureau of

Publicity, improve highways, take over the summits of mountains for park and forestry purposes, and pass laws that "keep our state free from crude and offensive advertising signs, from cheap and vulgar displays along the roadside, and from all that would offend good taste."[24]

Studying and Selling Vermont Early in the Depression

Taken as a whole, *Rural Vermont* was a vision of Vermont's future as a society and landscape carefully planned by experts for the use, to a great extent, of not just outsiders, but an elite class of outsiders. One newspaper, the Burlington *Free Press*, even found an unexpected benefit from the Country Life Commission's work, in that it had drawn a great deal of attention from metropolitan newspapers, which was "the finest kind of advertising for Vermont that did not cost you or us a cent, whereas we as a State are paying thousands of dollars to newspapers and magazines to keep people talking about Vermont and its attractions." Echoing the praise for the publicity garnered by Alonzo Valentine's Swede scheme in 1890, the article concluded, "As a publicity stunt alone the work of the Vermont Commission on County Life was well worthwhile. It will attract to our Green Mountain region many a seeker after homes and recreation."[25] State lawmakers strongly agreed that, in light of the Depression, the promotion of tourism was essential. The Bureau of Publicity's appropriation was increased from $15,000 to $25,000 in 1930, and raised again to $30,000 in 1932. When Walter Crockett died unexpectedly late in 1931 he was replaced as director of the Bureau by Harold H. Chadwick, the news editor of the St. Albans *Messenger*.[26] Chadwick found the bureau's work to be in a healthy condition. Tourists were spending less on their visits to Vermont, but the number of visitors had increased, such that Vermont had its most-ever number of tourists in 1931, while the bureau received one-third more inquiries than the year before.[27] Tourism appeared to be a depression-proof industry. Under Chadwick the BOP continued to advertise in out-of-state newspapers and distribute many of the publications it had released under Crockett's leadership, plus some new ones.[28] Author Dorothy Canfield Fisher contributed *Vermont Summer Homes* in 1932, a volume that explicitly specified the type of person the Bureau of Publicity wanted to welcome to Vermont. It was written as an open letter to "those men and women teaching in schools, colleges and universities; those who are doctors, lawyers, musicians, writers, artists—in a word those who earn their living by a professionally trained use of their brains." According to one historian, the volume is "almost fawning in its supplications, [as it] stresses the commonalities and compatibility between resident Vermonters and these select candidates for summer homes."[29]

In 1933, deciding there was a more efficient way of promoting the state, Chadwick consolidated many of the BOP's publications into a single volume, *Unspoiled Vermont*. The volume tantalized readers with the prospect of "any number of abandoned hill farms with magnificent views over unspoiled countryside which will exactly fit your dreams of the ideal summer home at the cost of only a few hundred dollars for repairs."[30] The Brandon *Journal* wrote that *Unspoiled Vermont* would make better known Vermont's hill farms to "the best class of visitors, the kind who not only spend money but take an intelligent interest in their adopted communities."[31] With more money available after the consolidation of pamphlets, Chadwick expanded the bureau's advertising campaign.[32] While per capita tourist expenditures continued to fall for the next couple of years, the number of tourists remained steady.[33] In 1934 the bureau saw inquiries from prospective tourists double, an indication that the "Unspoiled Vermont" campaign was working. It was also apparently appealing to the right sorts: Newspapers praised the slogan for its appeal to "desirable people." If Vermont was to weather the Depression by replacing native Vermont families with out-of-staters, the Bureau of Publicity chose to pursue people who fit an elitist mold.[34]

There was another committee of the Commission on Country Life addressing a topic that intimately affected the denizens of Landgrove: the Committee on Forestry. That committee's report concluded that Vermonters' "continuous drain" on the forests had had serious consequences. As a remedy its members recommended the expanded acquisition of forestland by the state, the reasons for which they thought "self-evident." "Vermont contains many natural attractions," the committee reported, and "these can be maintained useful and beautiful only if the forests along the roads and in highly scenic areas are under public ownership with a definite policy for their maintenance in a wild or natural condition." The report claimed that logging "can ruin forever a beauti-

ful stretch of highway or a waterfall." Additionally, the committee recommended that "roadsides already ruined should be improved as far as
reason allows."[35] Vermont's movement toward extensive public, bureaucratic management of forests took a massive step forward in 1932 with
the creation of the Green Mountain National Forest, projected to eventually comprise as much as 580,000 acres. The federal government began with the purchase of over 31,000 acres, which were mainly located
in Peru but touched on Landgrove as well. There was concern among
many locals that the loss of tax receipts on the land would cause hardships for affected towns, but many small timber companies and hill
farms owners were eager to sell.[36] The state's leaders, and indeed most
Vermonters, welcomed the National Forest as a way to mitigate damage
from future floods and to preserve scenery.[37]

The New Deal Comes to Vermont

Creation of the Green Mountain National Forest was one of the last
actions of the Hoover administration to have a significant impact on
Vermont. The consequences of the policies of his successor, Franklin
Roosevelt, were especially felt in the Landgrove region in two areas.
The first was the founding of the Civilian Conservation Corps in April
1933. Intended to undertake soil conservation and reforestation projects
while putting the unemployed to work, the CCC was immediately recognized by the state forester, Perry Merrill, as a precious opportunity
both to preserve and to improve Vermont. Merrill had already drawn
up plans for forestry projects suitable for federal programs and leapt at
the opportunity to locate CCC camps in Vermont. Merrill placed the
very first camp in the northeastern United States near the site of the old
Clark Lodge in Danby, west of Peru Mountain, and soon after located
a second camp in Peru.[38] The men placed in those camps were given a
number of tasks related to the care of the surrounding forest. To start,
after building their barracks, the CCC's "soldiers" commenced building a 15-mile road between Landgrove and Danby over Peru Mountain
to aid in the administration and protection of the National Forest.[39] A
third CCC camp was established soon after nearby in Weston.

Perry Merrill and other state officials recognized that the work of
the CCC could entail not only conservation but also development in

ways compatible with the state's emphasis on catering to tourists and sightseers. Merrill had previously positioned himself as an ardent advocate for the construction of parks and playgrounds to aid the summer business, and was now armed to act along those lines.[40] In a 1934 talk to Burlington's Rotary Club, Merrill outlined the CCC's work accomplished, under way, and projected. Among other projects, he mentioned the building of roads for the use of sightseers and picnickers as well as for fire protection and forest maintenance, and the construction of hiking trails and bridle paths. Merrill had encountered skiing while studying forestry in Sweden in the 1920s, and noted that those trails could be used for the sport in the winter.[41] "We who live so close to them do not fully appreciate the beauties of our State," Merrill said; "We have been slow to develop and commercialize them as we must if we are to keep up with other States."[42] In pursuit of this goal, Merrill authorized in 1934 the conversion of an old mill site on Peru Mountain into a camping ground, the first such facility built in Vermont by the CCC.[43] It was to be located on the banks of what was formerly known as Mill Pond, where a sawmill owned by Marshall Hapgood had stood for decades, and where Carl Westine had worked. The pond was renamed "Hapgood Pond," and the lumber camp was cleared away. By the summer of 1935, CCC workers had constructed the campground, dams and bridges over the Pond, facilities for swimming, and three miles of hiking trails. The Hapgood Pond camping area opened in the summer of 1935, its conversion from a place of work to a place of recreation complete.[44]

The Green Mountain Parkway Motivates Sam Ogden

The second topic that held the potential to affect the Landgrove area immensely arose in 1933. The federal government made relief assistance of $18 million available to Vermont for a large-scale public works project. Civil engineer William Wilgus proposed that the money be spent on a 250-mile road along the length of the Green Mountains, flanked on both sides by protected parkland. The massive project set off an immediate and heated public debate across the state. Both proponents and detractors couched their views of the Green Mountain Parkway in terms of its compatibility with, or potential to destroy, the mountain scenery through which it would pass; both framed it as a question of

preserving an "unspoiled" landscape.[45] The Burlington *Free Press* pointed to the CCC's road over Peru Mountain as evidence that such construction did not destroy the "natural charm" of the landscape around
it.[46] Others disagreed passionately. Particularly vociferous in their opposition were many members of the Green Mountain Club, who saw
the parkway as an existential threat to the Long Trail. The Bennington
Banner asked in response if it "isn't a bit selfish for the comparatively
few who enjoy the rugged beauty of the Green Mountain range to say
that nobody who isn't a hiker shall be allowed to partake of it?"[47] But
opposition to the project was not confined to hikers: Not only were
there widespread fears that it would damage Vermont's "unspoiled"
character, there were also concerns that the parkway's reliance on federal funds violated Vermont's traditions of independence and self-sufficiency.

Most important agencies in the state and region, such as the state
Chamber of Commerce and the New England Council, supported the
project, though, and in November 1933 the Burlington *Free Press* reported in a headline, "Mountain Parkway Project Seems Assured." The
president of the Chamber of Commerce said that 80 percent of the
state's newspapers favored the project, and that he could foresee "1934
and 1935 employment on the new highway for large numbers of hard-
pressed Vermonters; a century of progress for the State, and the enjoy-
ment of Vermont's beauties by many millions seeking relaxation and
recreation."[48] The New England Council, for its part, promised that the
parkway "would add to rather than detract from the attractiveness of
Vermont."[49] In light of the parkway and other projects both in process
and proposed, Governor Stanley Wilson, a supporter of the project,
decided that Vermont needed a State Planning Board to direct matters.
It was created in the legislative session of 1934, composed of representatives from the state's departments of highways, finance, forestry, agriculture, and fish and game.[50]

As surveying and planning for the Green Mountain Parkway proceeded in 1934, its construction looked inevitable.[51] No matter how
many of its proponents saw the parkway as entirely compatible with
preserving Vermont beauty, it held the potential to dramatically disrupt
the life Sam Ogden was creating for himself. He wrote many years
later that, "during the first years of our life in Vermont, we Ogdens
were engaged in such a scramble to secure an economic and spiritual

toehold in the country of our choice, that we had time for little else."[52] By 1934 the Ogdens were considerably settled in and stable. His family grew with the birth of a son, Duncan, in 1932. By and large, locals considered the Ogdens a welcome addition to town. Sam grew very fond of Charles Colburn, referring to him as "Uncle Charlie." A member of one local family later said he was grateful for the Ogdens' arrival, as it was "great that somebody was keeping [the village] alive."[53] Both Sam and Mamie hired local folks to work for them, for Sam in construction and for Mamie with household tasks, useful employment in the years of the Depression. The extent to which the Ogdens were part of the community is reflected by the faith locals put in them to serve in town offices. By 1934 Sam was the overseer of the poor and a justice of the peace, in addition to serving as a selectman and a town lister (along with John Dolph Neilson). He was also the town's tax collector, and as such was responsible for chasing after such habitually delinquent payers as Harry Neilson and Myron Tifft. Mamie was not only on the school board but had also organized a library, for which Sam's sister Helen, who had joined them in Landgrove, served as librarian.[54] Sam continued to purchase and renovate houses in Landgrove and sell them to friends, moving beyond the village to surrounding farms. Ogden left his mark on the town in another tangible way: Intensely disliking the name "Clarksville," and being in possession of the village, he insisted others call it "Landgrove Village."[55] At his direction, a system was built to pipe water into the village. The Ogdens arranged for ice, meat, and other groceries to be offered by cart to those who lived near their house. Life was considerably less primitive than four years earlier.

By then Sam Ogden's activities and acquaintances stretched beyond Landgrove. In 1932, he joined the Bennington County Republican Committee.[56] As a man with an acute interest in music, art, and literature, he was making friends with many of the interesting characters in the area. Just up the road in Weston lived Vrest Orton, an author who had been on the staff of H. L. Mencken's *American Mercury* before deciding to abandon urban life in 1930. The two became close friends. Ogden also became friends with Scott Nearing, a politically active ex-college professor who had settled nearby in Jamaica in 1932. Nearing and his partner Helen Knothe shared many of Ogden's back-to-the-land ethics, though Scott Nearing's radical left, pacifist politics contrasted dramatically with Ogden's conservatism, and Ogden did not share Nearing's ascetic vision of proper rural life. Ogden was instrumental in the founding of the Vermont Symphony Orchestra in 1934, for which he was an early and enthusiastic member of the flute section.[57]

With his life becoming comfortable and stimulating, Ogden now saw the Green Mountain Parkway as a horrifying threat. Plans for the road had it coming from the south into Peru, where it would cross over the top of Peru Mountain, and then northward into Mount Tabor. To his mind, the idea of building a parkway across the peaks of nearby mountains was anathema; Ogden wrote later, "The prospect of the ravishment of my beloved Green Mountains aroused all the ardor I was capable of."[58] Seething, Ogden ran for Landgrove's seat in the state legislature and won, perhaps not an especially remarkable feat considering that Vermont's legislature allotted each town, no matter its size, one representative, and Landgrove had fewer than 100 residents. Clearly, though, Ogden was respected by his fellow townspeople, and so off he went in the early winter of 1935 to join what he later called "the Great Green Mountain Parkway fracas."[59] He nervously gave his first speech in the State House on the issue. In the process of fighting the parkway he enlarged his circle of acquaintances. Ogden had many legislative comrades in the fight, including author Dorothy Canfield Fisher of Arlington, with whom he became close friends.

In his initial term in the legislature Ogden was appointed to the committee on Conservation and Development. It had been created in 1921 to handle matters related to the natural environment, such as the health and cleanliness of streams and forests, issues about which he was passionate.[60] Ogden loved serving in the legislature. He was delighted by how it disproportionately favored residents of small towns, where he thought virtue resided. He enjoyed meeting important and interesting people. He cherished the concept that he could make a difference in the preservation of the integrity and beauty of Vermont's environment. One of the first bills he submitted proposed an increase in the fee for fishing and hunting licenses, with the money raised going to improve the purity of streams and the fish stock.[61] Most of all, Ogden was committed to bitterly fighting the Green Mountain Parkway. Ogden was delighted when the legislature voted against the parkway's construction. But the project's supporters did not give up, proposing that Vermonters vote on it in a referendum on Town Meeting Day in 1936.

Ogden was in Montpelier for a number of reasons, though primarily to defeat the parkway and see Vermont's environment preserved and improved. He greatly valued the idea of small-town democracy, so much so that he was the only member of the house to vote against state cooperation with the Social Security Act, believing that families and local communities alone should provide for the poor. The vote earned him the nickname "Stand Alone Ogden."[62] Nevertheless, he was fully aware that preserving the environment took planning, regulation, and management. He became a legislative ally of State Forester Merrill, who in his biography called Ogden "one of Vermont's early conservation legislators." At Merrill's encouragement Ogden submitted a bill to control the methods of harvesting trees, which did not pass.[63] And Ogden approved when the legislature in 1935 combined the divisions of fish and game, forestry, and the Bureau of Publicity into a new department, the Board of Conservation and Development, at which time the bureau was renamed the Publicity Service.[64]

The title of the Board of Conservation and Development alone suggests the paradox in which Vermonters found themselves. Beauty, naturalness, and the image of an "unspoiled" state were assets to be exploited, but maintaining those attributes meant that growth needed to be regulated by political action and bureaucratic structures. This was illustrated in 1935 when the State Board of Planning issued a comprehensive study of the state, *Graphic Survey, a First Step in State Planning for Vermont*. The study's introduction described Vermont as historically having "an independent, self-reliant population," and insisted that "much of the same quality remains in the population of Vermont today." "Therefore," the report somehow concluded, "it is quite natural and appropriate that the government of Vermont should set up an official State Planning Board to look after the interest of the State." The board researched the state comprehensively, studying its geology, land use, highways, forests, industries, economy, and people.

The *Graphic Survey* noted that the state's population was relatively elderly, and vowed that the Planning Board would make it possible for the state to retain more of its young people. Indeed, the Planning Board called the question of how Vermonters were going to make a living in

1. Major Alonzo B. Valentine.
(Courtesy of the Vermont Historical Society.)

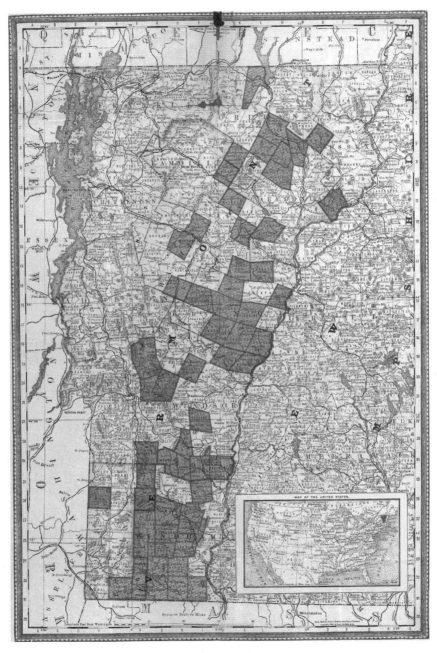

2. "Karte ofver Vermont" [map of Vermont]. Broadside taken to Sweden by
John Nordgren in 1890, and circulated in the United States by Valentine.
(Courtesy of Special Collections, David W. Howe Memorial Library, University of Vermont.)

3. Harry and Harold Neilson, John Neilson's youngest children, in 1898 in Landgrove.
(Courtesy of the Landgrove Historical Society.)

4. Carl Westine (right) and Carl Nyren drinking hard cider in a wagon in 1906 in front of John Neilson's house, around the time the Nyren family moved to Pawlet. The young man standing is Charlie Neilson, who drowned in Landgrove in 1914. The children are Willie Westine and Harry Neilson.
(Courtesy of the Landgrove Historical Society.)

5. The family of Edwin and Louise Anderson around 1903 at their farm in Londonderry. Sitting from left to right are Hazel, Louise, Edwin, son-in-law Alonzo Butler and Hilma, Esther and Helen. Standing are Carl, Charles, and Harry. (Courtesy of Earl Cavanagh.)

6. The McIntyre Mill crew posing. Carl Westine, the mill sawyer, is third from the right. (Courtesy of the Landgrove Historical Society.)

7. The Clark Hunting Lodge soon after its completion, from a postcard mailed in 1908. (Courtesy of Special Collections, David W. Howe Memorial Library, University of Vermont.)

8. The Westines sitting on their front porch on Uphill Road. Top row are Carl Westine, youngest daughter, Freda, and wife, Anna. Below them is Jennie, the oldest. In front are Nola Westine, Willie, nephew Julius, who later married Jennie, and Della Westine. (Courtesy of the Landgrove Historical Society.)

9. A group of students about 1909 at North School District #1. Freda Westine is in the front row on the left. Harold Neilson is in the second row on the right. Della Westine is in the back row on the left, and her sister Nola is on the far right of the same row.

(Courtesy of the Landgrove Historical Society.)

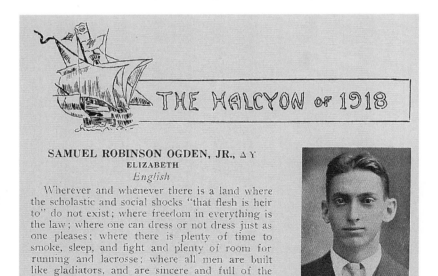

THE HALCYON of 1918

SAMUEL ROBINSON OGDEN, JR., Δ Υ
ELIZABETH
English

Wherever and whenever there is a land where the scholastic and social shocks "that flesh is heir to" do not exist; where freedom in everything is the law; where one can dress or not dress just as one pleases; where there is plenty of time to smoke, sleep, and fight and plenty of room for running and lacrosse; where all men are built like gladiators, and are sincere and full of the "milk of human kindness"; where Shakespeare and symphony concerts are given daily; WHERE WOMEN DO NOT EXIST—there you will find Ogden.

10. Sam Ogden's page in Swarthmore College's senior yearbook, the *Halcyon*, 1918.

11. Sisters Hilma Svenson Neilson and Anna Svenson Westine in the front yard of the Westine house, which Carl Westine bought from Axel Neilson in 1903.
(Courtesy of the Landgrove Historical Society.)

12. Sam and Mamie Ogden's house in Landgrove Village around 1932, with Sam standing in his front yard.
(Courtesy of Duncan Ogden.)

13. Four generations of Westines in 1934: Carl and Anna, daughter Jennie, Jennie's daughter Verna Westine Carleton, and Verna's son Donald.
(Courtesy of Andrew Carleton.)

14. Sam Ogden on the steps of the State Capitol Building
in Montpelier in the late 1930s.
(Courtesy of Duncan Ogden.)

15. Axel and Hilma Neilson with great-grandbaby, Nelsa Doane, in front of their house around 1942. Standing behind them are daughter-in-law, Mamie Beers Neilson, son, Alve Neilson, his son-in-law, Hugh Doane, and daughter, Elba Neilson Doane.
(Courtesy of the Landgrove Historical Society.)

16. Sam Ogden working on his anvil at his Rowen Forge, 1950s.
(Courtesy of Duncan Ogden.)

17. Sam Ogden proudly posing in front of the fireplace he built in his house, 1950s.
(Courtesy of Duncan Ogden.)

18. Sam Ogden riding the ceremonial first chair lift ride at the opening of the Mad River Glen ski area, 1948.
(Courtesy of Duncan Ogden.)

19. John Dolph Neilson, the son of Axel and Hilma Neilson, standing on the right. The photo was taken in 1958 at the time of the auction of the Neilson's farm, home, and equipment following its sale. John already had an apartment in South Londonderry and was working for an upholsterer. He would commit suicide a year later.

(Courtesy of the Landgrove Historical Society.)

the future the state's "most universal" problem, and mainly focused on one solution: recreation. Recreation, wrote the board, was not just "an important business" and "financial asset" that "ranks high with other assets." It was the key to the future, because "while other state assets tend relatively to decrease, recreation steadily increases."[65] The Planning Board's members appeared wistfully resigned to the decline of traditional industries. Their study found that recreation already provided twice as much income as quarrying and was on par with the dairy industry. But "whereas recreation, guided by progressive and imaginative planning, can develop into proportions now undreamed of, no such extension can be reasonably foreseen" for either dairying or quarrying. Dairying faced "severe competition," while quarrying possessed no "immediate prospect for material expansion." Recreation was "the only industry of the three which is in a position to move quickly forward." The report especially emphasized that winter sports showed great promise for expansion, and recommended their growth be encouraged through careful planning. The board praised the Publicity Service for its work, celebrating its effectiveness at attracting "the professional class," and illustrating its point by noting how Sinclair Lewis, Robert Frost, and others from "the literary and artistic world" had found in Vermont "a congenial, stimulating environment." It especially noted the concentration of the "professional and artistic class" summering in the southern part of the state. There, as elsewhere, the proliferation of summer homes was "a welcome and worthy phase of the development of recreation in Vermont."[66] The *Graphic Survey* concluded, "Aesthetically, as well as financially, uniform long-range planning is the prerequisite to the success of the recreation business in Vermont."[67]

Newspapers generally congratulated the Planning Board for the *Graphic Survey*. The Burlington *Free Press* called it "an attractive and thought-challenging effort to set forth the facts about Vermont, and at the same time to trace the outlines of a vision for the future." Harold Chadwick at the Publicity Service wasted no time acting on the Planning Board's recommendation about winter sports. In the autumn of 1935 he hired one Narada "Ted" Coomara of Craftsbury to make a first-hand study of the state's potential for developing ski resorts. Coomara, born in England to an Indian father and an English mother, had learned to ski while attending an elite boarding school in Switzerland.

His father had become a curator at Boston's Museum of Fine Arts, and Narada enrolled at MIT but dropped out after a year. He had ended up in Craftsbury because in 1930, when he was 19, engine failure had forced him to land his personal airplane there. Unfortunately for Coomara, the aircraft was carrying a load of liquor he was smuggling into the country from Canada. When court proceedings concluded, having lost his flying license and liking his new surroundings, Coomara settled down and started a ski club, giving lessons and selling handmade skis. After a tour of potential ski area sites, Coomara told Chadwick he had absolutely no doubt that Vermont held great potential for the development of a thriving ski industry. Chadwick duly reported to the state legislature this opinion from the man identified as his "Hindu Ski Expert."[68]

George, Lottie, and the Vermont Marble Strike

When the 1935 legislative session ended, Sam Ogden returned to renovating houses in Landgrove, expecting a pleasant and busy summer. His daughter Jane, however, began complaining of physical discomfort. Doctors provided a nightmarish diagnosis: She had developed sarcoma of her pelvis. Sam and Mamie quickly moved to New York City so Jane could get the best possible care, renting an apartment across the street from her hospital. Jane did not get better, however, and in early 1936 they brought her back to Landgrove. She died on February 29. A few days later, on the first Tuesday in March, Vermont voters decisively rejected the Green Mountain Parkway in the town meeting day referendum.

Sam and Mamie Ogden were not alone in having a traumatic winter of 1935 and 1936. Lottie Nyren Derosia and her husband George were living in Mount Tabor, George employed as a machine runner in a marble quarry in Danby owned by the Vermont Marble Company (VMC). For the previous year the International Quarrymen's Union of North America had been lobbying without success to get the VMC to sign an agreement providing a higher minimum wage and a standard 40-hour work week. In October 1935, the company declared that the workers in Danby would be put on a staggered schedule in which each employee would work for three weeks and then have one off. In response the workers voted to go on strike. The workers at the VMC's other operations voted to take a "holiday" in solidarity with those in Danby, and when the company tried to continue operating, violence broke out at the VMC's gates in Rutland. With the company and its workers unable to reach an agreement, the "holiday" grew in length, while the violence grew in frequency and magnitude. As October became November and violent clashes between those on strike and those who chose to work escalated, both sides dug in their heels.[69]

It is not known what part George Derosia played in the strike, but of particular concern to many contemporary observers was the condition of the Danby strikers and their families. Newspaper reports described them as ill-clothed and hungry.[70] The strike received a fair amount of attention outside of Vermont, not just because of its violence and bitterness, but also because of the seemingly anomalous reality that it was being waged in a state marketing itself as "unspoiled." The New York City magazine *Commonweal* ran an article bitterly denouncing the VMC and state government that was ironically titled "Unspoiled Vermont."[71] A group of residents of New York City, many of whom had summer homes in Vermont, formed the United Committee to Aid Vermont Marble Workers (UCAVMW) to offer support to strikers and pressure the company to negotiate. Led by Rockwell Kent, a writer and artist who owned a summer home in Arlington, the UCAVMW held hearings on the strike in West Rutland as a way to support the workers and attract sympathy to their cause. The committee had a negligible impact, however, and the strike dragged on. The VMC deputized the largest police force in Vermont's history to keep operations running, ejected some strikers from company housing, and shut off electricity to the houses of others.[72] In April 1936, power lines leading to the Danby quarry were dynamited twice, most likely because 16 employees there had returned to work. The strike dragged on to its conclusion in June, ending in bitter defeat for the workers. George Derosia went back to work, but the strike would linger long in local memory.[73]

What seemed remarkable about the strike to many outside observers was that it had happened in Vermont at all. Author Sinclair Lewis, the owner of a summer home near Rutland and author of *It Can't Happen Here*, a book warning of the rise of fascism set in Vermont because he considered it the most unlikely place to tolerate it, was shocked by the strike. A friend told him during the strike's darkest days that *It Can't*

Happen Here was not only prophetic, "but its dire prophecy was already *happening*, and practically on the doorstep of this luxurious farmhouse."[74] The conception of Vermont as largely consisting of luxurious farmhouses was inaccurate, though. As judged by the lives of Major Valentine's Swedes in the mid-1930s, life was more likely to be a hardscrabble existence of toil and hardship, as it was for George and Lottie. In 1935, Emma Anderson died at the age of 79 in Brattleboro. After working as a servant into her mid-70s, she lived out her last years as a resident of the Brattleboro Retreat, a psychiatric hospital. She left behind five children in the immediate area: son Charles, for example, was working as a sawyer in a basket mill in Westminster, while daughter Ellen lived in Brattleboro with her husband, a sign painter of Irish descent. The husband of another daughter, Esther Carey, was a Brattleboro truck driver. In 1936 Eddie Tifft, Lottie Derosia's ex-husband, died. He lived out his final days on a small farm in Peru, his occupation listed on his death certificate as "laborer." A year later his and Lottie's daughter Addie Tifft Guyette, long plagued by bad health, died at age 37 of a lung hemorrhage, leaving behind her farmer husband and five children. There were happy times, as well. Harry Neilson married in Landgrove in 1935 at the age of 43, to a woman from Weston. Helen Ogden, the town clerk, signed his marriage certificate. But life had not been easy for Harry: Since losing his father's farm in 1929, Harry had drifted between Weston and Landgrove, working as a farm laborer. It was practically inevitable that he would give up on Landgrove.

Meanwhile, after the tragic death of their daughter, Mamie and Sam set back to work. The previous summer the Ogdens had hosted five children of New Jersey friends for a few months, and in 1936 Mamie expanded that number to ten, the start of a yearly summer camp. In the coming years the camp grew, providing companions for the Ogden children and much-needed income. Alve Neilson's wife Mary did some cooking for the campers, specializing in birthday cakes that had small change embedded in them, and her daughter Arline worked at the camp at times.[75] Sam expanded his work renovating houses. He had a team of workers by this time, and was taking jobs outside of Landgrove. When visiting his uncle's farm as a boy, Ogden had been fascinated by the forge used to repair farm machinery and had learned the basics of ironwork.[76] Now finding himself in need of specialized tools, he decided to make them himself and built at his house what he named the Rowen Forge. The Ogdens' ties to their neighbors deepened. Sam's sister Helen married Landgrove farmer Lester Cody in 1937. Three years later, Mamie's sister Betty married William Badger, the son of the man who had purchased the first summer home in Landgrove only months before the Ogdens had arrived in 1929.

Those marriages were the first of many between members of the community that surrounded the Ogdens in the years to come, in a pattern reminiscent of the intermarriage between the Dorset families of earlier generations into which Valentine's Swedes had inserted themselves. Descendants of those Dorset families remained in the area, including in Landgrove. Ahial Crandall, a descendent of the family into which Henry, Moses, and James Tifft had married in the mid-nineteenth century, lived on a marginal farm in Landgrove. So too did Myron Tifft, a son of Moses. Myron and his wife Lutheria had a reputation not only for being peculiar characters, but for being untrustworthy. They were frequently suspected of stealing from their neighbors. Carl Westine once caught Lutheria sneaking out of his yard with a chicken; when he seized her, eggs poured out of her pockets.[77] Myron and Lutheria were impoverished; town lore has it that one winter's day, in the midst of an argument, Lutheria threw a knife at Myron. When he ducked and the knife smashed through a window, Lutheria castigated him for moving out of the way, saying that now they would freeze.[78]

The Arrival of Skiing

As tourism boomed in Dorset, the town of Myron Tifft's birth, there was increasingly less of a place for people like him. Landgrove had proven a refuge for a few decades, but change was coming there, as well. Sam Ogden was intimately involved in one of the crucial factors in that change. Early in the 1930s the Ogdens opened an inn in Peru, "Ogden's on the Mountain," for skiers who came in the winter to utilize easily accessible sections of the Long Trail. Sam would drop them off in his Ford station wagon at the top of the trail and pick them up again at the bottom. In 1934 the nation's first rope tow was constructed in Woodstock, Vermont.[79] The apparatus proved immediately popular, and downhill skiing took a leap forward. In 1935 the Vermont State Planning Board drew up a map of winter recreation spots, distributed by the Publicity Service, which prominently featured Peru. The first trail at what became Big Bromley ski resort was cut by the Works Progress Administration in 1936. The area's potential for expansion drew the attention of Fred Pabst, of the brewing family. In 1938 Pabst founded the Big Bromley ski resort; Sam Ogden helped to install its first rope tow.[80] Pabst's expansion of the ski area entailed, as a *Vermont Life* article on skiing described, "dynamiting, bulldozers, and thousands of man hours of hard work."[81] This was a drastic reshaping of the landscape, but one that Ogden and others thought consistent with the maintenance of an "unspoiled Vermont," unlike the Green Mountain Parkway. Later in the decade Ogden's on the Mountain burned down. Sam decided not to rebuild, but lost no interest in the growing ski industry. The Ogdens' house was large enough to sleep 14 boarders, and in these years they rented spaces to skiers.[82] A few years later Ogden told a newspaper that, while he had originally staked his future on creating a summer colony, "as soon as the winter sport interest started, I took it up immediately as I sensed it had great future possibilities."[83]

Sam, Mamie, and their sons became enthusiastic skiers. One day in 1937 saw Sam and Mamie skiing in Worcester, Vermont, with Dorothy Canfield Fisher and her husband, all of whom a newspaper described as "pretty fair shakes as skiers."[84] In 1938 Sam was elected president of the Eastern Amateur Skiing Association, and a later article on the early days of skiing remembered him officiating races, "always standing at the finish gate enveloped in an enormous raccoon coat, stop-watch in hand."[85] Ogden loved the small scale of Vermont towns, the participatory nature of their politics, the closeness of their communities, the idiosyncratic nature of their residents, and the integrity of Vermont's scenic beauty. Like other kinds of tourism, Ogden thought that, done correctly, skiing could be complementary to all he valued about his adopted state.

Managing the Landscape

Ogden had become quite a prominent figure in Vermont. As he went about his many activities he came to be called "The Gentleman from Landgrove."[86] In 1937 the board of the Vermont Symphony Orchestra, founded three years earlier as a venue for amateur and professional musicians alike, elected him its president. The orchestra was struggling, and Ogden, a devout music lover if not gifted himself as a musician, worked tirelessly to put it on stable footing.[87] He also pursued his political career with relish, becoming an increasingly influential member of the legislature. He was reelected representative from Landgrove in 1936, and when the session began he was appointed chairman of the committee on Conservation and Development. It was an important post: As chair of that committee Ogden would have a great deal of input on such environmental issues as how forests were managed, how streams and soil could be preserved and improved, and how tourism would be regulated so as not to destroy the scenic beauty on which it depended.

The legislative session of 1937 began with the inauguration of a new governor, George D. Aiken. Unlike the great mass of his predecessors, Aiken was not a lawyer or wealthy businessman, but instead the owner of a nursery and seed business. Raised on a farm, he had not attended college. Aiken was widely considered relatively progressive for a Vermont governor.[88] On the issues closest to Samuel Ogden's heart, the new governor had mostly sympathetic views. Aiken said in his inaugural speech that Vermonters "should look with satisfaction" at the hundreds of "small hill farms and village properties" bought as either permanent or summer homes by outsiders to the state. In a statement that distilled the paradox of using the state's beauty to promote growth, he said that Vermont "should not go to extremes" in promoting tourism but instead, "try to maintain a sound balance" between it and other parts of the economy. Nevertheless, he encouraged Vermonters to continue to develop recreational resources in such a manner that people from other states would "find Vermont most attractive." Aiken also spoke extensively about natural resources, advocating that Vermont take advantage of a recent federal law, the Fulmer Act, which provided federal funds for the purchase of forestland to be used as state parks. Aiken strongly endorsed the work of both the State Planning Board and the Board of Conservation and Development.[89] Ogden could safely feel that in the new governor he had an ally in his effort to preserve Vermont while attracting more people to it in a carefully thought-out and regulated way.

On at least one issue Ogden differed from Aiken: The governor advocated the separation of responsibility for fish and game management from the Board of Conservation and Development. Ogden opposed the move, fearing it would give hunters and fishermen too much influence over policy and lead to a reduction of conservation efforts. The Fulmer Act had proven extremely controversial in the legislature. Its detractors feared increased state reliance on the federal government, but Ogden heartily supported it, despite his faith in local control.[90] Submitting a bill enabling the state to employ the act's terms, Ogden explained it was a means to expand state forest areas to 100,000 acres. A report his committee issued to the full legislature asserted the act was "designed to check the willful and selfish exploitations by private interests of forest lands which have resulted in harm to the public welfare."[91] To quell fears it would impoverish rural towns by reducing their tax base, Ogden put into the bill a special provision to reimburse affected towns for losses in taxes from land acquired.[92] The committee he led also submitted an unsuccessful bill to establish county conservation boards to regulate the use of soil and streams, and county foresters to supervise timber cutting.[93]

Much of Ogden's work in the legislature entailed walking a fine line between using state and federal resources to defend and preserve Vermont's environment, while at the same time not robbing the state of its long-cherished traditions of local control and individual rights. This complex and contradictory demand was felt by others. Governor Aiken was typical of many when he said that, "a reasonable amount of publicly owned land, properly divided between the State and Federal government, is all right, but we must not forget the private owner of the land," adding that "I would like to see as many persons as possible own a little land. The more people there are who own a little land in this country, the better citizens we shall have."[94] It was a commonly felt dilemma. A speaker to a Vermont conference on wildlife in 1938 told his audience that, "Not only should Vermont capitalize on her advantages by continuing to tell people about them, but she should also strive to make her State even more interesting, more attractive. However, in doing this she should ever be most cautious not to sacrifice that individuality, that 'unspoiled Vermont' which she now possesses."[95] Vermonters were likely to want to hold on to Vermont tradition, as least as they individually saw it. But they also needed to be cognizant of the necessity of casting aside some elements of Vermont tradition so as to save other aspects of it.

Whatever the complications that arose from the mission Ogden and those like him shared, Sam was enjoying the people he met. He worked closely, and became good friends, with forester Perry Merrill. Governor Aiken was fond of Ogden. And Ogden was also enjoying an increasingly high profile. A 1938 Burlington *Free Press* article on Mamie and him titled "Restored 'Deserted' Village" congratulated him on giving Landgrove "a new lease on life." It credited him with having combated the town's "slow burning of decay" by buying 16 Landgrove properties in total and renovating them. "Gradually," the article described, "as their friends from New Jersey and Kentucky and their friend's friends came to visit them, the Odgens sold them the old houses...All have now been sold and are occupied during the summers."[96] A letter to the editor in a subsequent edition credited the Ogdens for "reviving [Landgrove] and making it attractive as a summer community, after it seemed to be on the way to complete abandonment." The letter's author further made a wish for more people with Ogden's kind of "vision and ability and determination" to come to other struggling towns so as "to save these communities and make them self-sufficient again." The *Free Press* speculated that many Vermont communities "could profit from the energy, ability and initiative of people like the Ogdens," and proposed the creation of a "special committee of Vermonters" who could make a tour of the state and identify villages that could profit from similar renovation. The committee could then draw on the Publicity Service's inquiries to find candidates to revive those villages, "but these would have to be weeded out with care. Those selected as the right sort of developers of summer home colonies should be visited personally by the committee" to ensure they were "the right sort of people." [97] Echoing Alonzo Valentine's program many decades before, only a certain kind of people would do for Vermont, adhering to not only class, but also ethnic and racial, specifications.

In 1938, the 35 or so voters of Landgrove again elected Ogden to the General Assembly. A newspaper profile of him at the beginning of the 1939 session called him one of the "Interesting Personalities" in the legislature, noting his identifying feature to be a green Tyrolean hat with a small feather.[98] He was spoken of as a potential Republican house majority leader, but instead was reappointed chair of the committee on Conservation and Development.[99] He again used the position to fight for a cleaner environment, and especially for measures to combat water pollution. The house killed a bill he wrote that would have created a state water resources board, despite support from Governor Aiken and the state's Planning Board.[100] Trying to walk the fine line between centralized management and local control, he opposed a bill establishing soil conservation districts with federal money, depicting it as an acceptance of a federal bribe in exchange for federal encroachment on local rights.[101] Ogden successfully sponsored a bill that pried a $1,000 appropriation for the Vermont Symphony Orchestra.[102] One of the most contentious issues into which he inserted himself was billboard restriction, which came before the committee he chaired. Support for billboard restriction had been gaining momentum as a means to improve scenery, the charge led by the two-year-old Vermont Association for Billboard Restriction. Many in the business community, and especially the owners of small enterprises, were adamantly opposed to greater regulation, but the Association's head, while admitting that it was impossible at the time to ban billboards entirely, insisted they must be kept out of scenic places.[103] Sinclair Lewis lobbied the legislature in favor of billboard restriction, stating in a letter that, "inasmuch as it is primarily the quiet beauty of Vermont which has attracted all such summer residents as myself, we patriotic outsiders cannot conceive the possibility of Vermont not making the most drastic rulings against the use of any roadside billboards whatsoever."[104] When the original bill in 1939 was withdrawn in the face of opposition, Ogden submitted a substitute bill that was less drastic but similar in purpose.[105] That bill passed, initiating legislation limiting the size and placement of roadside signs and resulting in the removal of many billboards statewide.[106]

As the 1939 legislative session wound down, Governor Aiken appointed Ogden to a prestigious post, the state's Planning Board.[107] Barely two months later, however, Aiken shifted Ogden over to the Board of Conservation and Development.[108] In this capacity he would help oversee matters under the purview of the fish and game director, the state forester, and the head of the Publicity Service. Ogden threw himself into the board's work, and among his early accomplishments on it was successful advocacy of the installation of the first ski chair lift on Mount Mansfield, and then the construction of the Mansfield Base Lodge there, where a plaque remains to this day listing Ogden's name alongside those of the board's other members.[109] A decade after buying his "deserted village," Ogden was moving in the state's highest circles. A newspaper photograph from April 1940 shows him at the opening of the Vermont's Sportsmen's Show in Burlington alongside Governor Aiken, Merrill, Chadwick, and the other members of the Board of Conservation and Development. He has the smile of a man delighted to be surrounded by important people, and confident in the knowledge that he too matters.[110] Further responsibilities were thrust on him in 1940, when Ogden was appointed one of Vermont's directors on the New England Council.[111] That appointment put him in contact with an ever-wider range of important people, and in a position to have an even greater impact on Vermont.

Ogden was one of Vermont's most visible and active citizens. When he had the time he continued to renovate houses in Landgrove and other nearby towns. He worked at Big Bromley ski resort in the winter, selling tickets and maintaining the machinery. He took up a teaching position at a private high school that opened nearby in 1937. He sold some of the wrought iron products of his forge. A significant part of the family's income came from the camp Mamie ran every summer. But if he could not take pride in the accumulation of wealth, he could be gratified at how dramatically Landgrove had changed in ten years. The houses were bright and orderly, and in the summer the village was full of interesting and entertaining friends. One book on Landgrove describes the village then as populated by "the painter, sculptor, puppeteer, musician, photographer, doctor, architect, writer, and gourmet cook."[112] Ogden stood at the center of this community of interesting, creative people. In his 1937 book *Let Me Show You Vermont*, Charles Edward Crane called Landgrove "one of the most interesting summer-home developments I have seen in Vermont." Noting that Sam and Mamie had "bought practically all of the little village of Landgrove," Crane called the town "a passion with the Ogdens, not always profitable, but they have found heaps of livin' in their country experiment."[113] In the late 1930s, Dorothy Canfield Fisher's pamphlet *Vermont Summer Homes* largely consisted of Ogden's renovations, and Fisher summarized their work by writing, "Mr. and Mrs. Samuel R. Ogden studied the possibilities of this oldtime Vermont place and attained this charming result."[114] A profile years later declared that, "The Ogdens have ruled Landgrove ever since they bought up most of the village during early Depression days, restored its abandoned houses and sold them gradually to fellow expatriates from New Jersey, thereby creating a backroad cul-de-sac of culture, creativity and common interest."[115] This was at least true of the summer. During the decade between 1930 and 1940 Landgrove's full-time population dropped from 104 to 64.

If Ogden had created an identity for Landgrove, the town was representative of much about which many Vermonters felt ambivalent. With increasing intensity in the late 1930s, Vermonters debated the state's identity and future as they weighed the consequences of 40 years of its marketing as a peaceful retreat from the modern world, and especially a decade of attachment to the slogan "Unspoiled." Over the 1930s the number of farms had dropped less dramatically than in previous decades, to 23,582, but farmers faced worsening problems related to overproduction, declining consumer demand, and inefficient systems of milk collection and distribution.[116] Many traditionally important sectors of manufacturing, such as textiles, timber, and quarrying, had declined during the Depression and faced an uncertain future. The federal government was winding down the Civilian Conservation Corps, which had done much to stabilize Vermont's economy.[117] Tourism had been a bright spot during that difficult decade. The Vermont Chamber of Commerce proclaimed in 1940 that, "Vermont has pioneered in the promotion of her unique attractions to that well-to-do class who can contemplate ownership of a summer home. Numerous Vermont towns have already been revitalized by this transition of abandoned or non-productive farms into improved summer residence properties." The chamber declared that the "possibilities in this direction are limitless. The surface has hardly been scratched as yet."[118] But staking so much of Vermont's future in that direction received resistance. A particularly heated episode in that debate resulted from a 1941 Bennington *Banner* editorial proposing that greater effort be taken by state government to preserve natural beauty. It touched off what the *Banner* called an "editorial controversy" that "raged throughout much of the state press as to the state's 'Unspoiled Vermont' program." The Rutland *Herald*, Burlington *Daily News*, and St. Johnsbury *Caledonian-Record* shared the opinion that the "Unspoiled" narrative resulted in stultification and stagnation. It mainly was attractive to old and wealthy people who were opposed to developing the state, limiting opportunities for its young people. Keeping Vermont "unspoiled," they argued, demarcated the present and future of the state as being in the hands of some people and not others.

Sam Ogden inserted himself into this debate. Writing to the Rutland *Herald*, Ogden insisted that the state's priority should be to preserve "Vermont's unquestionable charms." In response to claims his opposition to development might label him a "fuddy-duddy," Ogden not only embraced the term but proposed the creation of a "Fuddy-Duddy Club," nominating Dorothy Canfield Fisher as honorary president. Ogden rejected the idea that there were only two kinds of people, "those who don't want change, and those who find Vermont and Vermonters a bit dull and lethargic about making changes in their way of doing things." He was instead "an exponent of the theory that there are fundamental values in Vermont which it would be a pity to lose in any promotional effort to change it to what some people might call 'a more progressive state.'" Ogden wrote, "This charm and this way of life have nothing to do with stagnation or with quaint somnolence. People who have found Vermont a good place in which to live are not trying to escape from progress. They are merely defining progress differently from those who think the word is synonymous with speed and intensity of action."[119] Ogden concluded, "In the river of life there is a place for the rapids. But constant travel in the rapids is devitalizing. It is the calm quiet places where the river flows evenly and steadily that the surplus strength and power is developed to do the constructive work of the world."[120] Vermont, he believed, was uniquely that kind of place. The *Banner's* final word on the controversy crystallized the search for the elusive balance between tradition and progress to which 50 years of the state's evolution had led it: "We can work for all these things. We can all try to be progressive, not static. But we can at the same time attempt to keep the state from literally becoming spoiled unnecessarily."[121] Ogden, perhaps, understood better than many the challenge of balancing progress and tradition. But as he also knew, there were times one had to choose between them. As admirable or desirable as Ogden's vision might or might not be, the reality was that that vision foresaw a society and landscape planned for and organized largely around the desires of only certain kinds of people.

Away From, and To, the Soil

By 1941 traces of Valentine's Swedes remained in Landgrove. Axel and Hilma Neilson were still there, as were their sons Alve and John Dolph. Alve supplemented his farm income in those years by working for the state Forest Service.[122] The farmhouse of Axel's brother John, which had lain uninhabited since its sale in 1929, was purchased in 1938 by a professor of anatomy at New York University. In 1940 Anna Westine died at age 74, and Carl moved to Stratton to live with his daughter Jennie, whose husband and two sons worked in a sawmill. Their Landgrove house on Uphill Road was purchased as a summer house in 1941. Son Willie Westine died in Chester in 1938 from chronic asthma, leaving behind six sons still at home. Carl and Anna's daughters Nola and Freda lived nearby, their husbands and sons working for various small sawmills and manufacturing firms.

Others of the second generation continued to move away from the Landgrove area. Harry Neilson finally gave up around 1940, moving to Bellows Falls to take a job at the machine-tool company Jones and Lamson. His brother Harold had moved even farther, to Brewster, New York, where he worked at a CCC camp. Mostly this second generation of Valentine's Swedes continued living the modest lives they had made for themselves. Anna Nyren Fountain lived in Wilder, taking in the laundry of students at Dartmouth College, where her husband worked in maintenance. Her daughter Lillian remembered that her parents had very good credit: "Their jobs weren't fancy, but they would be the first to get an electrical refrigerator." Anna liked Vermont very much and had a fulfilling social life. She enjoyed her walk to church each Sunday morning, where she would encounter a neighbor who was from Germany, and the two would speak to each other in their native languages. All of Anna's siblings came to visit periodically, and she visited them: Lottie in Mount Tabor, Carl in Arlington, and Oliver in Rutland, still living with his niece Mildred and her husband John, who worked as a machinist in a furniture factory. Mildred is remembered by relatives as having been a kind woman, but John, though not a big man, was rowdy, in the habit of going to beer joints and picking fights. Carl and Lottie were reaching retirement age, but Oliver, a very bright man who Lillian describes as "very interested in everything, very up-to-date," was enjoying the mature years of a successful, if stressful, career as the assistant superintendent of Prudential Insurance's Rutland office. The lives of the children of Valentine's original five Landgrove families tell many different stories, but a unifying theme is the movement away from agriculture. Judging by their lives, as by the trajectory of Vermont's agricultural economy, Vermont's future was not in its soil.

Sam Ogden came to the opposite conclusion. Tending his extensive vegetable garden was a central joy of his life. When Mamie was running her camp he often put the children to work doing tasks such as weeding, believing that connection to the soil and living things was an essential experience. Sam decided he knew enough about gardening to write a how-to book. Published in 1942, *How to Grow Food for Your Family* spread his name further.[123] He gave the first copy to George Aiken's successor as governor, William Wills. A review of the book went out over the Associated Press wire and appeared in newspapers across the country. With World War II begun and the government's push for citizens to plant "Victory Gardens," its publication benefited from good timing.

Sam Runs for Congress

Sam Ogden's political ambitions reached their zenith in 1942. Vermont's lone congressman was Charles Plumley, first elected in 1934 and a passionate opponent of the New Deal. For example, Plumley had warned that the CCC "would engender hatred and strife and breed all forms of isms except Americanism."[124] With a flamboyant oratorical style and an aptitude for garnering attention, Plumley had positioned himself as one of the most strident anti-Communists in Congress. George Aiken, now a United States senator and the leader of the progressive wing of the Vermont Republican Party, hoped to find a contestant who could give Plumley a good challenge in the primary election, but the most likely candidates refused to run. In August, just one month before the primary, Samuel Ogden decided he should take up the mantle, against the advice of his friends.[125] Ogden promised a "whirlwind fight" against Plumley.[126] The contest drew a fair amount of attention, in part because it was that year's only contested primary in Vermont.

Publicity went beyond Vermont's borders when *Life* magazine published a brief profile of Ogden in a late-August edition. A picture of Sam at his forge was accompanied by a caption that read, "Town Builder: Samuel Robinson Ogden, 46, is a blacksmith, architect, food and conservation expert and Swarthmore College graduate who has rebuilt the resort town of Landgrove, Vermont, much of it with his own hands. Ogden is running in the September 8 Republican primary against Charles Plumley, Vermont's only representative, who is noted for Red-baiting and anti-labor speeches."[127]

Ogden's campaign was associated closely with the progressive Aiken wing of the Republican Party, though Sam by no means considered himself a liberal. He received endorsements from labor unions, largely because of his association with Aiken, who had treated unions well, and as a rejection of Plumley.[128] The influential Rutland *Herald* gave Ogden a glowing endorsement. The Newport *Express* saw the contest as perfectly illustrative of the division between the party's liberal and conservative wings, but in response the Brattleboro *Reformer* wrote that, "The question of liberalism vs. conservatism cannot properly be introduced into the consideration of the two men." The paper saw Ogden's candidacy more as an attempt by Aiken to have greater influence over the party. To the *Reformer*, Ogden was "a fearless fellow who does his own thinking and isn't in the habit of taking orders from anybody."[129] As was frequently the case with candidates born out of state, there was some grumbling about Ogden's nativity; the Bennington *Banner* predicted that Ogden would mainly attract "the summer colony vote."[130] The *Free Press* insisted, however, that "his length of residence in the state as well as his interest in its affairs entitles him to the name of Vermonter in every sense of the word."[131] Ogden was also opposed by many sportsmen, and by small timber-lot owners angry about his support for utilization of the Fulmer Act.[132]

On primary election day, Plumley trounced Ogden by a two-to-one margin. Aiken felt satisfied that Ogden had run a colorful campaign and, as Aiken put it, brought "a lot of the Old Guard faults out in the open."[133] The Brattleboro *Reformer* was of the opinion that, "you can't move into Vermont, live here, however efficiently and nobly for thirteen years, and have a ghost of a chance to go to Washington."[134] All tallied up, Ogden had spent a total of $995.40 on the campaign.[135] A month after the primary election Samuel Ogden enlisted in the Army. He sent a letter to Governor Wills offering his resignation from the Board of Conservation and Development, but Wills left the seat open for him, much to the distress of the sportsmen who had grown to dislike Ogden's activist approach to fish and game issues.[136] In late October, Ogden made an appearance at the annual meeting of the Vermont Guild of Oldtime Crafts and Industries, for which he was a trustee and his dear friend Vrest Orton was secretary.[137] With that done, Sam Ogden went off to serve his country.

CHAPTER 7

Vermont in a State of Twilight: 1942 to 1959

The World War II Years

WORLD WAR II was hard on Landgrove: Five of its young men, either full- or part-time residents, died in the war. Sam Ogden served his two years as an army captain stateside and was able to continue serving institutions like the Vermont Symphony Orchestra and the Vermont Historical Society.[1] The war also gave him time to think about his next literary project. For years, summer residents of Landgrove had been telling him how much they admired his life. The constant refrain he heard from his urban friends was that they worked hard but felt as if they were not getting anywhere, spending money without taking pleasure in their purchases. They could not imagine trading the city for the country, however. Such a move was too complicated, the hardships too daunting, the sacrifices too extreme. Sam decided there was a place for a how-to book for those who might follow his example but for timidity. It would be a good thing, Sam thought, to impress upon people how fulfilling rural life was.

As many of the children of Valentine's five Swedish families had served in World War I, so their grandchildren went off to World War II. Of particular note was the service of Norman Anderson, whose father Harry had died when he was four. Norman served bravely in the European theater, and by the time he retired from the military many years later as a lieutenant colonel he had received two Purple Hearts, three Bronze Stars, two Silver Stars, and the Army Commendation Medal. The service of other descendants was more prosaic. Willie Wes-

159

tine had served overseas during WWI, and now four of his sons enlisted in the military. Glenn Westine enlisted in December 1942 at the age of 18 in the Corps of Engineers for the duration of the war. He had a grammar school education, and his occupation was listed as "unskilled construction." Freda Westine Wilson's son Stanley also enlisted, as did Jennie Westine's son Caspar, who at the time of enlistment was described as a "semiskilled chauffeur and driver" with two years of high school. Military service was good for Lottie Derosia's youngest son Richard, who she raised in the rough atmosphere of lumber camps. Having only a grammar school education, in 1940 he was living with his older brother Charles in Hancock, Vermont, working as a woodcutter, and family memory recalls him as being exceedingly lazy prior to the war. His service as a warrant officer did much to give him more discipline.

In the meantime the war served to burnish Vermont's image as a reservoir of old American values. The Publicity Service was not alone in crafting this image of the state. Beginning when he moved to Arlington in 1939, Norman Rockwell's paintings, and especially those on the cover of *The Saturday Evening Post*, had depicted small-town Vermont as a special world characterized by the finest values and forms of neighborliness produced by traditional American communities. During the war Rockwell produced his famous "Four Freedom" paintings, which projected a flattering impression of Vermont and Vermonters' values.[2] Rockwell used Arlington residents as models for his paintings. Among them, according to family lore, was Carl Nyren, still working as a machinist in Arlington at the age of 71.[3] Rockwell's paintings depict a world in which long-term shared experiences, the raw material of strong communities, are the foundation of human interaction. For all the hard times she had endured, Carl's older sister Lottie had known that kind of community. She and husband George had moved in 1940 to Granville, in Addison County, where they took up a farm. If her first marriage had been a disappointment, the second was full of love, including the love she gave to the step-grandchildren they raised. She was frequently visited by her children, and was especially close to her daughter Mildred. In 1944 George Derosia died, and soon after Lottie moved to Arlington. In his life George had worked at various times in lumber camps, in marble quarries, and in farming. These had been the foundation of Vermont's economy at one time, but in the preceding decades they had become steadily less significant. The World War II soldiers descended from Valentine's Swedes could justifiably imagine they were fighting to preserve a very special kind of society in Vermont. The question was to what extent that society would have a place for them in the future.

In Sam Ogden's absence, Vermont state government continued to work on matters of particular interest to him. The 1943 legislative session witnessed a hotly debated bill to divorce the three responsibilities of the Board of Conservation and Development—publicity, forestry, and fish and game—into three separate departments. The measure was supported by the state's fish and game clubs and other sportsmen's organizations, whose members continued to feel badly treated, excessively regulated by the board, and excluded from helping to shape its policies. Supporters of the board as it was then constituted responded that it was efficient, and Vermont was too small a state to need or support three separate departments. As one representative put it about the discontented sportsmen, taking out their frustrations with some fish and game officials by destroying the department was akin "to burning the barn to get a couple of weasels."[4] To the dissatisfaction of sportsmen, the bill failed after being the most contentious topic of the session. Fish and game interests grew even more unhappy when, at the very end of the session, the Board of Conservation and Development was replaced by a new five-member board named the Department of Natural Resources, which, while having expanded responsibility for the state's geology and landscape, had no more representation from fish and game interests. As the session neared its end, according to one newspaper, "considerable heated arguments raged" about the reorganization.[5] State government, sportsmen widely felt, was favoring outsiders over natives in the use of natural resources.

In 1944 Harold Chadwick of the Publicity Service published a ten-year study titled *Vermont's Tourist Business*. Chadwick's examination revealed that while in the late 1930s tourism had declined, 1941 had been the best year ever. The war had caused the number of tourists to fall again, but the average expenditure by those who still came had jumped. Apparently, fewer but wealthier people were coming. Chadwick had distributed questionnaires in the previous few years to tourists, asking what particularly attracted them to the state. Among the reasons, he found that city people were "tired of the social whirl and desire to get away from large crowds." Chadwick's study also documented the rising importance of winter sports to Vermont tourism. He congratulated the work of state government in encouraging the improvement of ski areas, which had led to larger patronage at many resorts, including Peru's Big Bromley. Chadwick happily promised that, "soon after the war, winter sports should be well over a million-dollar business."[6]

When Landgrove's representative in the legislature died in the spring of 1944, Mamie Ogden was appointed his replacement.[7] In the fall, having finished his army service, Sam returned home and resumed his political activities. He replaced Mamie in the house in the election of 1944 and was again appointed chair of the committee on Conservation and Development. And again, in that position, he drew the ire of those who thought there was too much governmental interference in Vermonters' use of their own land.[8] Ogden submitted a bill providing for more regulation of Vermont forests by the Department of Natural Resources. At a public hearing on the bill that filled its room to capacity, Ogden argued that greater regulation was obviously needed, and it was better for the state rather than the federal government to impose it. Opponents were distressed by the prospect of yet more regulation and rules over what they could do with their land; one speaker said he "felt just the way the Vermont hillbilly did—when he wanted a Vermont forester on his land, he would ask him to come." The bill ultimately was defeated.

Ogden had more success restructuring state agencies. He was a sponsor and a vocal proponent of a bill that renamed the Planning Board the Vermont Development Commission. It was to an extent only a rebranding, made in large part because Governor Mortimer Proctor wanted it to create, as he said, "more opportunities for work and more incentive for young people to stay in Vermont."[9] The Development Commission was also given responsibility for handling matters related to flood control. Additionally, the Publicity Service, then located in the Department of Natural Resources, was switched to the Development Commission. Ogden argued that moving the Publicity Service would consolidate promotion and give a different direction to the state's publicity efforts. In opposition, a legislator protested that the legislation was "in effect subsidizing the hotel business."[10] Ogden and his allies would most likely not have seen a need to apologize for that.

The reorganization passed, and at the conclusion of the legislative session Ogden was appointed to the new Development Commission. It had been appropriated $55,000 for publicity and $20,000 for other activities, compared to $45,000 total to the Planning Board the year before. The publicity funds were intended not just for recreation, as many legislators felt had been too much the case since the 1910s, but also to promote Vermont's agricultural and industrial opportunities.[11] The Development Commission quickly took up the business of promoting tourism. After three years with no such publication, the commission made available upon inquiry in 1946 a winter sports promotional folder. Advertising Vermont as a "scenic wonderland of winter sport," it especially highlighted four ski areas—Snow Valley, Pico, Stowe, and Big Bromley—that had operated during the war.[12] The commission also took upon itself the task of gathering and distributing to newspapers reports on ski conditions at Vermont resorts.[13]

From the beginning, the Development Commission's work was controversial. By the end of its first summer it had come under some public criticism for perceived inaction, to which its members responded that 70 percent of its work had been in the area of flood control, which its members pointed out was not even related to actual development of the state.[14] The commission also became a political issue in the fall of 1946. Ernest Gibson, a close friend and political ally of George Aiken, was seeking to be the first candidate to ever unseat an incumbent governor in a Vermont primary. That incumbent, Mortimer Proctor, ran newspaper advertisements promising "New Horizons for Year 'Round Recreational Development in Vermont," predicated on an increased appropriation for the Development Commission's publicity activities. Gibson, on the other hand, ran on the promise of dramatically modernizing state government, and he made reform of the Development Commission one of his key issues. Gibson proclaimed that Vermont was plagued by "dying towns" in danger of becoming ghost towns. He saw the solution as bringing industrial development to such places, something he thought the Development Commission and its predecessors had not sufficiently done.[15] In a shock to Vermont political tradition, Gibson won the August 13 primary. He prepared to shake up the Development Commission once he was elected governor.

The Birth of Vermont Life Magazine

Ernest Gibson complained that the Development Commission was thus far a disappointment, but it was doing more than just flood control. In early September 1946, the commission published the first edition of a new state magazine, *Vermont Life*.[16] The director of the Development Commission and its board members, including Sam Ogden, had decided earlier in the year that an official state magazine would be a great addition to their promotional efforts, and the news that such a publication would be forthcoming was announced at the beginning of April.[17] Resistance to the idea came from the state auditor, who considered the magazine of dubious worth in light of its cost, but the Development Commission won the day.[18] The magazine's staff was composed of associates of Sam Ogden: The president of the Vermont Historical Society, Earle Newton, was appointed editor-in-chief, and Ogden's good friends Vrest Orton and Walter Hard Sr. were appointed to the advisory board. Upon appointment Newton promised that the magazine's goal was to "set forth the Vermont way of life, and show opportunities for industry, agriculture and recreation."[19]

If it was Gibson's goal to have the Development Commission place more emphasis on promoting industry, he might have been disappointed by the magazine's first edition. Its articles collectively depicted Vermont as a rural ideal. There was one piece on the history of the machine-tool industry of Windsor and another on the Vermont Industrial Relations Council, an organization created to solve labor disputes in, as its handbook stated, a peaceful "Vermont way."[20] But from the front cover depicting an autumn landscape to the back cover showing a haying scene, the clear message of the magazine was that Vermont was a beautiful, pastoral state composed of small towns, farms, and recreational attractions. Its purpose was clearly stated in an introductory letter from Governor Proctor: "If you are one of those who has not yet had an opportunity to know at first hand our beautiful countryside, the friendliness of our people, and the 'Vermont Way of Life,' this magazine will be a preview of what you may expect." The way of life on display was clearly one that differentiated the state from urban, industrial places, not one endeavoring to become like them. Newspaper reviews of the magazine celebrated that angle. To the Bennington *Banner*, *Vermont Life* deserved to be hailed with approval by out-of-state people "who consider Vermont a sort of scenic paradise, unspoiled by urban civilization," noting that "the magazine is frankly slanted to appeal to prospective visitors and summer residents."[21] The Rutland *Herald* described the Vermont depicted by the magazine as composed of "lakes, streams and attractive villages," and called the first edition "evidence of the pictorial appeal found in this state." Within two weeks the Development Commission announced that all 12,000 copies of the magazine were sold out.[22]

This Country Life

The society depicted in *Vermont Life* was crafted to contrast with the general direction of America. To Samuel Ogden, the society on show was not an illusion created by bureaucrats and writers. Already pondering a book on living in the country, Ogden was put into action when a number of returning servicemen found their way to his Landgrove home to ask for advice about how they too could live in the country. They were an echo of the same disillusionment with modern life he had experienced in the wake of the First World War.[23] Within a few months he had finished what became his best-known work, *This Country Life*. Published in the summer of 1946, the book did not pretend that rural life was without "care, grief and want," all things Ogden had known well since moving to Landgrove. Ogden made it clear that he was not writing to those who measure success in terms of the accumulation of material possessions. *This Country Life's* measure of success is instead a fulfilling, useful life characterized by a happy family, meaningful work, and civic engagement. The book walks prospective back-to-the-landers through not only what to look for in selecting a house, but also how to improve and maintain one, such as by renovating chimneys. Ogden identifies potential ways to make a living in rural places, including hosting guests, with special mention of the potential held by winter sports like skiing. The book also described such practical matters as how to tend a garden, how to ensure one's children receive a quality education, and the proper way to behave so as to smoothly ingratiate oneself into a rural community.

For all its practical advice, *This Country Life* was primarily Ogden's effort to lay out his philosophy of life. When running for Congress in 1942, he had been accused of being naïve for calling farming "a way of life" rather than another form of employment, but the book reiterated that belief. He wrote, "In the country, life seems to be more direct and normal and satisfying, and country living seems to me to erect bulwarks against the mistakes and follies of the age." The satisfaction Ogden promoted is drawn from a self-directed life. If one wants food, he grows it; if one needs tools, he makes them; if one wants a good school, he creates it. Most of all, if one wants good government, he gets engaged in it, and the magic of rural places was that the small scale of government makes it possible for each citizen to contribute to communal life and local affairs. Ogden wrote that, "the closer the machinery of government is to the people, the more meaning it has; and the more active the participation in the responsibilities of government, the better the citizen. For these reasons, living in the country, or in a small rural community, brings one to better citizenship." To Ogden, the opportunity to become a member of the community and to get close to the workings of governing was "one of the strongest reasons for a return to the soil." He thought that involvement in public affairs happened naturally in rural places. Ogden's bottom line was that country living is superior because, as far as possible in modern society, people were in control of the forces that affected their lives.

This Country Life was well received, with reviews appearing around the country. The review that went out over the Associated Press wire called it "a practical, entertaining and beautifully illustrated book for those who live, and want to live, in the country." The Pittsburgh *Press* described it as "a recipe for changing city slickers into real farmers... full of advice in a rambling, simple style, through gardening and its wormy troubles, how to operate a forge, how to make flies for sportsmen, tips on how to raise dogs, and so on." For all its advice, "it is not a dry book," the review concluded, "but more in the vein of a mellow-philosopher who tries to lure the dusky denizens of a metropolis into a better life."[24] It was a review, one assumes, of which Ogden approved.

Postwar Politics

In 1946, for the fifth time, Samuel Ogden was elected Landgrove's representative to the state legislature. As expected, Ernest Gibson was elected governor. Gibson had spent the campaign attacking the work of the Development Commission, saying it was his goal to "vitalize" it, and his criticisms continued after election day.[25] In response to the commission's director telling Vermont's Tourist Association that its members' business would soon outstrip agriculture as the state's biggest revenue producer, Gibson responded that the commission should be spending its time surveying small towns as to their industrial prospects, and then searching for people willing to invest in those towns' development.[26] Industry and not tourism, Gibson believed, should be the foundation of Vermont's economy. Gibson also desired a complete overhaul of the Department of Natural Resources, which at the time was responsible for conservation, fish and game, forestry, and the study of the state's geology.[27] These moves in economic development and conservation were part of Gibson's larger, extremely ambitious program of reform touching on education, health care, welfare, and other issues. Gibson's inaugural address reiterated his belief that state government desperately needed comprehensive modernization. He proposed that the Development Commission be relieved of its responsibility for flood control and devote its work to two areas. First, he declared that "the time is now ripe for the State to secure for itself small industries that will fit our State" and reverse the depopulation of small towns. Perhaps influenced by Ogden, he also softened his rhetoric on tourism, describing Vermont as "on the verge of a big recreation boom," especially in regard to winter sports, and demanded that investors in ski resorts be rewarded with adequate road maintenance and cooperation from all departments of state government, specifying particularly the Forest Service. In both regards he challenged the Development Commission to be "the nerve center for industry and industrious Vermonters."[28]

At the beginning of the legislative session Ogden was once again appointed chair of the committee on Conservation and Development.[29] Feeling it a conflict of interest to be directly concerned with legislation affecting the Development Commission, Ogden resigned from the commission. Gibson held the position vacant for him, calling Ogden an "outstanding member" of the commission.[30] During the 1947 session three contentious issues particularly occupied Ogden's time. The first concerned further billboard restriction, something Ogden strongly supported. His committee produced a bill that Ogden speculated would ban 80 to 90 percent of existing billboards. He campaigned hard for passage of the bill, promising that he was ever-mindful of "a reluctance to admit that a man cannot use his own land as he pleases."[31] The Vermont Association for Billboard Restriction was grateful for his leadership on the topic. Most of the state press supported billboard restriction, as well; one reporter warned that failing to act would cost the state many millions of dollars because people come to Vermont "to enjoy views created by time and nature rather than by high-pressure soap salesmen."[32] But Ogden's efforts earned a great deal of enmity from other groups, led by the Vermont Outdoor Advertising Company. Sam's friend Earle Newton, in his 1949 book *The Vermont Story*, singled out Ogden as a putting an especially heroic, underdog's effort into the fight, in the face of the "high powered and lavishly financed campaign of the advertising interests."[33] After a series of heated hearings, the restriction bill was defeated.

The second issue was Vermont's great political football: management of fish and game. Ogden's committee proposed the creation of a board, appointed by the governor, which would have the authority to comprehensively regulate fish and game. When it was presented, sportsmen and the legislators representing them howled. One legislator called Ogden's bill "the most dictatorial bill ever written." Another said about members of the Natural Resources Board, "they took half the rights, now they want all the rights." One representative from a small town complained in general about what he saw as the proliferation of boards in general, saying, "all we have to do is get a few more boards like this and we can go home and stay indefinitely." In the end, a representative added an amendment to Ogden's bill that allowed the establishment of the board but struck out the rest of the bill. Ogden lamented that his bill, "the result of long, painstaking and honest effort," was now "in a secondary position to a bill which was shipped up overnight." In the end, again, Ogden lost.[34]

On the third issue Ogden had more success. The Development Commission's responsibility for issues related to the health of Vermont's waterways and flood control had allowed it to get very little else done.

Ogden's solution was the creation of the Vermont State Water Conservation Board. A Water Resources Board had been established in 1944, but it had no legal status or enforcement powers. Ogden wrote and submitted the bill creating the new board, and to the satisfaction of him and others who wanted Vermont to become more "unspoiled," the bill passed.[35] It had been a busy legislative session for Ogden, with mixed success, but as one reporter put it, he had "cut a lot of weight with the '47 House," especially earning him a greater reputation as one of the state's leading conservationists. With the session over, he returned to his place on the Development Commission, which the legislature had reorganized at Gibson's request. It now had four divisions under the director: research and planning, publicity, industrial development, and geology.[36]

Soon after he resumed that position, the five members on the Development Commission's board came up for reappointment by the governor. Having loudly made his dissatisfaction with the previous commission known, Gibson now had a chance to revamp it. He declined to reappoint four of its members; the only one who remained on the board was Samuel Ogden, who Gibson made the chairman.[37] Going forward, Ogden and the commission's director had greater resources with which to work. At the governor's urging, the legislature granted it a much larger appropriation, raising it to $200,000 a year. Of that sum, $100,000 was devoted to publicity activities, and half of that was consumed by *Vermont Life*.[38]

A major reason for the increased appropriation, and for Gibson's reorganization of the Development Commission, was his desire to see it do more to attract industry. The commission set to work compiling statistics on the state and its towns, largely for the purpose of identifying industrial growth areas and potential manufacturing sites.[39] *Vermont Life* did not reflect that emphasis, however; it continued to depict Vermont as standing in contrast to industrial society. For the Summer 1947 issue of the magazine, Sam Ogden wrote an article titled "On Country Living" that condensed his book of the year before. The article implored the reader, "if you have any ideas for a small industry, contact the Director of the Vermont Development Commission in Montpelier." The statement was an awkward fit in the article, though; most of it was devoted to extolling the beauty and quality of life in a state that diverged from urban, industrial places. Ogden wrote, "the most difficult step to take in changing from city living to country living is a shift in point of view and a change in values." Compared to city life, he wrote, country life was "normal and satisfying." He concluded, "It is my sincere hope as I sit here before a fire of four foot logs this morning, while the blizzard rages outside, that others may find as I have found, satisfaction and serenity among the Green Mountains of Vermont." Such was the anomalous nature of the Development Commission's work. It endeavored to make Vermont more industrial, even as it sold the state as an escape from the world touched by industry. However paradoxical its work might be, the commission's board and employees pressed ahead.[40]

The Development Commission continued to churn out quarterly issues of *Vermont Life*, despite the magazine consistently losing money. The magazine complemented the Publicity Service's extensive promotional efforts, which still included the distribution of free pamphlets and the placement of advertisements in metropolitan newspapers. A new aspect of the commission's publicity campaign was the production of movies. The first of these, produced in 1947, was *Our Amazing Beavers*. Three more followed in 1948.[41] One, *Thanks to Vermont*, focused on the state's agricultural products and methods and was mainly aimed at young Vermonters. The other two were aimed directly at tourists. *Background for Living* is a series of recreational scenes—golfing, boating, horseback riding, skiing, and others—with a soothing voiceover extolling Vermont's many attractions. The movie asks, "What can Vermont mean to you?" and gives a number of answers, one of which shows footage of Sam Ogden at his forge while the narrator intones, "For Samuel Ogden, it has meant the creative satisfaction of restoring a once-vigorous community to life, largely by the work of his own hand." Interspersed through the half-hour movie is a story about a very Caucasian, very middle-class family of four searching for a home because, as the narrator tells us, Vermont also means "A gracious farmhouse against the hillside, a bit of lakeshore, a refuge for days of ease upon retirement, or a fine old house on a tree-bordered street." At the conclusion of the movie the family finds the perfect house. Making it clear that he has the power to decide who is allowed to live in town, their crusty real estate agent tells them in a heavy Vermont accent,

"This isn't a big town, and we don't have room for folks who don't fit in, but you folks do."

The third movie was *Ski Vermont*, a companion piece to *Background for Living* showing scenes of the sport.[42] Copies of these movies were made available for free by request from the Development Commission, and in the coming years the agency paid to have it shown on the new medium of television. In 1951, when *Ski Vermont* won an award, it was estimated that it had been seen by a million people. By then, promoting skiing had become a significant part of the Development Commission's work. In 1948 it conducted a study of the impact of the ski industry on Stowe, and upon the report's recommendations the resort launched a major construction project over the next couple years, flattening some slopes, making others steeper. The commission lobbied the state to devote more Highway Department resources to building new access roads to ski areas, and to prioritizing keeping existing access roads open and in good repair. Members of the Highway Department were unhappy with that emphasis, wishing instead to prioritize roads used to a greater extent by state residents. In his history of Vermont skiing, Perry Merrill explained that while it was the state's policy in the late 1940s to provide highway access to ski areas, "Highway Department officials were opposed to the policy and did all they could behind the scenes to frustrate its implementation."[43] Nevertheless, the Development Commission generally got not only the roads it wanted, but also funds for parking lots and base lodges.[44] The commission carefully tracked the income produced by the ski industry, and promoted it through such things as "Why Ski?" essay contests.[45] When the manager of one resort gave a talk in December 1948 declaring that Vermont led all states in skiing, he singled out the Development Commission as especially deserving of praise for doing much to promote the sport.[46]

Though the expansion of the ski industry required extensive manipulation of the landscape, it included the kind of tree cutting of which Sam Ogden and others on the Development Commission approved, and was strictly regulated by state permits. The commission's members felt quite the opposite about how Vermont's forests were otherwise being treated. When speaking on the subject, Ogden was careful to emphasize his personal opposition to the general spread of state controls into personal affairs, but, as he told an audience at a Vermont forestry conference in 1949, "we cannot escape the conclusion that forest management is a public responsibility." To Ogden, no individual had the right to exploit the land he owns so that it was ruined: "Ownership of land can only be regarded as trusteeship," he stated, and "The record shows that we are and have been despoiling the state's resources and violating the laws of nature, and it is being done more through greed than ignorance."[47] Ogden reiterated the point a few weeks later in a similar forum, declaring that good forestry practices could not just be voluntary, and calling for forest harvesting to be "regulated by law and the law implemented by force."[48]

For a man who strongly felt that the role of government should be limited, Ogden was unafraid of calling for its use when he thought necessary. When a committee was formed in 1950 to advise the Development Commission on promotional efforts, Ogden told them that "there is a never-ending supply of scenery to sell tourists, but Vermonters should be concerned with the damage done to this scenery through stream pollution and the scattering of waste and rubbish along highways."[49] If there was to be development, Ogden believed, it could not defile the environment or change Vermont's essential character. Change had to be managed, and not just in forests and streams. His friend Earle Newton wrote in 1949 that as Development Commission chairman, Ogden had "no vast plans to lure great industries into the state, nor to promote a great wave of indiscriminate tourist travel. [Ogden] represents the wise synthesis of the native and the new-comer in his desire to see the state develop along progressive lines without a sacrifice of its individuality and its more or less unique way of life."[50] The elusive, perfect balance between past and future was out there, Ogden believed. If working toward it required the loss of some personal liberty, it might be unfortunate, but was necessary.

Landgrove in Its Prime

Sam Ogden stayed plenty busy in these postwar years, exclusive of his political activities. Particularly special to him was his ongoing service as president of the Vermont Symphony Orchestra. World War II had caused the symphony's suspension, but in the years following the war's end Ogden led an expansion of its schedule and opened smaller chapters of the main orchestra in various parts of the state; he and Dorothy Canfield Fisher presented the charter to the new Bennington chapter in 1947. By the late 1940s, the orchestra was making a profit.[51] Sam ended his long tenure as president of the VSO in 1952, but his love for classical music did not diminish in the slightest.[52] Though he considered himself a poor musician, Sam loved playing cello and flute, and participated in amateur performances in his and others' houses. These amateur performances were elevated in quality when Sam struck up a close friendship with Nathan Milstein, a world-class violinist. Milstein bought a house in Londonderry, and for a number of years hosted other equally prestigious classical musicians, much to Sam's delight. Alice Pitcher Dibble, whose parents owned a summer home in the village, remembered later that, "in the village, night and day, you would hear music on Victrolas, and chamber music Sunday afternoons in the Ogdens' living room. Sam was a sort of pied-piper, gathering musicians. Milstein, [pianist Alexander] Brailowsky, [pianist Vladimir] Horowitz, and other musical neighbors all participated."[53] To Sam Ogden's delight, Landgrove had become a magnet for artistic, creative people.

Landgrove's evolution in such a short period of time from an isolated, stagnant place to a thriving, artistic community drew some outside attention. *The American Home* magazine profiled Landgrove in 1947, writing that, after being "abandoned and neglected for over sixty years, its houses gray and forlorn, this village gained new life and charm thanks to the ingenuity of a city-bred architect and wife." The result was that, "from early spring until late fall, every house overflows with community-spirited owners and the friends…Everywhere, an atmosphere of friendly warmth and happiness permeates throughout this tiny community, restored from neglect and decay by one who had both courage and vision." *American Home* concluded, "city-bred Samuel and Mary Ogden have made a fine art of country living, and have helped and are helping others to find the same freedom of spirit and abundant living which they so highly prize."[54] Two years later the cover of the same magazine featured a photograph of the Landgrove home recently built for Barbara Comfort, a landscape and portrait painter from Greenwich Village who attended France's Ecole des Beaux Arts.[55]

Landgrove certainly was doing well. The town carried no debt and its school was well regarded.[56] Landgrove was associated with an artistic set of people with urban sensibilities, yet enjoyed an identity as an oasis of country living, as if a municipal mirror of the products on the shelves up the road in Weston at the Vermont Country Store, Vrest Orton's replica of his father's old dry-goods store.[57] Much of that identity revolved around Sam Ogden. A 1950 article on Ogden's forge in the magazine *Craft Horizons* emphasized "the extreme simplicity" of his methods working with "true wrought iron" that Sam ironically imported from Sweden. Through the forge's window one could get "a glimpse of the Vermont woods," while inside Ogden used only tools "gathered from old blacksmith shops all over the countryside." The article went on to describe how Odgen had revitalized the deserted village, where "the ring of hammer on the anvil and the smell of smithing coal in the air were the first signs of a rebirth of activity."[58] This balance between the village's "rebirth" and its pastoral character was echoed two years later in a *Yankee* magazine article titled "The Blacksmith's Village." After recounting Ogden's discovery and renovation of the village, it detailed how he had sold houses "to friends and people who, like the Ogdens, wanted to exchange the confusion of city life for the simplicity and basic virtues of the country." Describing Landgrove Village as "an ideal setup for a summer development," *Yankee* wrote that Ogden did not mind not having made a "financial killing" because what he wanted was "good neighbors, converts to country life, so he sold his houses without material profit."[59]

In some ways Landgrove was indeed replicating the patterns of a traditional rural village. Marriages between young Landgrovites continued. The aforementioned Alice Pitcher, for example, was married in 1947 to Thomas Dibble, whose family also had a village summer home. In other ways it was growing increasing distant from such types of communities. The *Yankee* magazine article also contained a picture of Lutheria and Myron Tifft captioned "the last of the old timers." The Tiffts were not, in fact, the only "old timers" left in Landgrove. Axel and Hilma Neilson remained on their farm along the Landgrove Road, along with their son John Dolph, and son Alve still lived nearby. They were the last of Valentine's Swedes in Landgrove. Of the five couples that were the seedbed of the 1890s "Swedish colony," Axel and Hilma were the last alive. Carl Westine died at his daughter Jennie's house in nearby Chester in 1949. Jennie's nephews, the sons of her brother Willie, also lived in Chester, most of them commuting to jobs in Springfield, such as at the machine-tool company Fellows Gear Shapers.[60] John Neilson's son Harry worked at Springfield machine-tool concern Jones and Lamson at the same time, and one assumes they would be glad to encounter each other, having grown up together. The same is true of Jennie Westine's sister, Nola Westine Carver, who lived in Brattleboro, where her husband Charles worked for a heating and plumbing business. She most likely encountered Hazel, Ellen, Esther, Charles, and Carl Anderson, who had lived in Londonderry at the same time as Nola 40 years earlier and now also lived in the Brattleboro area, as did Mary Neilson Capen, the youngest child of Axel and Hilma Neilson.[61] Having grown up together in a rural village, they were reuniting in industrial centers.

These people's move to factory jobs in population centers is illustrative of the continuing evolution of Vermont's economy. The Andersons' sister Hilma and husband Lon Butler still lived on a farm in Danby, but by the early 1950s they had retired from dairying. Ceasing to farm was hardly unique to them. In 1945 there had been 26,490 active farms in Vermont, but by 1950 there were only 19,043.[62] Between 1940 and 1950 Vermont's rural farm population declined by 23 percent while its rural nonfarm population increased by an equivalent amount.[63] The costly transition from the old milk can to bulk tanks that was on the horizon promised to further compound those trends. Other traditional industries faced a similarly precarious future. Textile factories had been an important part of the state's industrial economy for a century, but antiquated facilities and competition from lower-wage states drove most of them out of business in the postwar years. The largest private employer in the state in 1946 had been the American Woolen Mill in Winooski, but it closed in 1954. The number of sawmills in Vermont was also declining precipitously.[64] The Connecticut River Valley's machine-tool companies in which the Westines worked were struggling to cope with postwar conversion; hundreds of workers were laid off in the years following the end of the War.[65] The machine-tool industry would rally for a while in the 1950s, but Vermont's economic future was clearly uncertain.

For a short time the conversation about Vermont's future played out in a monthly magazine to which Sam Ogden contributed. *Town Meeting* was published between March 1950 and April 1951. The discussions in *Town Meeting* give a portrait of a society under stress and uncertain of its future. When one contributor, a native Californian, denied that Vermonters had unique characteristics and asserted the state was not "an island unto itself," Ogden was outraged. Identifying himself as "an individual, not as Chairman, Vermont Development Commission," he wrote that the idea that Vermonters were not special was "characteristic of the 'liberal' point of view" that he found "completely unrealistic." Ogden declared that, "in reality we live in a world of differences...All human relationships are immediate and personal and if these relationships are conducted with love and understanding, with tolerance and good taste, with wisdom and complete acceptance of the golden rule, the need for a resident of Brattleboro to hope for the day when Vermonters would be undistinguishable from Texans would disappear." Ogden was the exception, though: The magazine's articles reflect a general feeling that those things that had distinguished Vermont and Vermonters for generations were endangered. Its pages overflowed with articles like "Does Vermont Face an Economic Crisis?" and "Shall Vermont Go Forward?"

One topic that especially concerned contributors to *Town Meeting* was the impact of tourism and summer homes. An officer of the Vermont Farm Bureau wrote that he had heard from many farmers who objected to the Development Commission's campaign to sell farms as summer homes. Farmers considered themselves in "cultural conflict" with the newcomers, and whereas Vermont had been characterized by an egalitarian spirit in the past, newcomers, "being more aggressive, seem to feel it is their special destiny to bring the benefits of their kind of society to the 'backwoods' of Vermont." Citing "this looking down upon Vermonters by newcomers" as the source of great antagonism, he concluded, "It is very infuriating to have your way of life looked down upon, particularly when you have a great regard for it."[66] Sam Ogden's friend Scott Nearing shared these farmers' dissatisfaction. In his book *Living the Good Life*, Nearing wrote that during most of his 20 years in Jamaica, he and almost all his neighbors had lived independently. He wrote, "In a word, each household was a law unto itself and was based upon a solid economic foundation—a piece of the earth from which, at a pinch, it could dig its own livelihood."[67] But Nearing saw that way of life as threatened by forces he and his neighbors could not control, one of which was tourism. If Vermont built a "vacationland economy," he warned, locals would be forced to abandon their economic independence. But as undesirable as tourism's impact on the economy was, "The social consequences of turning the countryside into a vacationland are far more sinister," because communities were built on people "living together and cooperating day in, day out," something impossible in a town dominated by transients from away. A second threat to locals' way of life, their "freedom as individuals," was aimed directly at the work Sam Ogden did: Nearing wrote that his neighbors "were suspicious of organized methods and planning. They would have none of it."[68] Scott and Helen Nearing decided they had had enough of it themselves in 1952 and moved to Maine.[69]

Sam Ogden's Stand

Sam Ogden's feelings about the consequences of planning and tourism were far more mixed. He enjoyed his work as chairman of the Development Commission. Considering the period of transition in which Vermont found itself, he could reasonably conclude that the state's economy desperately needed development, and therefore the work of the Development Commission was becoming more important. As he went about that work Ogden struggled with the challenge of striking a balance between the need to regulate and the desire to preserve personal liberty. He agreed with his close friend Dorothy Canfield Fisher when she wrote in her 1953 book *Vermont Tradition* that, "the basic, primary concern of Vermont tradition is...based on the idea that group life should leave each person as far as possible to arrange his own life."[70] In order to maintain the conditions that allowed one to arrange their life, however, extensive planning was necessary. This was illustrated by a 1951 Development Commission report that Ogden largely wrote. The report recommended that Vermont prioritize industries that would not add to the pollution of streams or mar the beauty of the landscape, and cited the need for planning in regard to proper land use and for local zoning laws. It also recommended the elimination of billboards, touted the preservation of covered bridges, and encouraged highway engineers to "take into consideration the charm of the scenery when relocating roads and bridges."[71]

Thus Ogden believed the Development Commission played an essential role in helping Vermont negotiate encouraging development while preserving tradition, and he entered the 1951 legislative session looking for an increase in the commission's appropriation. The new governor taking office, however, believed that Vermont did not need a Development Commission at all. Lee Emerson had made abolishing it one of his campaign promises, pointing to its expense in light of the Korean War. He reiterated the promise to abolish the commission in his inaugural address, proposing that its activities be distributed to other agencies and funding for those activities be cut in half. In protest Ogden resigned from the commission. In an open letter to the governor and the legislature he warned that, without the Development Commission, "such research as is necessary for the wise and intelligent operation of the State will not be done." Furthermore, the amount Emerson proposed spending was wholly insufficient and would constitute money wasted. The remaining members of the commission quickly passed a resolution thanking Ogden for his service, saying that they "sincerely and very deeply" regretted the end of his "most devoted and useful services" to the organization. "No one claiming Vermont as his birthplace has been more keen in discernment of the needs of the state, both material and spiritual," they wrote, "and no one has devoted more earnest and conscientious effort to help in every forward endeavor to spread the knowledge of Vermont life and make Vermont a better place to live."[72]

Ogden's resignation was politically dramatic, his protests vigorous, and the state's press followed the battle over the Development Commission's fate closely. Ogden pressed his case to save the commission in numerous forums. One late January article covering a speech by Ogden was headlined, "Ogden Opens Up on Emerson." Emerson named a replacement for Ogden, but before the house could act on the appointment, an appropriation bill was introduced that kept the commission as it was, though cutting its funding to $75,000. In response to it Ogden withdrew his resignation, putting Emerson in an awkward position. The governor implicitly accepted the resignation by appointing a replacement.[73] When hearings were held on the bill, Ogden led the opposition, declaring the reduced appropriation entirely insufficient. In the end the commission was granted $100,000, which Ogden testified was the bare minimum it needed to function. While the commission moved forward with less funding and a new leader, Ogden left it convinced that its work promoting Vermont, both recreationally and industrially, was essential to the state's future.[74] He also knew the state's environment and scenery were endangered by too much success along those lines. Vermont's traditional small-town life and communities were not just assets to be sold, but things to be cherished and preserved on their own merits.

Ogden had come to Vermont in search of a meaningful life 22 years before, and the degree to which he had found it was inseparable from its rural character. If the community that he had in large part created was composed of mostly artists and professionals from away, it also benefited from people like John Dolph Neilson. A lifelong bachelor who had always resided with his parents, John was a local character. Quiet and amiable, he had served in a number of town offices, such as on Landgrove's election commission alongside Sam Ogden. For over 30 years he had been performing roadwork for the town when necessary. John had persisted where so many other natives of the town, the people Ogden had found in 1930 to be so peculiar and engaging, had left. But Landgrove, and Vermont, as a whole, had changed since then. Ogden had personally engineered the community along the lines long promoted by the Bureau of Publicity: It was a community composed largely of "desirable" people, defined in class, ethnic, and racial terms. In the late 1880s Alonzo Valentine had sought to engineer Vermont's human landscape in that way. To a fair extent, in Landgrove, Sam Ogden, who had turned his back on the multi-ethnic, multi-racial New York City area, had succeeded.

The Coming of the Interstate Highways

One significant change for Vermont came when WCAX, the state's first television station, went on the air in 1954. The state's citizens had long cherished their tradition of small-scale, town-based politics. Television initiated the era of what political scientist Frank Bryan calls "antenna politics."[75] Political images and reputations would now be created much less by personal contact on the local level. Another adjustment Vermonters had to make in the mid-1950s was to the proliferation of bulk tanks on dairy farms. They were not yet required, but it was hard for farmers without them to compete. But the greatest turning point of the decade was the 1954 announcement that the federal government would be undertaking a massive public works project to build four-lane highways across the country. The poor condition of Vermont's road network had been a concern for four decades, but the prospect of the interstate highways brought their own anxiety. State officials had to figure out how to pay the state's share of the cost. Additionally, many Vermonters were to be displaced where the path of construction ran through houses and fields. And once the highways were completed the state would be within an easy day's drive of an enormous number of people, putting more pressure on local communities and resources. When construction began in 1957, Vermonters could look at the project with a mixture of hope and apprehension.

Those people who owned and worked at ski resorts probably felt less apprehension than most. The industry had grown substantially since World War II. When Mad River Glen opened in 1948, Samuel Ogden of Landgrove, Development Commission chairman, looking ebullient and nattily attired in a newspaper photograph, was given the honor of taking the triumphal honorary first chair lift ride.[76] Dressed inadequately, he claimed afterward to have nearly frozen to death by the time he reached the top. A number of large ski resorts opened in the following years, including Mount Snow, Ascutney, and Jay Peak. When young New Yorker Preston Leete Smith approached Perry Merrill, now in his third decade as state forester, about starting a ski resort, Merrill pointed him in the direction of Vermont's second-highest mountain. Merrill arranged for 3,000 acres of forestland in Sherburne, 40 miles from Landgrove, to be purchased from the Vermont Marble Company. The plan to develop Killington ran into intense opposition from the State Highway Department, which threw every obstacle it could into the path of construction of access roads to the area, diverting money intended for Killington to other projects that to a greater extent served state residents. Despite the resistance the resort opened in 1958. Soon after a business executive named Frank Snyder, on his way home from a ski weekend at Stowe, eyed Stratton Mountain, 11 miles to the south of Landgrove, and formulated plans to develop it for skiing.[77] Sam Ogden, who still worked at Bromley and was good friends with its owner, would soon have a second large resort in close proximity to his home.[78]

Resistance to Centralization:
The Home Rule Committee

Change was coming quickly to Vermont in the 1950s, and many of its residents often wondered if they were losing much of the independence and autonomy they had long prized. In recent decades there had been an expansion of the reach of government, both state and national. The interstate highways, primarily funded by the federal government, were perceived by some as a threat to state independence. What portion of the highway project Vermont's state government was required to shoulder caused the state to go into much greater debt, which some Vermonters thought was tantamount to surrender.[79] For many Vermonters, too much control over educational policy had been taken away from small towns, and the state's encouragement of school consolidation and union schools seemed a violation of tradition. This general feeling of a loss of autonomy was manifested in the founding in February 1956 of the Committee for Home Rule in Vermont Towns. The moving spirit behind the organization was Herbert G. Ogden, a newspaper publisher who was no relation to Sam. He dedicated the committee to "the principles of individual responsibility, self-help and self-government, upon which Vermont was founded." Herbert Ogden decried the "the tendency for governmental power to concentrate in Montpelier."[80] The committee commenced publishing a bi-monthly bulletin, and by mid-summer Herbert Ogden reported that the group had over 200 members and was still growing rapidly.[81] With determination, the committee's members readied themselves to fight for their version of Vermont tradition.

As the 1958 legislative session approached, the members of the Committee for Home Rule promised that they would speak for "those Vermonters who have come to realize that their towns have been steadily stripped of their powers of self-government while the central government in Montpelier (or Washington) has become ever more powerful." Unless this trend toward centralized power was halted, the committee warned, "the unique advantages of a democratic form of government will be lost to Vermont." Early in the session the committee held a public hearing to announce its two main goals: keeping more tax money in the towns in which it originated, and keeping small schools open. About relief from the "ever-increasing tax burden" the group claimed was forced on small towns, one legislator sympathetic to the Committee for Home Rule's goals identified the main problem to be the conversion of farms into summer homes. As for schools, the committee insisted the last elementary school in a town should only be allowed to close after a vote by the townspeople. One attending legislator was less than impressed by the committee's recommendations, calling them "destructive rather than constructive."[82] During the actual legislative session the organization made little headway on taxation, but its members got the law on the closing of schools they desired.[83] That victory did not placate Herbert Ogden, however. Later in the year he quit the Republican Party, for which he had been chairman in his town of Hartland, grousing that the party "has sought to ape and even outdo the Democrats in their fruitless search for the welfare state."[84]

Sam Ogden undoubtedly understood the philosophy of the Committee for Home Rule, if not perhaps some of its proposals, and he was never a member of it. Sam had always considered himself a conservative, and was growing more conservative as he aged. At least in principle, he did not like change that impinged on the independence of small towns, one of the aspects of Vermont he most highly prized. As was obvious from his service on various state agencies, however, he thought it necessary that extensive research and planning be conducted to keep Vermont's small towns vital and independent. In 1957, while the Committee for Home Rule railed against the concentration of power in larger political entities, Sam was appointed to the United States Department of Agriculture's 18-member advisory committee on soil and water conservation.[85] Samuel Ogden's paradoxical ideas and actions are illustrative of the crossroads at which Vermont found itself late in the 1950s. It would have been hard to find a Vermonter who did not prize the state's democratic traditions, but it could not be denied that Vermont was facing severe economic and institutional challenges that required large solutions and expertise. How to reconcile those two realities was the trick with which Vermonters grappled, and there were no easy answers.

The Death of John Dolph Neilson

Service on the soil and water advisory board took Sam Ogden to Washington frequently, and gave him cause to make appearances around Vermont, as he had been doing for nearly three decades. But the time he valued most was that which he spent in Landgrove. Late in the 1950s residents of the town were engaged in preliminary discussion about adopting a zoning ordinance that would put restrictions on new construction, so as to keep Landgrove looking as much as possible as it did. But Landgrove could not entirely remain the same. For 20 years, Sam's sister Helen and her husband Lester Cody had operated a farm they appropriately named Stony Hill Farm, for it was up a road from the village, away from the better farmland in Landgrove's valley. Lester Cody was described by Sam's son Duncan as a "real mountain man," good with horses and at logging operations, and he had helped Sam with many of his house renovation projects. By the late 1950s, state regulators were mandating that dairy farms install bulk milk tanks. The Codys could not afford that expense, and like many other marginal hill farms, Stony Hill Farm was driven out of business.[86] When the 1950s had begun the state contained 19,043 farms, most of them dairy farms. In 1959 that number was down to 12,099.[87]

Other eras ended in Landgrove in the late 1950s. Myron Tifft died in 1954 and was followed by his wife Lutheria four years later. The Tiffts had been a numerous family in the area for over 100 years, and had extensively intermarried with local families, including Major Valentine's Swedes. Now, for the first time since before Eddie Tifft married Lottie Nyren in 1893, there was no Tifft presence in Landgrove. In the late 1950s. Lottie resided in Arlington, living in a space above a store. She spent much of her time sitting on a bench in front of the store and was a familiar and much-loved figure. Her daughter Mildred drove down from Rutland to see her frequently, and she had many other relatives in the area. Her grandson Robert Tifft lived in Arlington and became acquainted with Arline Neilson, the daughter of Alve, who had worked at Mamie Ogden's summer camp. She had moved to Arlington and married a Peru native in 1955, worked at the Hale Furniture Company, and had acquired the nickname "Mountain Rose."[88] Robert remembers that she was "a hell of a good woman" who dressed and worked like a man. Their acquaintance was entirely coincidental. Over the many years they knew each other, they were unaware of their mutual connection to Alonzo Valentine's scheme to regenerate rural Vermont.[89]

Evidence of the scheme was diminishing in Landgrove. Hilma Neilson died in 1955, her husband Axel followed in 1956, and their son John Dolph was unable to keep the farm going. Karl Pfister, holder of a Ph.D. in organic chemistry and employed in New Jersey by Merck, bought the Neilson farm from John Dolph in 1958. Pfister's uncle had become friends with Sam Ogden during World War I and had purchased a house in Landgrove decades before. Now Karl Pfister's family joined the circle of friends and relatives who took such great pleasure in each other's company. Summer afternoons were famous in Landgrove for their impromptu cocktail parties on various porches. The Fourth of July was a particularly grand occasion, with Sam Ogden leading the camp children on a parade through the village. Christmas was also a special time, as townspeople attended midnight services in the church without the benefit of heat, a tradition started by Mamie Ogden.

As for John Dolph Neilson, after the sale of the farm he moved to a rented apartment in South Londonderry. He worked for a local upholsterer, driving a car that locals joked was "old enough to vote." He had always lived with his parents, and now with them gone the motivating force in his life had been removed. At 2:30 on the afternoon on March 15, 1959, John Dolph Neilson walked into a mill yard in Londonderry and shot himself in the head.[90] Counting parents and children, there had been 32 of Major Valentine's Swedes in Landgrove and Weston in 1900. Now only Alve Neilson was left.

CHAPTER 8

Entering the Interstate Era

Landgrove at the Dawn of the Interstate Era

In October 1961, the Bennington *Banner* ran a lengthy profile of Sam and Mamie Ogden comprised of three separate articles. The *Banner* was to begin running Sam's weekly column "Sparks from the Forge," which he had been writing for the Rutland *Herald* since 1956, and wanted to acquaint readers with him. The first article was headlined, "Landgrove Was Rebuilt from Decay by Sam Ogden." It reported that the town's residents did not want too many people knowing about Landgrove because "they like the place the way it is and don't want a lot of curiosity seekers coming by." As evidence of how true that was, the article reported that when *Life* magazine had wanted to write a story about Landgrove, Sam had turned it down. Sam described Landgrove as, "a congenial, compatible and unique sort of community." The second article, titled, "In 32 Years Here, Vermont Has Been a Virtual Career," recounted Sam's political, philanthropic, and literary career. The third, "They Discovered Successful Country Living in Vermont," emphasized Sam and Mamie's active roles in town affairs. It concluded by summarizing the terms of the proposed zoning ordinance on which residents were to vote at a special town meeting a few weeks later: establishing a minimum area for lots, a ban on billboards, strict standards for building expansions, and discouraging mobile homes and junk yards. The village having been saved from "dying a natural death" and the town rejuvenated, its residents now wanted to preserve it as it was.[1] Of course, the human landscape of Landgrove had dramatically changed in the previous 30 years. Whether Sam acknowledged to himself the irony of now preserving a town increasingly bereft of the kind of people who were the customary repositories of Vermont traditions and values, he was deeply satisfied with what Landgrove had become. The articles' collective message was summed up as, "In many ways, Samuel Robinson Ogden *is* the town of Landgrove."[2]

Soon after the *Banner's* profile, Sam and Mamie flew to Europe on a mission to promote travel to the United States. Sam promised a reporter that during the tour, which was sponsored by Pan American Airlines, Greyhound Bus, and a sightseeing association, he would put in a good word for Vermont whenever he could but would refrain from any mention of Landgrove.[3] Publicizing Vermont, if not Landgrove, remained one of Ogden's main endeavors. In 1960 he joined the editorial board of *Vermont Life*, in which he began publishing a regular column, "VL Reports," composed of essays and book reviews. Ogden also had a professional interest in promotion of the state. Still scrambling to make a living at the age of 63, Sam acquired a real estate license in 1960. But it was much more than that: Ogden genuinely wanted to help ensure a good future for the state that he had made a "virtual career," and tourism, now a year-round industry, looked as much as ever to be an essential part of that future.

At the same time, Ogden was ever cognizant of the need for limits to promotion. A 1961 edition of "Sparks from the Forge" laid out some of his concerns about the over-commercialization of Vermont, and especially the tendency to market to the wrong kind of person. He criticized the Vermont Development Department, which replaced the Development Commission in 1960, for a lack of discernment in the quality of those to whom it marketed the state. The department, he wrote, had "let down the floodgates in its new policy of reaching the masses." The danger, Ogden warned, was the loss of Vermont's unique character. When the editors of the Rutland *Herald* objected in an editorial, arguing not only that Vermont would be fine, but also that it should not be marketed as a "19th-century backwater," the Bennington *Banner* joined the discussion.[4] The *Banner* agreed with Ogden that Vermont's character was endangered by the wrong type of commercialization: "Whom we entice into Vermont," it admitted, "is a controversial question." It continued, "Vermont can be engulfed and suffer some of the worst aspects of excessive commercialization, industrialization, and—let's coin a word—touristization." Vermont could indeed be promoted as a "quaint 19th-century backwater," as there were plenty of residents "who haven't got out of the

19th century." At the same time the *Banner* believed the state could be advertised as one that welcomed new industries and was "as modern as the twentieth century," holding up as evidence farms that operated according to the most up-to-date business methods and technology. The *Banner's* editors concluded, "Vermont is quaint. Vermont is modern. Take your pick, but Vermont does have a flavor and it ought to be saved. The secret is sensible controls that prevent the worst blights of modern metropolitan civilization and preserve the advantages of country living."[5] This ideal vision of Vermont's future could perfectly well be articulated: a state of affairs where the past and the future, tradition and progress, existed in appropriately complementary measures side by side. The questions were, exactly what would that look like, how could the state get there, and who were the right kinds of people to help in that effort?

Sam Ogden was still eager to participate in the difficult decisions needed to be made to help Vermont negotiate a path between stagnation and over-development. His many decades of experience doing that were appreciated by at least one *Banner* reader when "Sparks from the Forge" began appearing in the paper. In a letter to the editor she wrote, "If Vermont is in danger of over-industrialization or undue commercialism, Sam can with his wealth of experience make valid suggestions as to a wise course for us to follow in this high-speed age."[6] Ogden agreed with that assessment of himself. Soon into his tenure on the *Banner's* editorial page, Ogden recalled his successful role in "the Great Green Mountain Parkway fracas," writing that ever since 1935, "I have been in the midst of the fray doing whatever I could to help preserve that previous and indefinable essence of Vermont, which constitutes its most important economic asset, an essence which seems to be more readily recognized by outlanders than by natives."[7]

Ogden saw striking the right balance between preservation and development as Vermont's central challenge. Accomplishing that just in the Landgrove area was challenge enough. The Big Bromley ski resort, which Sam had helped build and then operate for over 20 years, was doing good business four miles away. In 1960, the Magic Mountain ski area opened a little more than a mile from his house. The next year, the much larger Stratton Mountain ski resort, the prospect of which had helped drive Scott and Helen Nearing to Maine, opened 11 miles away.[8] Many residents of the area felt consternation about various aspects of these developments, including the rising taxes needed to pay for the construction of access roads. A Stratton resident who had served as the town's state representative, Malvina Cole, suggested in a letter to the Bennington *Banner* in 1962 that the resorts themselves should pay those costs, contending that many locals did not experience any direct benefit from ski access roads, specifying machine-tool workers, sawyers, and dairy farmers.[9] While acknowledging that the ski industry contributed to the Vermont economy, she noted, "so do machine tools, lumber products, and dairy farming. And they do not demand special roads from the state."[10]

Long deeply invested in the ski industry, Ogden felt fully qualified to dismiss such complaints. In a response to Cole titled "Biting the Hand That Feeds Us," Ogden wrote, "Perhaps I am mistaken in assuming that Mrs. Cole regards either an increase in her bankroll, or in the well-being of her fellow citizens, or an increase in the activities in the community, as being desirable changes." Ogden insisted that nothing in decades had been as good for the regional economy as the ski industry. Forcing ski operators to pay more in taxes would put them out of business, Ogden insisted. Whereas when the industry was young skiing had had few supporters, Ogden wrote that "everyone is on the bandwagon except...a few disgruntled individuals like Mrs. Cole."[11] Cole responded indignantly within days. Not only had she not experienced "an increase in her bankroll," she wrote, her taxes had increased, and a week before a bank had refused her a loan. Without greater state supervision, she wrote, the ski industry would further cause others "to suffer as we have in the name of progress. But at state expense, and at the expense of community and resident families." She mentioned an acquaintance who had quit working at Stratton "because he didn't want to be pushed around," and another friend who had quit because of the low wages Stratton paid. Among other indignities, Cole continued, such wages left Stratton's workers unable to afford to eat in the new restaurants that served skiers. Furthermore, she argued, the industry's dependence on snow conditions caused stressful layoffs. Finally, Cole expressed concern about the environmental consequences of so many ski resorts close by.[12]

The exchange ended there. If Ogden, one of the state's leading conservationists for three decades, was moved by Cole's environmental plea, he did not say. But Ogden did frequently use his column to critique the condition of Vermont's landscape. In a January 1962 column he lamented that in Vermont, "in place of landscaped parks and gardens, of trimmed and tree-lined roadsides we have piles of junk, beer cans and billboards."[13] Ogden emphatically disliked the expense and the impact of the interstate highways, both scenic and environmental. On this topic he was joined by the president of the Committee for Home Rule in Vermont Towns, Herbert Ogden, who at the time was waging what one newspaper called "a one-man campaign against the interstate highway," demanding a state referendum to halt the project.[14] Whatever disagreements there might be, such as those illustrated by the exchange between Cole and Sam Ogden, concern was widespread that, no matter the extent to which progress could benefit Vermonters, they were losing control of their state.

At least one state resident did not mind the interstate highways one bit. Anna Nyren Fountain, sister of Lottie Nyren Derosia, now in her mid-70s, lived in the village of Wilder, in the town of Hartford, through which I-91 was to pass directly. Her daughter Lillian remembered that Anna thought the highway was wonderful when completed. It made it so much easier and quicker to get around. Anna was widowed by then, but her three children remained in the area; in those years one of her sons, Leland, operated Lee Fountain's Electrical and Refrigeration Service in nearby White River Junction. Anna no longer drove, but frequently had one of her sons drive her across the state to visit her sister Lottie, who in her mid-80s was still a familiar sight outside the Arlington store where she had worked for many years. Anna also frequently visited her brother Oliver, who had retired from Prudential Insurance late in the previous decade. Oliver had a cerebral hemorrhage in July 1961, and died on January 23, 1962. His long career had provided him with a nice home in Rutland, but the stress of it had worn on him. I-91 also went right past Brattleboro, where six of the original Anderson family lived. Agnes Anderson Brown, in her working life a waitress in western Massachusetts restaurants, had moved to Brattleboro after the death of her husband in 1949 so she could be nearer her siblings. On the night of February 13, 1962, she fell on ice. Taken to the hospital, she died during the administration of spinal anesthesia, though the main cause of death listed on her death certificate was "Chronic alcoholism with delirium tremens." Agnes's oldest sister, Hilma Butler, who had arrived in 1890 at the age of four and lived on a farm in Danby, also died in 1962. She left behind one son, Clarence, who had spent most of his working life operating a derrick in a Danby marble quarry. Capping off a rough spring for the children of Major Valentine's Swedes, Jennie Westine died at her house in Mount Tabor in May. At the time of her death one of her sons was a carpenter, the other a farm laborer.[15] This dwindling second generation of Valentine's Swedes had produced a third, and by and large they were the kind of people who Malvina Cole feared were not favored by the state's priorities.

The Hoff Era Begins

November 1962 brought a dramatic change to Vermont's political traditions: Philip Hoff was elected governor, the first Democrat to hold the office in over 100 years. As a passionately devout Republican, Sam Ogden was appalled by Hoff's election, but not just because of party affiliation. During the campaign Hoff had offered a host of proposals to modernize the state, many contrary to Ogden's most firmly held beliefs. His proposals generally sought to make state government more efficient and effective by centralizing authority. Hoff advocated the consolidation of schools on both the elementary and secondary levels. He also proposed that the state's smallest towns should have some of their government functions merged in the name of efficiency and cost savings. Perhaps worst of all to Ogden, Hoff proposed the reapportionment of the state's General Assembly on the basis of population rather than its traditional one-town, one-vote model. That was utterly anathema to Sam Ogden.

Hoff also called for more and better planning, and that had drawn Ogden into the campaign. In the summer of 1962 the chairman of the Development Department called its recently released policy statement the first of its kind. Asserting that the chair was "100 per cent wrong," Ogden pointed out that under his leadership the commission had produced a similar statement in 1951, calling the new policy statement "of dubious value because it does not relate development to the overall good of the state." To smooth things over, the department's chair publicly thanked Ogden for giving him advice. With help from people like Ogden, he continued, "we will be able to develop Vermont along these lines, blending modern advancement with a retention of those traditions we so endear." Candidate Hoff made political capital out of the incident, thanking Ogden for reminding Vermont that "do-nothing" Republicans had not acted on the 1951 statement and were ill-equipped "to reinvigorate Vermont's dwindling rural communities."[16] That a Burlington resident would claim to know what was best for Vermont's smallest towns, especially when more state responsibility for them was his solution, galled Ogden. In response to Hoff's repeated call for more planning, Ogden, the one-time member of the Planning Board wrote, "As far as I am concerned, governmental planning tends to infringe on the rights of the individual, and every move in this direction must be taken with care and deliberation."[17]

The early months of the Hoff administration dismayed Ogden on a number of counts. He deplored what he called, "The capricious wave of voter petulance which washed a Democratic governor into office." He dismissively criticized all those who proposed the consolidation or elimination of small towns' autonomy, "on the presumption that they are outmoded units of government, expensive, duplicative, inefficient, and as such, constitute a burden to the state."[18] Ogden repeatedly wrote in 1962 and 1963 "Sparks from the Forge" articles that the major problem facing Vermont was a lack of information, and insisted that the state needed to be studied extensively before action was taken. Whatever their political differences, on that count he and Phil Hoff agreed. Hoff established a Central Planning Office in 1963 to coordinate the work of 15 new resource management and development panels.[19] For the chairman of the review panel on scenery and historic sites Hoff appointed Samuel R. Ogden. Upon the completion of its work in December, the panel issued a report that Ogden was largely credited with writing. It began with historical quotes about the need to preserve scenery, such as from an English visitor to Vermont in 1910 who begged the state's residents, "Do not permit any unsightly buildings to deform beautiful scenery which is a joy to those who visit you. Preserve the purity of your streams and your lakes…Keep open the summits of your mountains." The panel's report found that "the almost inescapable conclusion to any study of land use in Vermont is that the problems of the state are but many facets of one huge problem: How are we to get along in the modern world without sacrificing the values and assets we treasure most dearly? This is truly a problem in conservation—of people, natural resources, scenic beauty, historical sites, land, water, tree bogs, wild flowers and birds—anything you can mention." To avoid such sacrifices, the panel recommended the creation of a land use commission and the formulation of a "master plan of such ingenuity, simplicity and dramatic imagination that it will find acceptance from the top to the bottom of our state." The report continued, "A wise use of our land and water which will conserve its beauties and resources for future generations requires that a master plan can only be worked out for the state as a whole. Piecemeal planning is foredoomed to failure. Such a master plan must be not only laid down but strongly implemented by legislation." Ogden described "Our ancient motto" as "eat it up, wear it out, make it do." Ogden called for a revision of that ethic: "We have nearly eaten it up, worn it out, and made it do so long that we are going without the things that make a fruitful future possible." If Vermont did not adopt a new model, Ogden warned, its economic, educational, and environmental future was imperiled.[20]

The scenery report was received positively in the press. One newspaper called it "a voice crying out in the wilderness, for the wilderness."[21] Governor Hoff was impressed by the report and used its findings to advocate for the creation in 1964 of the land use commission. The coordinator of Hoff's planning activities specifically cited "the existing interest in land by out of staters" as the primary reason why an extensive zoning and conservation program was needed.[22] The proposal for such a commission and its accompanying regulations went nowhere in the 1964 legislature, however. In the small-town-dominated legislature the amount of regulation and planning entailed by a land use commission, and the threat to local control it constituted, held little appeal. The Hoff administration let the commission go without a fight. The environment was not a big priority when there was so much else to get done.[23]

Founding the Vermont Natural Resouces Council

If state government was not going to do enough in the area of conservation, private agencies would have to pick up the slack. That was the consensus of the Vermont Conservation Conference, a meeting of conservationists at Goddard College in February 1963. There was consensus among attendees about little else. It was a variety of people who gathered to discuss how Vermont's resources could be best preserved and developed, and as Sam Ogden wrote soon after, "Almost immediately it became apparent that here were conflicting interests, cross currents, telescopic views, microscopic views and divergent opinions as to the whiteness of black or the blackness of white; there was distrust of the 'grass roots,' distrust of the upper layers, distrust of the specialist, of the generalist, of the activist, of the conservative and of the liberal."[24] Not despite but because of these differences, a fruitful discussion followed that resulted in agreement that a new organization was needed to coordinate conservation efforts in the state. That agency was founded at a subsequent June meeting that was chaired by Ogden. The Vermont Natural Resources Council was made possible by a series of compromises between two groups, the first led by Perry Merrill and members of the Vermont Nature Conservancy, the second a panel created in February whose members were appointed by Ogden. They adopted as their united goals to coordinate the work of state conservation groups, to act as a clearinghouse for governmental and private agencies, and to advocate for conservation measures in state government. Ogden was elected the first president of the VRNC. He relinquished the presidency a few months later but remained a member of its board for years.[25]

As his involvement in the VRNC indicates, Ogden remained a resolute advocate for conservation as he approached his late 60s. Writing about the new anti-pollution book *God's Own Junkyard* in "Sparks from the Forge," Ogden declared it to be of more importance to Vermont than any other state because "with us, the major problem is one of prevention, rather than of cure." Calling resistance to protecting the environment false independence, he wrote, "As a rock-bound conservative I deplore any action which erodes personal rights, but I concede that in this area we must do some hard-headed thinking as to what personal rights consist of."[26] In these years he gave talks on conservation around the state with titles such as "Beer Cans, Billboards and Battered Wrecks."[27] He felt that far too much his pleas that Vermonters act to save their state from environmental ruin were met with blank stares and indifference.

Such indifference to conservation joined an accumulating set of complaints about society that Ogden harbored in the mid-1960s. On the national level he perceived rising disorder and contempt for tradition everywhere. He opposed the 1963 March on Washington, for example, not because he supported segregation, which he deplored, but because "it attempts to set up mob rule in the place of orderly legislative procedures."[28] On the state level, for the time being at least, he thought sanity mostly prevailed, but he worried about society's seemingly cease-less movement in the direction of consolidation and change. He ex-pressed particular contempt for efforts to consolidate schools. Fighting at the time for school regionalization measures that the legislature had rejected, Vermont's education commissioner called Vermont's system of school districts "obsolete" and insisted that "streamlining measures must be undertaken to modernize Vermont's education system."[29] Holding up the successful record of Landgrove School as evidence, Ogden responded in early 1964 that "the eventual obliteration of the one-room school will come not as a result of its failure as a pedagogic institution, but as a result of the determined plans of the educationists to get rid of it."[30] Legislation to expand school consolidation was de-feated in 1964, but Ogden now perceived the traitorous spread of con-solidation even to Landgrove.[31] Formal discussions in town began in 1965 to merge Landgrove's school with that of Londonderry and to build a new facility. At a meeting attended by 27 of the town's 41 voters, Ogden led opposition to the new school in the face of supporters com-prised primarily of people with school-age children. In a letter to the Rutland *Herald*, one of the latter called Sam Ogden not the "Voice of Landgrove," but instead the "Voice of Part of Landgrove," and de-scribed the preservation of one-room schoolhouses as akin to favoring kerosene lamps over electricity. Ogden argued strenuously against con-solidation, but the demographics of Landgrove were working against him. Of the town's 41 voters, 31 were in their upper 50s or older, and there were only four young married couples. As one parent put it in a letter to town residents, Landgrove was "primarily a town of old folks except for some summer residents and winter skiers."[32] Town officers had largely consisted of the same handful of people for decades. Land-grove's town government was on an obviously unsustainable path.

Landgrove, like the rest of Vermont, existed in a metaphorical in-between space in these years. It existed in between the desire to cater to tourists' desires for a traditional, "unspoiled" landscape, and the need to have a working landscape. It was trapped between the desire to preserve small-town government and local control and the need for regional and statewide planning to prevent other kinds of change. It romanticized cherished decentralized institutions and traditional ways of doing things but also recognized the unavoidable necessity of consolidating institutions and running them with greater oversight and efficiency. This state of affairs was cogently described in a 1964 article in *Vermont Life*, the magazine Sam Ogden had been instrumental in founding and for which he still served as an editor and wrote articles. "The Two Faces of Vermont," written by Dartmouth professor, and Thetford, Vermont, resident, Noel Perrin, depicted a state torn by growing tension between two groups, one that saw Vermont as the last stand of a traditional way of life that must be preserved at all costs, the other pushing the state toward greater modernization. The movement in the last five years, Perrin wrote, was decisively in the direction of modernization, leaving Vermont's "last-standers" to fight a battle they were destined to lose. By Perrin's definition, Sam Ogden was in many ways the ultimate "last-stander." But the equation was more complicated than Perrin's formulation: The tension existed not just between people, but also within them, and the trend toward modernization went back a lot longer than five years. Whether native Vermonters of either a city or rural background, newcomers of all kinds, or tourists, everyone wanted to preserve what they perceived to be best about Vermont tradition, but in various areas of life saw the need for change. That everyone was plagued by these internal tensions did not create unity, however; they only made the tensions more stark and bitter. But Perrin was certainly right that, in 1964, modernization was on the way.[33]

Sam's Nightmare: Legislative Reapportionment

If there was one aspect of Vermont that Sam Ogden idealized and cherished the most, it was the state legislature's apportionment. For nearly two centuries each town, no matter its size, had sent a representative to the General Assembly. The result was a large body deeply divided between its rural majority and its urban and business interests. For Sam Ogden the body was the essence of true democracy, reliant primarily on the wisdom and virtue of small towns. When Philip Hoff, as a gubernatorial candidate, had advocated reapportioning the legislature by population, Ogden had scoffed. Hoff believed that the solutions to local problems could only be found on a regional and statewide basis, which was virtually impossible under the General Assembly's current organization.[34] In his first term the assembly had been the primary obstacle to the implementation of many of his objectives. As he worked on his reelection campaign in 1964, prospects for accomplishing things in his second term became much brighter. In June the United States Supreme Court ruled Vermont's form of apportionment unconstitutional and ordered it to reapportion the house.[35]

Sam Ogden was utterly aghast. "June 15 was a calamitous day for representative government, which, in the United States of America, has provided the framework for the most stable state that the world has ever known," he declared in "Sparks from the Forge." "The conviction of the constitutional draughtsmen was that wise and virtuous men should represent the people, not mountebanks. This is a principle which the new liberalism rejects in toto." The Bennington *Banner*'s editors disagreed, calling "divisive and disruptive" the fact that the will of the majority was constantly thwarted by a minority which, "despite what Sam believes, has no special endowment of virtue or wisdom," adding that Vermont was marked by a parochialism that generally failed to meet the problems created in the state by population shifts. The decline of small towns and growth of urban areas, the *Banner* concluded, "have led to problems which the controlling minority has either failed to recognize or chosen to ignore." Such reasoning moved Sam not in the slightest. Governor Hoff sent out feelers to Ogden to see if he was willing to serve on the panel being created to make reapportionment proposals. Ogden agreed to serve, but was not surprised when he was not asked. "The governor knew where I stood when he asked me," he wrote, "and must have known that what he might expect from me would be a minority report to the effect that there should be no acquiescence to the order of the federal court at this time."[36] Ogden declared the court decision to be unconstitutional and advised the state to refuse to abide by it. In "Sparks" article after article he expressed disgust at the court decision, wondering why, if the one-man, one-vote principle was necessary in Vermont's house, it did not equally apply to the United States Senate. He accused supporters of reapportionment of thinking the state's founders were fools. He called the effort to reject reapportionment "a sober and rational effort to preserve sanity and decency in government."[37]

It made no difference. In 1965 the legislature adopted a new configuration of 150 members, apportioned by population. Governor Hoff, having been reelected the previous autumn, signed the bill on June 17. On that very same day, residents of Landgrove, Londonderry, and Weston voted in a special election to join in a union elementary school. The ballot item was approved. June 17, 1965, was a very bad day for Sam Ogden.

Planning, Preservation, and the New Vermont

After the reapportionment of the General Assembly, Governor Hoff was able to get a lot more done, and there was much in his opinion that needed to be done to respond to the changes overtaking Vermont. The symbol, and the greatest agent, of those changes, the interstate highways, continued to work their way north through the state. Sam Ogden had no time for the interstates. In a 1964 article he called them "death traps"; a year later he wrote, "I have often maintained that the world would be a better place if there were no automobiles." Much else offended him. He lamented the loss of Landgrove's school, a "superb community institution" that had been "swallowed and digested by a monster accoutered with all sorts of modern devices, whose fantastic and unjustifiable costs have docilely been underwritten by the taxpayers…while the bulldozers snort and the bankers rub their hands and the architects detail their ignoble plans." To Sam, the new school was "an unwelcome, unwarranted and piratical assault" on the town's taxpayers. In these and other areas of life, Ogden was bewildered by the foolishness he saw all around him.[38]

Yet while Sam Ogden dismissed with disgust what many others considered progress, the Hoff Administration continued the practice of branding Vermont as a place where traditional America endured. In 1965, the Development Department initiated an advertising campaign organized around the slogan, "Vermont: The Beckoning Country." Advertisements were placed in out-of-state newspapers offering upon request a free, lavishly illustrated booklet promoting four-season vacations. When launching the campaign the Development Department was careful to emphasize that it was avoiding a "hard sell" approach.[39] Its director described the booklet as "a prestige publication, typifying the character of Vermont" that did not "resort to the over-commercialism, over-exaggeration and the hard sell contained in some vacation-travel promotion material.[40] It was soon obvious that the "Beckoning Country" slogan had resonated, as measured by the volume of requests for the publication and the increased number of tourists.[41] And as always the necessity remained of making the state's appearance approximate the image being sold. As one newspaper noted in 1966, it would not do for natives to continue to joke when driving past old cars abandoned by the roadside, "so that's the beckoning country."[42]

The Hoff Administration's response to the dissonance between image and reality was the establishment in 1966 of the Scenery Preservation Council. There was some legislative resistance to the council—one representative submitted an amendment specifying that its members must have lived in the state at least ten years, saying he resented "the way newcomers and suntanners invariably come into Vermont and want to remake the state."[43] The amendment was defeated. The council's work produced two landmark studies in 1966 that were released through the Central Planning Office: *Vermont Scenery Preservation* and *The Preservation of Roadside Scenery through Police Power.*[44] Those studies illustrate how roadside beauty had come to occupy a central place in the discussion about the future of Vermont scenery. The classic Vermont landscape of unspoiled farmland, forests, and quaint villages, it was increasingly believed, must be protected in some cases and in others restored. According to historian Blake Harrison, the Hoff Administration's increased attention to environmental issues is representative of a larger shift in Vermont from the principles of conservation to those of environmentalism, driven by the recognition that tourism "was becoming a threat to the entire scope of rural land and life as much as a beneficiary of it."[45] As Sam Ogden, former state planner and skeptic of state planning, knew, preserving Vermont was going to require extensive planning, zoning, and regulation.

In at least one regard, Sam Ogden found satisfaction in the Hoff Administration's expanded interest in issues related to the environment. Ogden had become a soldier in the war against billboards in the late 1930s. After a period of dormancy, the Vermont Association for

Billboard Restriction had been reborn in 1951 as the Vermont Roadside Council, and since then Ogden had served as one of its directors.[46] Before 1967 he frequently used his newspaper column to rail against both the visual blight of billboards and the lobby defending them.[47] When the adoption of more stringent billboard restriction rules came to the fore in 1967, Ogden was delighted. In a letter to the editor of the Bennington *Banner* he wrote that, "the interests of billboard advertisers are only in billboard advertisers; they obviously care not a whit for Vermont as a place to live nor as a place for the rest of the nation to come and enjoy restful beauty."[48] He was joined as a prominent critic of billboards by old friend Vrest Orton, and by former U.S. Senator Ralph Flanders, at whose house Ogden could be found on the frequent occasions it served as headquarters for the Roadside Council.[49] Testifying before a House committee on the proposed legislation, Ogden insisted that "the essence of Vermont's attraction is its scenery, not its signs."[50] After a bitter legislative struggle, the legislature adopted laws that essentially banned billboards and most other roadside signs.[51]

Landgrove in the 1960s

Sam Ogden turned 70 the year the billboard ban was adopted. His Landgrove project had been a success, but as he looked around the village in 1967, fewer of his old friends could be seen. "Pitch" Pitcher, one of the first to invest in Ogden's project, died in 1960. But some of the old crowd was still around, augmented not just by their children but by their grandchildren. Some were products of what were called "camp-house marriages," kindled during summers spent together at Mamie's camp. Now nearing 70 herself, Mamie still held her camp every summer, though her daughter-in-law Sally did a lot of the work. The main restrictions on the children's movement took the form of signs in the house that read "Big Sam's books. Do not touch," and "Big Sam making a tape recording. Do not enter." Otherwise the camp retained its traditional unstructured format. The children, none older than age 12, still were given the freedom to swim and explore the woods largely unsupervised. The tradition of Fourth of July parades continued, with the children marching through the village, led by Sam carrying an old rifle.[52] By the late 1960s Sam considered himself retired, but in addition to his many activities around the state he had found the time to do more writing. In 1967 he published a book of poetry titled *Vermont's Year*, comprised of 12 poems, one for each month. One review described it as written for those "who choose the wooded way to the concrete expressway."[53]

Also semi-retired now was Alve Neilson, whose fiftieth wedding anniversary in 1965 had been an event in Landgrove. He and his wife remained highly regarded members of the community. Alve's last cousin, Harry Neilson, died in 1966. Harry lived in Brattleboro near the end of his life, and one wonders if in those years he knew any of the Brattleboro-area Andersons around whom he had grown up, such as Charles, the first American-born child of Major Valentine's Swedes. Charles's eight children by his second wife all lived in the Brattleboro area, as did his sisters Esther, Ellen, and Hazel and their children.

The State That Beckoned Too Much

As these people daily did the type of hard work that kept Vermont going in the present, the debate about Vermont's future continued to rage around them. The "Beckoning Country" campaign had not only been successful; many Vermonters were deciding it had been too successful. According to a Massachusetts newspaper, the campaign's success bore much of the responsibility for Vermont being overrun with outsiders who had brought irrevocable change to the state. Vermont was "losing its grip on its unique and secluded way of life," the article claimed, "with Vermonters being forced to join the mainstream of 'rat race' living with its traffic problems, honky-tonks and the night and day confusion of the man-made world." "The boom is on in Vermont," the article continued, and "Money, most of it coming from outside, is flowing into the state to develop the Green Mountains into income-producing enterprises. The results…include huge scars on the sides of majestic green mountains and acres of former farmland now dotted with lush motels wrapped in urban tinsel that are out of keeping with the state' pastoral scenery." The article bemoaned that, "The Beckoning Country is a way of life fast disappearing…Everyone wants to own a part of Vermont, and to own a toehold in Vermont is a status symbol to be envied. Land speculators, recognizing this, are buying up tracts of land by the hundreds and thousands of acres—where they can still find land—holding it until the price goes up." The state tax commissioner was quoted as calling the land rush "hair-raising" and wondered if government planning and control could come quickly enough and keep pace with the rapid economic development. The article concluded that, "Paradoxically it is the native Vermonter who most resents the intrusion of outside influences and it is also the native Vermonter who most strongly protests any control of growth...Native Vermonters highly value their individual rights of decision and they see proposed controls as curbing their freedom."[54] In a state that had committed itself to reconcile freedom and unity nearly 200 years before, attempting to balance regulation and individualism seemed a zero-sum game.

By these years, Sam Ogden was harboring his own misgivings about the impact of tourism, and especially skiing. He articulated these in a 1967 newspaper article titled, "Winter in Vermont," which began with an acknowledgment of the good that skiing had brought to remote towns in the form of increased tax revenue. "But there are times when doubts creep into my mind," Ogden wrote, "and mind you, this is the mind of one who has played some part in the development of winter sports in Vermont." In numerous towns like the isolated Landgrove he had discovered in 1929, "the most remote roads are peeling down for speeding automobiles with their racks of skis. A rash of chalets and A-frames has sprung up as though some bizarre quirk of nature had contrived for the proliferation of great toadstools in the woods, and on the slopes of the mountain, once the exclusive domain of the wild things, smooth stretches like the lawns of rich men reach up to the very summits. Then to confound the poor creatures of the woods even more, great pipes squirt atomized streams out over the grass so that whether nature wills it or not, there shall be snow." But for all his qualms about the impact of skiing on nature, he saw the effects on the communities to be much worse. "Surely," he concluded, "if we Vermonters are wise we will contrive ways to control these aspects before it is too late. Landgrove is amidst three [ski] mountains and the citizens of the place have wisely decided that a zoning ordinance is necessary."[55]

He distilled these doubts about tourism further in a 1968 *Vermont Life* article titled "Changing Vermont." Ogden wrote that the recent "stimulation of growth" the state had experienced had "certain drawbacks," if "perhaps far from ruinous." But the future looked bleak to him. He wondered, "How long can we proceed along these easy ways before we do become ruined? Many of our mountain peaks are now scarred with the worm-tracks of ski trails—white in winter and pale green in summer. New highways are being blasted through the hills, pre-empting fertile fields and the homes of men; and commercial ventures are springing up without regard for what might be proper design or fitting location or even economic feasibility." Ogden went on to decry "the proliferation of road signs, the disregard for beauty on the part of highway engineers, the eyesores of public dumps and auto graveyards, the pollution of our streams, and the ravishment of wild areas." He lamented that skiing provided few good jobs, and that most of those it did create were occupied by outsiders to the state. The article resonated enough that the Vermont Development Department had it reprinted in a 1969 coffee-table collection of *Vermont Life* articles and photographs titled *Vermont: A Special World*. There is irony that the article was printed in publications supported by state funds and run by the Vermont Development Department. There is also obviously some irony, or even hypocrisy, in Ogden's disdain for "the worm-tracks of ski trails." In 1972 the president of the National Ski Area Association, in a talk on how environmental laws held back ski area expansion, held up the phrase as an illustration of his industry's challenge. Calling Ogden "a well-respected syndicated columnist from Vermont by the name of Sam Ogden—who, by the way, had worked as a cashier at Big Bromley ski area for years," he held Ogden's article up as an example of the "hostility" his industry faced.[56] But Ogden was hardly alone in wondering if change in Vermont had been too fast and too large.It was clear to him that Vermont was at a dangerous crossroads. He reiterated his concerns in a 1969 "Sparks" article that praised the former publicity director, Harold Chadwick, for recognizing that the promotion of tourism should be limited to "the decent exploitation of her beautiful scenery," marketed to "a special and select group of professional and retired people." Unfortunately, Ogden believed, that policy had been abandoned when he resigned from the Development Commission in 1951, after which a drastic change had occurred: The state adopted "the high-powered promotion which the press and the chamber of commerce boys were yammering for." Such people were those "who mistakenly believe that their pocketbook is best fattened by the influx of barbarians."

Ogden concluded that he was "afraid that until it becomes apparent that more money is to be made by preserving Vermont as an oasis in the desert, any successful effort to make it so will never take place."[57]

Ogden was not alone in fearing that the things for which he had once advocated wholeheartedly were in danger of going too far. His friend Walter Hard Jr., the editor of *Vermont Life*, wrote a similarly pessimistic article for the magazine in 1969 titled, "Shall Her Mountains Die?" and that, too, was reprinted in *Vermont: A Special World*. Most tellingly of all, the Development Department abandoned the "Beckoning Country" promotional program in 1969 because it had been simply too successful. A representative letter in the Burlington *Free Press*, in response to the program's abandonment, expressed relief that "Vermont is finally waking up to the fact that the Beckoning Country beckoned too much."[58] The Development Department's director announced that not only was his agency dropping the Beckoning Country theme that "has rubbed many Vermonters the wrong way," but also that going forward his agency was going to perform less promotion and focus more on planning. Noting the department's shift to local and regional planning, the *Berkshire Eagle* of Massachusetts called it "Small wonder… that those in state government who must take the long view are concerned lest Vermont's beckoning become an invitation to what could turn into a skin game, to the distress of everybody but the hit-and-run promoters who make fast bucks on ersatz Alpine villages."[59] The Development Department's replacement slogan was the rather uninspired "Ski Vermont First." As had been a running theme for some Vermonters for over five decades, the hope was that it would attract tourists, but not too many, and only of the right kind.

Vermont the Vanishing

Regional planning and regulation continued apace. The Hoff Administration created a state Land Use Commission in 1967, and it came under withering criticism from some legislators and citizens for constituting a statewide zoning body, at a time when only about 70 of Vermont's 260 municipal governments had zoning regulations.[60] In this, as in many other areas of life, centralization of authority appeared to threaten Vermonters' tradition of independence.[61] This was the state's essential dilemma, a fact that Governor Hoff understood well. In 1968, his administration's Planning Council issued a study of the state titled *Vision and Choice: Vermont's Future, The State Framework Plan*, that acknowledged Vermonters' reluctance to cede personal liberty, but argued that dramatic and immediate action needed to be taken if Vermonters were going to control the destiny of their state. Controlling the state's future sounded attractive to Vermonters, but the question was, at what cost?

Sam Ogden was trapped in these paradoxes, and the seeming regret he felt for at least parts of the very change he had helped bring about comes through in his newspaper articles. In the late 1960s he grew more bitter about the world around him, and more resistant to change. In 1967, he recounted a recent interaction he had had with a woman in Montpelier who told him, "I find not only that you are tiresome in your infatuation with the past, but that you are not even consistent." Another woman from what he called a "distinguished family" told him that she believed he found virtue only in the past. Her impression was that he thought nothing of modern times was any good, nor was there any gleam of hope for the future. Ogden's responded that he only cared about "the pursuit of truth and the unmasking of the false and bogus. It is a revealing commentary on the dogmas of our Western civilization which have to do with ideas of progress and with the conviction that the latest point in time represents civilization's great advance."[62] The late 1960s seemed to him in no way America's greatest advance; he perceived society collapsing all around him. In "Sparks from the Forge" articles he railed against an extensive list of topics: abortion, marijuana, the obsession with consumerism, the Vietnam War and war protesters alike. He denounced the "half-ass liberals, our ignorant intellectuals, our pseudo-conservationists" who were guilty of the "brainwashing of youth. Their goal is to make ignominy and nothingness acceptable."[63] He saw the situation in Vermont as no better. When a *Vermont Life* article appeared in 1969 that was critical of Vermonters' racial attitudes, Ogden dismissed the concern as soft-headed nonsense.[64] He continued to deplore the interstate highways, writing that, "the fact remains that the sinking of our hard-earned dollars in this ostentatious luxury was a monument to the persuasiveness of the salesmen and to our own stupidity."[65] Perhaps most painful, he thought the Vermont model of democracy he had cherished was irreversibly dying. In his opinion there was no turning back after reapportionment: "The 'one man one vote' changes have been brought about under the banner of democracy, but as is already apparent, the effect is to concentrate power in the hands of those who seek to wield it, and to disenfranchise the minorities."[66]

This dark view of the world around him was the inspiration for Ogden's next book. *America the Vanishing* is a collection of essays from authors such as Audubon, Muir, Thoreau, and Rachel Carson that collectively described, as the subtitle reads, "The Price of Progress." Covering the period from the colonial era to the 1960s, the essays condemned Americans' foolish, destructive approach to nature. "Without intending to adduce proof that the old days of living in the country in America were the best ones," Ogden wrote in the introduction, "I found that the author of the excerpts, which I chose from books in my library, were unmistakably making just that point."[67] A St. Louis newspaper wrote that implicit in each selection was "a dark portent for the future."[68] The Bennington *Banner* called the book a "disapproving commentary on what [America] has become," and predicted that, as it was "as contemporary and up-to-date as tomorrow morning's headlines," it might be used in upcoming college teach-ins focused on the environment.[69] The Camden (NJ) *Courier-Post* speculated that the book's limited audience would be "a strange alliance of the real old-timer and the hippie, both of whom are looking for Ogden's sort of peace in an unspoiled, remote place." When Ogden made an appearance on Vermont Public Television to promote the book, the topic was "the tension between development and the preservation of the 'traditional Vermont,'" and the station described *America the Vanishing* as "both a nostalgic memorial to what was and a disappointing commentary on what is."[70] It was a timely book. As the 1970s began, many Vermonters felt the state was at a crossroads.

The Arrival of Act 250

Sam Ogden's "sort of peace," if produced by personal independence and local democracy, was what many Vermonters, in various ways, had been making strides to save from extinction. In other ways it was also the thing that those same strides had the potential to make impossible.

Under the leadership of Governor Hoff, great progress had been made on the centralization of authority, and on careful planning on a regional and statewide basis as a means to control and shape change.[71] Hoff left office in 1969 and was replaced by a Republican, Deane Davis, who promised to pull back from the activism of the Hoff years. In terms of environmental planning, zoning, and regulation, however, the Davis Administration exceeded its predecessor. Making the environment a top priority, Davis appointed a Governor's Commission on Environmental Control to study the state's environment and economy. The work of what was commonly called the Gibb Commission led in 1970 to the enactment of Act 250.[72] Act 250 was not just the product of the commission's work, but the logical culmination of Vermont's evolution going back to the 1890s. It is a comprehensive land-use law that divides the state into environmental districts, each possessing a board to review the impact of proposed development, according to a set of criteria. Following Act 250's passage, the Vermont Natural Resources Council received funding from the Ford Foundation for a project designed to inform Vermonters about the law, and to stimulate citizen participation in the preparation of the statewide plans the law entailed.[73] In his newspaper articles, Sam Ogden was strangely silent about his feelings toward Act 250, and his surviving family and acquaintances do not recollect them. It is safe to say that he either absolutely loved Act 250, or absolutely hated it.

Because of Act 250, Vermont's landscape could much more effectively be managed and preserved, though opposition to the law would take various forms in the years to come. A salient question was, would it be a landscape managed in a democratic and participatory way that preserved personal independence? Act 250 could preserve the physical landscape, but could it equally preserve the human landscape? Act 250 was driven by the desire to limit the kind of growth that pushed residents out. As one correspondent to a newspaper wrote in 1969, in a letter proposing that Vermont's new slogan be "Vermont: the Taxing State," the more outsiders came to the state, the harder it was for those who already lived there to stay.[74] But if enormous caps were placed on development, there might not be enough jobs for state residents, and Vermont might be in even more danger of becoming a plaything for a narrow, well-off group of people. A letter to the editor of the Bennington *Banner* wondered what would happen to "bulldozer operators, brush burners, chain saw men, and all other manner of trades," lamenting "the ravishes wreaked on the working man" by regulation.[75]

Ogden's Landgrove—in its common ethic of preservation, in its pioneering zoning laws—was a model for what Act 250's impact might be. As a beautiful town with strict zoning occupied by a few, mostly elderly residents, would Landgrove be an attractive model, or would it be a cautionary fable, of the future? As it was, the town was finding it difficult to fill all of its offices, as the handful of people who had served the town for decades grew too old or tired of their responsibilities.[76] The land rush of the 1960s had threatened the integrity of Vermont's traditional landscape. As a solution Act 250 empowered state government much more to determine what could and could not be done to that landscape. The limits placed on development presented their own challenges, however, such as whether the law would prevent the construction of a sufficient supply of affordable housing, already a pressing problem in the state. One 1970 newspaper article titled, "Most Vermonters Can't Afford Their Own State," distilled this problem, claiming that "Vermonters see thousands of acres of beautiful open land within commuting distance, but they can't afford to buy a square foot of it." *Vermont Life* ran a similar article bemoaning the fact that "Most native Vermonters can no longer afford their own state," and another one titled, "Who Owns Vermont?," accompanied by a tasteless drawing of a Middle Eastern man in a keffiyeh leaning on a water pump.[77] A law that sought to preserve open spaces had the potential to make other problems worse.

In the wake of Act 250 Herbert Ogden of the Committee for Home Rule proposed that the state enact a nonresident income tax to make it more expensive for outsiders to own a piece of Vermont, asking if it made sense "to lure more and more newcomers to the state when the main lure is open spaces?" Quoting Ogden Nash he wrote, "progress may have been all right once, but they let it go on too long."[78] Herbert Ogden had devoted his time over the previous two decades to defending the independence of small towns from the encroaching control of state government. In 1972 he ran for and was elected to the state senate as a means to fight more effectively for the cause of local control. At the time, Herbert Ogden was also the chairman of the state chapter of the

Sierra Club. Described as "a strong conservative on most issues and an ardent advocate of environmental protection," Herbert Ogden heartily supported Act 250.[79]

The Death of Mamie

Through 1970 and 1971 Sam Ogden's "Sparks from the Forge" articles grew angrier and more reactionary. Racism and anti-Semitism increasingly crept in. In one representative piece Ogden wondered how 66 percent of professional athletes could be black "unless questions of race are involved," and noted that the "anthropologists and scientists and geneticists who so vigorously maintain that there are no relationships provable between the intellectual accomplishments of individuals and race are practically all Jewish."[80] Much about the world by then disgusted him, but he had a lot to live for: the village he had redeemed, his family, and especially his beloved wife, Mamie. Christmas Day in 1971 was, in Sam Ogden's own words, "one of the happiest" he had experienced, when suddenly Mamie was stricken with a heart attack and died almost instantly. Sam was inconsolable.[81] For a short while he continued to write increasingly incendiary "Sparks" articles. One in May 1972 claimed, "We insist on living by untruths. AntiChrist is in the driver's seat and where it will all end up is not pleasant to contemplate. Best thing to do is to ignore the whole business and let the blacks take over."[82] Readers of the *Banner* began to label his articles "trash," and the editors of the paper apologized for his "tasteless and offensive" opinions. Soon after Ogden gave up the column. He retired as an editor of *Vermont Life* in 1972, as well.[83]

Ogden remained a trustee of the Vermont Symphony Orchestra and was honored at an October 1972 performance for his nearly 40 years of service to it.[84] He still worked in his garden, and had acquired the stature of an authority on organic farming in a new generation of books on the subject.[85] He frequently received visits from young people who had bought a Vermont farm or joined a commune and who, inspired by *This Country Life* or one of his organic gardening books, wanted advice on how to successfully go back to the land. Despite his distaste for hippies, Sam invariably received them politely, patiently, and helpfully. But he found there was little in which he could still take pleasure. One thing that was quite meaningful to him was a visit in 1972 to the Maine home of his old friend Scott Nearing. The two in many ways were political opposites, and the same skiing industry that Ogden had strenuously promoted had played a major role in driving Nearing away from Vermont 20 years earlier. Nevertheless, they shared many of the same values, and it was a pleasant visit that meant a lot to Sam. He wrote an article about it for the Bennington *Banner* in which he said, "I esteem Scott Nearing as highly as any man on earth. He is a great and good man, and [our] fundamental differences in basic viewpoints could never detract from my regard for him. I presume it works both ways, for we have been friends for many years." Ogden wrote that Nearing's choice of a home was excellent, as it was "far from any city folks' summer estates, far, even, from any civilization."[86]

The article about Ogden's visit with Scott Nearing was published in late November 1972. A few days earlier Sam entered his garage by himself. He had been despondent, feeling his family did not appreciate the depth of his despair and demoralized by health problems. He attached a funnel to the exhaust pipe of his car and connected it to a tube, which he placed in the car window, rolling up the glass. When he started the car the funnel became dislodged, and while he was in the act of replacing it a family member happened upon him. He was rushed to the hospital and survived. While lying in his hospital bed, despite trembling hands and difficulty talking or thinking clearly, Ogden began writing.[87] His thoughts appeared two months later in the *New York Times* under the title, "When Mamie Left." "All I wanted after she died was to die too and hoped that somehow I might find her and be with her again," he wrote, but "it was in the hospital that I made my great discovery. I discovered that all the values which my unbearable grief had twisted into a pattern of evil could be set aright once I looked at them through Mamie's eyes; and this, by grace of God, I managed to do. Now I resolved to live with as much joy as I could accomplish, doing the things that I knew she would want me to do."[88] After returning home, Sam continued to relinquish activities he had long performed. He announced at town meeting in 1973 that he would no longer serve as moderator. For the citizens of Landgrove, the announcement felt like a melancholy end to an era.[89]

The Last of Major Valentine's Swedes

In 1973, Lottie Nyren Derosia, age 97, broke her hip. She had repeatedly said that she was going to go dancing on her 100th birthday, but now that was in doubt. Her sister Anna had died earlier that year, leaving her as the last survivor of the Swedes who Major Valentine recruited in 1890. She still had a lot to live for. She had continued to keep house for the owner of the store in Arlington until her late 80s. When she finally stopped working, she moved in with her son Carl. Her children all lived nearby; her son Richard, raised partially in the Sandgate lumber camp, worked in maintenance at Castleton State College. Her Swedish heritage was important to her, and the fact that she never learned to read in English did not bother her. She remained charming, kind, cheerful, and clear headed, singing songs in Swedish to her great-grandchildren, as she had done for her children and grandchildren. She taught her grandson Robert to count to ten in Swedish but declined his request she teach him Swedish profanities. When Lottie died in 1976, two days short of her 100th birthday, she had four children, three step-daughters, ten grandchildren, 16 great-grandchildren, and seven great-great-grandchildren, nearly all of whom lived in Vermont. Alonzo Valentine had not been entirely wrong in his belief that his recruitment program would help repopulate Vermont.

Charles Anderson, the first child born to the Swedes upon their arrival in Landgrove, also died in 1976. He left behind 12 children, four from his first marriage and eight from his second. Most lived in the Brattleboro area. One son, Donald, was a Korean War veteran and worked as an auto and truck mechanic. Another son, Robert, worked at the Putney Paper Company after serving two tours of duty in Vietnam as a Marine. For all the derision Alonzo Valentine's recruitment scheme received in its time, it had succeeded in his goal of providing Vermont with good citizens. They paid their taxes. They served honorably in the military. They worked for some of Vermont's largest employers. They opened small businesses. They helped to build Vermont. They were Vermonters.

In 1977, Alve Neilson, age 83, sold his Landgrove farm and retired to New Port Richey, Florida. He had been the last descendant of Valentine's Swedes to live in Landgrove, but the memory of Valentine's experiment did not end when he left. Karl Pfister, to whom Alve's parents had sold their farm, moved to Landgrove full-time in 1971. In the process of working on the town's 1976 bicentennial commission he organized an exhibit of old Landgrove photographs. Among the earliest and most generous contributors of photographs was Verna Westine Carleton, Jennie Westine's daughter. In the years to come Alve Neilson was consulted by telephone frequently on matters of Landgrove history, a task he was happy to perform. It is in great part due to the work of Pfister and other town historians, including Sam Ogden's son Duncan and his wife Sally, and Priscilla Grayson, who had been introduced to Landgrove by Mamie's summer camp, that so much of the history of the town survives.

At the time of the 1976 national bicentennial, Sam Ogden was nearing his 80th birthday. He did not get out much, or even know many of the people in the village. Sam thought it was high time he completed writing projects he had long planned. As early as the early 1930s, he had been sketching out essays on his own life. He also wanted to write on the history of Landgrove, and to that end had done research on the town and interviewed some old-time residents in the late 1960s. In 1976 he published a short book on the early history of Landgrove, and then set about completing a work very important to him. *The Cheese that Changed Many Lives* is neither strictly a history of Landgrove nor an autobiography, but instead an idiosyncratic, wistful combination of the two. He writes of various Landgrove events before his arrival, including Charlie Neilson's drowning in 1914. He also recounts his discovery and rehabilitation of the village, and bits and pieces of his life since. There is a lot on Mamie, for whom his undying love is utterly touching. He spells out some of his philosophy on the natural landscape, writing that, "uncontrolled growth means death."[90] He is regretful about much of the change overtaking the world, writing, "it must be obvious that the old days and the old ways of the rural backwoods community are by now a thing of the past."

But for all his discomfort with the direction of Vermont, and American society in general, Samuel Robinson Ogden was hopeful about the future and satisfied with his life. Chief among all things dear to him, after his family, was Landgrove Village, his beloved creation. In a world that he thought had gone crazy from its obsession with progress and material comfort, in his mind Landgrove remained a real community, an oasis of sanity, civility, and virtue. "I hope," he writes, "that the denizens of Landgrove will hang on; nay, more than that, will, in fact, construct a community whose brightness will shed light on other places, a light which may be ever increasing, infectious and contagious, for if this world is to be saved, this is the sort of thing which will have to happen more and more frequently all about us."

CONCLUSION

W HEN SAMUEL OGDEN DIED IN 1985, his Rutland *Herald* obituary called him a "dyed-in-the-wool Vermonter."[1] During his life, Ogden had himself insisted many times that he deserved the title of "Vermonter."[2] While there are those who emphasize nativity as an essential qualification for the designation, Sam most certainly had earned it. When Vermont was established in 1777 its founders, embattled on all sides, needed to make Vermont an exciting idea that captured others' imaginations. They chose as its motto "Freedom and Unity," adopting a mission statement that Vermont would be the place that would reconcile the most fundamental contradictions of the human condition: Members of the Vermont community would be free to pursue personal gratification, but not at the expense of a commitment to communal well-being. Vermont would prove that life need not be a zero-sum game. That mission of achieving balance has remained a constant throughout the state's history, though it has evolved in its specifics. In Sam Ogden's time the tensions between contradictory factors manifested themselves in struggles over preservation versus development, over tradition versus progress, over natural versus managed. Ogden cherished small-town democracy, but he acted on a statewide scale to see decisions ever more determined by centralized bureaucracies. He wanted to protect the landscape built by state residents, but encouraged and enabled its change, much for the use of outsiders. He was enamored with the people he first found in Landgrove, yet shaped the town in a way that made it so those people were progressively scarce. He grew increasingly disenchanted with the direction of American society, yet became a bit of a guru to a younger generation he did not understand. Anyone who was that much of a bundle of contradictions deserves association with a state defined by its ongoing struggle to find balance between contradictory impulses.

Charlotte Nyren Tifft Derosia was also not born in Vermont, but she too became a Vermonter. Despite her economic hardships, life of hard labor, failed marriage, and other difficulties, she persevered in the state, even as its direction, propelled forward by both public policy and private enterprise, served to marginalize people like her. The economy, and indeed the society she encountered upon arrival in 1890, was very different by the end of her long life, but to this day southern Vermont is blessed by the presence of a large number of her descendants. They quietly do the hard work that is Vermont's bedrock. It is work that belies any notion of Vermont as being somehow "unspoiled." Vermont was, and need remain, a working landscape.

In that way, despite all the changes that have transpired since the Gilded Age, Vermont is about continuity. Another form of continuity has to do with the importance of a strong sense of community. The world of East Dorset in the 1870s was homogenous and driven by consensus, and for all the challenges and shortcomings of life there, the Tiffts, Reeds, Beebes, Crandalls, and others found their lives so attractive that they were determined to persevere while so many others left. Over 100 years later, a 2004 newspaper article on Landgrove described it as "the ultimate gentrified Vermont community of former flatlanders." That description is quite unfair. Many people who live there, whether part- or full-time, have long-term, deep attachments to the town and their neighbors. It is also a homogenous, consensus-driven community. In the article one Landgrove resident is quoted saying that people elsewhere "are searching for this sense of community."[3] But it is a fact that community, which is not physical but rather arises out of shared experiences, is a fragile thing. A 2009 profile of neighboring Peru exemplifies this danger. One resident was quoted as saying that, "There are hardly any Peru people left. Some died, some moved away. People from the cities, especially after 9/11, moved in, drove the price of land so high our young people can't afford to stay here. Both my daughter and my son wanted to stay, but we couldn't find an affordable plot for them. We've become the suburbs of Connecticut, New York and New Jersey. That's just the economics of things."[4] Progress and change can be good, but as many Vermonters have long recognized, they need to be controlled and given direction. If they are not, then outsiders who come to Vermont looking for a special sense of community will find it largely extinct, obliterated by people like themselves. Vermont remains an experiment to perfect balance, and along that journey it must be remembered that people of all kinds must be a presence and play a part in that experiment.

The ironies to this story are obvious, but two main ones merit being spelled out. First, Alonzo Valentine brought Swedes to Vermont because he thought that many of the people living there, namely French Canadian immigrants and the Yankees he thought dissipated, were a blight. Those were the wrong kind of people, and the Swedes were the right kind. But by giving tourism the boost it did, the recruitment program played a role in the process that gradually shaped Vermont in a way that marginalized Valentine's Swedes and their descendants. Second, Sam Ogden came to Vermont looking for something dramatically unlike the urban world he knew and thought ugly, dehumanizing, and controlling. He found in Vermont the beautiful landscape and independent living he sought, but in order to save the things he valued it was necessary for him to build and serve bureaucratic institutions that threatened the existence of the human scale of democracy he cherished. Of course, a great deal of the transition that Vermont underwent was inevitable. The state was not going to remain economically dependent on dairy farms, quarries, lumbering operations, and heavy manufacturing. Vermont was evolving, and action was necessary to steer the state in the most desirable direction. There are no villains in this story, least of all Sam Ogden, who devoted himself to the good of the state and the town he loved. He and many of the other people from the beginning of this story to its end did what they thought best to help Vermont negotiate its twentieth-century transitions in the healthiest possible way. But if there is a lesson to this story, it is that, sometimes, when you think you are doing what is in the best interest of everyone, you might reassess whether what you are doing might mostly be in the best interest of people like yourself.

Entering from Londonderry, the Landgrove Road runs from south to north through town. In the center of town along that road there is a graveyard. It sits across the road from the old Farmers and Mechanics Hall that Mamie and Sam helped to turn into a first-rate rural school.

Behind the graveyard is Utley Brook, named for the first settler in town. Beyond the brook are fields that end where mountains rise up. Few structures are visible, and those there are harmonize with the natural landscape. It is a quintessentially beautiful Vermont scene, one that probably looks a great deal like the view that Major Valentine's Swedes had when they arrived, impoverished, in 1890. The enormous amount of zoning, planning, and regulation required to keep it looking that way has made it a physical landscape designed for people unlike them.

In the south part of the cemetery lie the graves of Samuel Robinson Ogden and Mary Campbell Ogden. They are surrounded by the graves of friends who joined them in Landgrove—the Pitchers, the Dibbles, and others. Up a hill farther to the south sits the village to which Sam and Mamie came in 1929. It is composed of tidy, handsome houses that comprise Sam Ogden's greatest lasting monument. The village is largely quiet in the winter, but in the summer it bursts into life. Its residents are a friendly, gracious, generous, interesting, accomplished, and creative lot. Their careers generally take them away from Landgrove, but for them the town is always home, a place full of strong communal bonds built on generations of shared experiences, deep friendships, and a web of intermarriage. It is in some ways similar to the kind of community that throve in Dorset in the 1870s, the one composed of Tiffts, Crandalls, and Reeds. In other ways it could hardly be more different.

In the north part of the cemetery is another group of headstones. John and Louise Neilson are buried there. Axel and Hilma Neilson are there, along with their son, John Dolph. The graves of Anna and Carl Westine are there, as well. Heading north up the Landgrove Road one passes the houses in which they lived and raised their families. The original structures can still be discerned, though additions have expanded them into fine vacation homes. The houses and the gravestones are the last tangible remnants of a human landscape that has vanished.

NOTES

Introduction

1 Historians have been interested in the story of Alonzo Valentine's Swedes for a number of reasons. The story illustrates the degree to which the state's Gilded Age elite saw its farming districts as in a state of crisis. Controversy over the program is also evidence of the deep divisions between urban and rural perspectives that characterized Vermont society, manifest in both state politics and in society at large. It suggests the extent to which state leaders did not perceive that the purchase of farmsteads as summer homes, rather than as working farms, would be to a large extent the future of rural Vermont. It speaks volumes to the extent to which the state's urban-minded leaders profoundly misunderstood the sources and character of the strong communal bonds that knit together the residents of small towns. Perhaps most of all, the story illustrates the pervasive anti-Catholic bias of the era, particularly as it applied to immigrants from Québec and their descendants. See J. Kevin Graffagnino, *Vermont in the Victorian Age: Continuity and Change in the Green Mountain State, 1850-1900* (Bennington and Shelburne, VT: Vermont Heritage Press and Shelburne Museum, 1985), 119-21; Blake Harrison, *The View from Vermont* (Burlington, VT: University of Vermont Press, 2006), 58; John Lund, "Vermont Nativism: William Paul Dillingham and U.S. Immigration Legislation," *Vermont History* 63 (Winter, 1995): 15-29; Michael Sherman, et. al., *Freedom and Unity: A History of Vermont* (Barre, VT: Vermont Historical Society, 2004), 310.

2 In typical accounts, most of the Swedes quickly moved on from where the state settled them, never establishing the cohesive colonies that Valentine hoped would attract more Scandinavians.

3 Paul M. Searls, *Two Vermonts: Geography and Identity, 1865-1910* (Durham, NH: University of New Hampshire Press; Hanover, NH: University Press of New England, 2006), 72-73.

4 Andrea Rebek, "The Selling of Vermont: From Agriculture to Tourism, 1860-1910," *Vermont History* 44 (Winter 1976): 17; Sherman, et. al., *Freedom and Unity*, 310.

5 Sherman, et. al., *Freedom and Unity*, 310; Graffagnino, *Vermont in the Victorian Age*, 121. The best source on the outcome of the scheme is Dorothy M. Harvey's article "Swedes in Vermont," which first praises Valentine's program, and then, in a brief section on the program's results, specifically identifies three families as having persisted for a few decades in the town of Weston. Dorothy M. Harvey, "The Swedes in Vermont," American Swedish Historical Museum *Yearbook* (1960), 23-43.

6 See, for example, Dona Brown, "Vermont as a Way of Life," *Vermont History* 85 (Winter/Spring 2017): 43-64.

Chapter 1

1 St. Paul (MN) *Daily Globe*, 2 June 1884.

2 Jacob G. Ullery, comp., *Men of Vermont: An Illustrated Biographical History of Vermonters and Sons of Vermont* (Brattleboro, VT: Transcript Publishing Company, 1894), 406-408.

3 The original senate bill put the number of commissioners at five, but the thrifty house revised that number down to a single commissioner. *Report of the Commissioner of Agricultural and Manufacturing Interests of the State of Vermont* (Rutland, VT: The Tuttle Company, Official State Printers, 1890), 4 (hereafter, *Report of the Commissioner*); *Journal of the House of Representatives of the State of Vermont, Biennial Session, 1888* (Montpelier, VT: Argus and Patriot Job Printing House, 1889), 24 November 1888; Burlington (VT) *Free Press*, 15 March 1889; Boston *Evening Journal*, 30 March 1889; Boston *Evening Transcript*, 11 November 1904.

4 Harold F. Wilson described railroads as "the strongest single factor affecting life in northern New England" from the 1840s to the 1870s. Harold F. Wilson, *The Hill Country of Northern New England* (Montpelier, VT: Vermont Historical Society, 1947), 29-45.

5 Addison County, for example, where conversion to sheep had been most vigorous but which remained predominately agricultural, experienced only marginal growth overall in the 1830s. On average Addison County towns lost 12 percent of their population in the decade that followed; see P. Jeffrey Potash, *Vermont's Burned-Over District: Patterns of Community Development and Religious Identity, 1761-1850* (Brooklyn, NY: Carlson Publishing, 1991), 105. Shoreham declined from 2,137 residents in 1830 to 1,674 in 1840. Thomas W. Arnold, *Two Hundred Years and Counting: Vermont Community Census Totals, 1791 to 1980* (Burlington, VT: Center for Rural Studies, University of Vermont), 15.

6 Harold A. Meeks, *Time and Change in Vermont* (Chester, CT: Globe Pequot Press, 1989), 104.

7 Randolph Roth, *The Democratic Dilemma* (New York: Cambridge University Press, 1987), 267.

8 Lewis C. Aldrich, *History of Bennington County* (Syracuse, NY: D. Mason, 1889).

9 Cephas Sheldon died in Kalamazoo, Michigan; Sylvester died in Johnson Creek,

Ohio; Ebenezer died in Kewanee, Illinois; William died in Flushing, Michigan; Eliphalet died in Addison, Shelby County, Indiana.

10 State of Vermont, Vermont Vital Records. New England Historic Genealogical Society, Boston, Massachusetts.

11 Emmons applied for a veteran's pension in 1833. Emmons was born in Stafford, Connecticut, in 1760. He went into service as a six-months solider belonging to the town of Wilbraham and served in the continental army of the US in 1780. Rufus P. Stebbins, *An Historical Address, Delivered at the Centennial Celebration of the Incorporation of the Town of Wilbraham*, 15 June 1863 (Boston: G. C. Rand and Avery, 1863).

12 U.S. Department of the Interior, Census Office, Seventh Census, 1850, Dorset, Bennington County, Vermont.

13 Already by then, rural and urbanite Vermonters were respectively pursuing, as historian Hal Barron writes without overstatement, "fundamentally different patterns of life." In the antebellum decades this manifested itself in controversies over such things as temperance, education reform, land use, Masonry, and the desirability of progress. Hal S. Barron, *Those Who Stayed Behind: Rural Society in Nineteenth-Century New England* (Cambridge: Cambridge University Press, 1984), 8.

14 Ibid., 15, 31-36.

15 U.S. Department of the Interior, Census Office, Eighth Census, 1860, Dorset, Bennington County, Vermont; Certificate of Marriage, Moses Tifft to Sophronia Crandall. Vermont Marriage Records, Vermont State Archives and Records Administration, Middlesex, Vermont (hereafter VSARA).

16 Ullery, *Men of Vermont*, 406.

17 As will be detailed later, Agnes Beebe was the mother of Alonzo Butler, who married Hilma Anderson, and grandmother to the husband of Hilma's sister Hazel.

18 Tyler Resch, *Dorset: In the Shadow of the Marble Mountain* (Dorset, VT: Dorset Historical Society, 1989), 142.

19 William R. Cutter, *New England Families Genealogical and Memorial*, vol. 3 (New York: n.p., 1915), 847-49.

20 Burlington *Free Press*, 26 December 1873.

21 Victor R. Rolando, *200 Years of Soot and Sweat* (Burlington, VT: Vermont Archaeological Society, 1992), http://www.vtarchaeology.org/wp-content/uploads/200_years_ch6_optimized.pdf.

22 Sara Gregg writes, "The importance of the Green Mountain forest was impossible to ignore, in part because of the scale of clearing during the nineteenth century; by the 1880s an estimated two thirds of the state had been cut by loggers and farmers...yet even during the period of peak harvest, native Vermonter [George Perkins] Marsh sought to raise public awareness with *Man and Nature*." She continues, "During the last decades of the nineteenth century the volume of lumber production dropped steadily, and land that had been logged in the boom years of the 1870s and 1880s increasingly returned to forest." Sara Gregg, *Managing the Mountains: Land Use Planning, the New Deal, and the Creation of a Federal Land-*

scape in Appalachia (New Haven, CT: Yale University Press, 2010), 61-63.

23 C. H. Possons, *Vermont: Its Resources and Industries* (Glens Falls, NY: C. H. Possons, 1889), 209.

24 Barron, *Those Who Stayed Behind*, 131.

25 Ullery, *Men of Vermont*, 406.

26 *Proceedings of the Vermont Historical Society, 1903-1904* (St. Albans, VT: Vermont Historical Society, 1904), 88.

27 Aldrich, *History of Bennington County*, 542-45.

28 Walter H. Crockett, *Vermont, the Green Mountain State*, 5 vols. (New York: Century History Company, 1921-23), 4: 45, 104. The total cash value of all Vermont farms fell from $139,367,075 in 1870 to $109,346,010 in 1880. After 1880, while southern New England's fortunes declined, Vermont and Maine experienced little change relative to the rest of the country. Peter Temin, *Engines of Enterprise: An Economic History of New England* (Cambridge, MA: Harvard University Press, 2000), 159.

29 U.S. Department of the Interior, Census Office, Tenth Census, 1880, Dorset, Bennington County, Vermont; Christopher M. Klyza and Stephen C. Trombulak, *The Story of Vermont: A Natural and Cultural History* (Hanover, NH: University Press of New England, 1999), 87-88. For example, wheat production fell from over 450,000 bushels in 1870 to 337,000 in 1880. That trend would continue; between 1865 and 1900, Vermont's wheat production fell 92 percent, and corn production fell 30 percent. Grace Wood, in *Wells, Vermont*, describes wool prices as falling from $1 per pound in 1865 to 40 cents a decade later, and to 5 to 8 cents per pound in the 1890s. Grace E. P. Wood, *History of the Town of Wells, Vermont* (Wells, VT: self-published, 1955), 15.

30 J. H. Putnam, "The Depopulation of Our Rural Districts: Cause, and Some Suggestions in Regard to a Remedy," *Report of the Vermont Board of Agriculture* (Montpelier, VT: J. & J. M. Poland, 1878), 132-39. On fears of rural decline, see Richard W. Judd, *Common Lands, Common People: The Origins of Conservation in Northern New England* (Cambridge, MA: Harvard University Press, 2000), 64-67.

31 The conception of this lost, resplendently pastoral republic constituted in the late Gilded Age, writes Joseph Conforti, "a new geography of the imagination." See Dona Brown, *Inventing New England* (Washington, DC: Smithsonian Books, 1997), 139-40; Joseph Conforti, *Imagining New England* (Chapel Hill, NC: University of North Carolina Press, 2001), 204.

32 Meeks, *Time and Change in Vermont*, 178-79.

33 *Journal of the Senate of the State of Vermont*, 1888 (Montpelier, VT: Argus and Patriot Job Printing House, 1889), 349-57.

34 Boston *Evening Transcript*, 7 August 1889.

35 Wilmington (VT) *Deerfield Valley Times*, 10 January 1890.

36 Burlington *Free Press*, 15 March 1889.

37 The Vermont Planning Council, *Vision and Choice: Vermont's Future* (Montpelier, VT: The Vermont Planning Council, 1968), 25. Throughout this book, the Planning Council's 1968 calculation of the historical number of farms will be used. Other calculations of farm numbers are available, but those of the Planning Council ac-

curately depict historical trends in Vermont farm numbers, and its sole use will provide consistency.

38 Burlington *Free Press*, 15 March 1889.

Chapter 2

1 In 1907 a newspaper wrote, "Personal friends of Maj. Valentine will recall with what confidence and enthusiasm he entered upon this experiment, and how, for the time being, he put his whole heart and energy into it." Brattleboro *Vermont Phoenix*, 16 August 1907.

2 St. Albans (VT) *Messenger*, 24 August 1891; Jacob G. Ullery, comp., *Men of Vermont: An Illustrated Biographical History of Vermonters and Sons of Vermont* (Brattleboro, VT: Transcript Publishing Company, 1894), 406-408.

3 Boston *Daily Journal*, 30 March 1889.

4 The problem, Valentine believed, was that the commissioner's position was so poorly funded by the penurious state legislature that town listers could not be compensated for accumulating the information Valentine asked of them. Alonzo Valentine, *Report of the Commissioner of Agricultural and Manufacturing Interests of the State of Vermont* (Rutland, VT: The Tuttle Company, Official State Printers, 1890), 5-6.

5 Ibid., 15-16. Among other business endeavors, Valentine was then engaged in an enterprise in Nebraska with Bennington businessman John G. McCullough. Correspondence about this enterprise is held in the collection of Valentine's papers at the Bennington Museum, Bennington, Vermont.

6 Alonzo B. Valentine, "Swedish Immigration," *The Quill* 1 (September 1890): 23-28; *Report of the Commissioner*, 23; Dorothy M. Harvey, "The Swedes in Vermont," American Swedish Historical Foundation *Yearbook* (1960), 40; J. Kevin Graffagnino, *Vermont in the Victorian Age: Continuity and Change in the Green Mountain State, 1850-1900* (Bennington and Shelburne, VT: Vermont Heritage Press and Shelburne Museum, 1985), 119-21.

7 Matthew F. Jacobson, *Whiteness of a Different Color: European Immigrants and the Alchemy of Race* (Cambridge, MA: Harvard University Press, 1999), 39-78.

8 Erica K. Jackson, *Scandinavians in Chicago: The Origins of White Privilege in Modern America* (Champaign, IL: University of Illinois Press, 2018). See Arthur Comte de Gobineau, "An Essay on the Inequality of Human Races," in Michael D. Biddiss, ed., *Gobineau: Selected Political Writings* (New York: Harper and Row, 1970), 161.

9 Pittsburgh *Daily Post*, 13 August 1889.

10 The 11-page pamphlet was titled "Nordgren & Bergstrom, hufvudagenter for Bay State Companiets land i Nebraska och Wyoming" (1888).

11 Boston *Evening Transcript*, 13 September 1889.

12 *Report of the Commissioner*, 5.

13 Troy (NY) *Weekly Budget*, 25 August 1889.

14 Boston *Evening Transcript*, 12 August 1889.

15 Cleveland *Plain Dealer*, 9 August 1889.

16 New Haven (CT) *Register*, 14 August 1889.

17 Boston *Evening Transcript*, 7 August 1889; "Vermont Wants to Be Recolonized," Baltimore *Sun*, 10 August 1889; "Vermont Invites Immigration," Detroit *Free Press*, 13 August 1889.

18 Troy *Weekly Budget*, 8 September 1889.

19 Boston *Daily Journal*, 27 September 1889; Hapgood recounted his accompaniment of Valentine in the Bennington *Banner*, March 30, 1910.

20 Wilmington (VT) *Deerfield Valley Times*, 23 August, 20 September 1889; Boston *Daily Journal*, 27 September 1889.

21 Grand Forks (ND) *Herald*, 25 September 1889; Wheeling (West Virginia) *Daily Register*, 26 October 1889.

22 For example, "Swedish Colonists for Vermont," *New York Times*, 29 September 1889.

23 "The Abandoned Farms of Vermont," Baltimore *Sun*, 15 October 1889; Chicago *Daily Tribune*, 30 October 1889; Cincinnati *Commercial Gazette*, 2 November 1889; Greymouth, New Zealand, *Grey River Argus*, 19 November 1889.

24 Bennington (VT) *Banner*, 19 November 1889.

25 Boston *Daily Journal*, 18 October 1889.

26 Macon (GA) *Telegraph*, 26 September 1889.

27 *Deerfield Valley Times*, 27 June 1889; Dallas *Morning News*, 6 November 1889; St. Albans (VT) *Messenger*, 10 October 1889; St. Albans *Messenger*, 21 December 1889 (reprint of article in the Boston *Herald*).

28 Boston *Evening Transcript*, 12 October 1889.

29 Ludlow *Vermont Tribune*, 20 September 1890.

30 Montpelier (VT) *Argus and Patriot*, 15 January 1890.

31 Reprinted in the St. Albans *Messenger*, 22 August 1889.

32 *Vermont Phoenix*, 8 November 1889; St. Louis *Republic*, 2 February 1890.

33 St. Albans *Messenger*, 21 May 1921.

34 Montpelier *Argus and Patriot*, 18 December 1889.

35 The Montpelier *Vermont Watchman* wrote, "The phrase is just right. The farms were abandoned by their former owners, and the buildings have in many cases gone to decay or been sold to the insurance company that held a risk on them." *Vermont Watchman*, 4 September 1889. Valentine himself had no apologies for using the word. At one point in September 1889 he foresaw the location of colonies when writing, "Off to the east, through Windsor and Windham counties, nearly to the Connecticut River, lies farm after farm, unoccupied and abandoned. In Peru and Landgrove, to the west and south the same condition prevails." *Deerfield Valley Times*, 20 September 1889.

36 *Deerfield Valley Times*, 20 September 1889.

37 Burlington (VT) *Free Press*, 25 November 1889.

38 *Burlington Independent*, 8 November 1889.

39 St. Albans *Messenger*, 25 September 1889.

40 Quoted in the *Deerfield Valley Times*, 25 October 1889.

41 Montpelier *Vermont Watchman*, 21 October 1889. The *Watchman* called the charge of discrimination "sheer nonsense." E. L. Bass, ed., *Report of the Nineteenth Annual Meeting of the Vermont Dairymen's Association* (Montpelier, VT: The Watchman Publishing Company, 1889), 86.

42 Hal S. Barron, *Those Who Stayed Behind: Rural Society in Nineteenth-Century New England* (Cambridge: Cambridge University Press, 1984, 132-35.

43 Londonderry (VT) *Sifter*, 3 October 1889.

44 Boston *Daily Journal*, 18 October 1889; Troy (NY) *Weekly Times*, 31 October, 7 November 1889.

45 *Report of the Commissioner*, 23-24.

46 The Landgrove Historical Society possesses a copy of the map.

47 When Nordgren applied for a passport in November 1889 for his recruitment trip, he listed his place of birth as Varmland.

48 The contemporary spelling of the district is "Alga," but on a variety of United States documents for decades after, as far forward as Oliver Nyren's death certificate in 1962, Valentine's Swedes always spelled it "Elgo."

49 Ingvar Andersson, *A History of Sweden* (New York: Prager, 1956), 181-82.

50 "Olaf Olson," IAGenWeb Project, http://iagenweb.org/boards/boone/biographies/index.cgi?read=303099, posted 15 October 2010.

51 St. Albans *Messenger*, 2 May 1890; *Report of the Commissioner*, 25.

52 Springfield (MA) *Republican*, 30 December 1889; *New York Times*, 15 December 1889.

53 Bennington *Banner*, July 24, 1890. For a description of the extreme difficulty of acquiring land in Sweden, including in Varmland, and for this being a major cause of emigration from Sweden, see Franklin D. Scott, *Sweden: The Nation's History* (Carbondale, IL: Southern Illinois University Press, 1988), 370-71.

54 *Vermont Phoenix*, 17 January 1890.

55 Reprinted in the St. Johnsbury (VT) *Caledonian Record*, 9 January 1890.

56 Quoted in the Rutland (VT) *Herald*, 9 January 1890.

57 *Report of the Commissioner*, 49; *Vermont Phoenix*, 17 January 1890; Burlington *Free Press*, 21 January 1890.

58 Edwin Rozwenc, *Agricultural Policies in Vermont, 1860-1945* (Montpelier, VT: Vermont Historical Society, 1981), 35-37.

59 Ullery, *Men of Vermont*, 68

60 Rutland *Herald*, 18 January 1890.

61 Vermont State Board of Agriculture, *Eleventh Vermont Agricultural Report by the State Board of Agriculture, for the Years 1889-1890* (Montpelier, VT: Argus and Patriot Print, 1890), 32, 36, 44, 54, 108; Burlington *Free Press*, 24 January 1890.

62 St. Johnsbury *Caledonian Record*, 6 February 1889.

63 *Deerfield Valley Times*, 21 March 1890.

64 Boston *Morning Journal*, 8 March 1890; Springfield *Republican*, 10 March 1890

65 New York *Herald-Tribune*, 19 April 1890; Springfield *Republican*, 13 April 1890; Boston *Daily Journal*, 23 April 1890.

66 New York *Herald-Tribune*, 10 March 1890.

67 Boston *Daily Journal*, 23 April 1890.

68 Topeka (KS) *Capital*, 1 February 1890.

69 Providence (RI) *Journal*, 23 April 1890.

70 New York *Herald-Tribune*, 19 April 1890.

71 U.S. Commission of Immigration, "Passenger List of Steamship British Princess from Liverpool," August 5, 1890. There has long been confusion about the Swedes' arrival in America, with the date given as either April 23 or 24, and the location as New York. The Boston *Daily Journal* may have contributed to this inaccuracy immediately, reporting on April 25 that the Swedes had arrived in New York on the 23rd aboard the steamer *Philadelphia* of the American Line. No ship by that name landed in New York in 1890, but the *British Princess*, which landed in Philadelphia, was one of the American Line. Valentine etched this information into stone when his report to the legislature repeated the same inaccurate date and location. Boston *Daily Journal*, April 25, 1890.

72 St. Albans *Messenger*, 26 April 1890.

73 *Deerfield Valley Times*, 2 May 1890. The newspaper already had been downplaying local expectations in the spring, reporting in March that Wilmington would receive no more than six families. *Deerfield Valley Times*, 14 March 1890.

74 Dorothy Harvey wrote, "Two of Weston's residents recalled with pride that their fathers had driven teams over the mountain to help bring back Swedish arrivals at Danby depot." Harvey, "The Swedes in Vermont," 23.

75 *Deerfield Valley Times*, 2 May 1890.

76 St. Albans *Messenger*, 2 May 1890. *Deerfield Valley Times*, 16 May 1890.

77 *Deerfield Valley Times*, 13 June 1890.

78 San Francisco *Bulletin*, 22 July 1890; Chicago *Herald*, 9 August 1890.

79 *Deerfield Valley Times*, 28 September 1889.

80 Fort Worth (TX) *Weekly Gazette*, 26 September 1889.

81 According to Harvey, the Swedes had first "tried their hand at the Weston farms, but soon found it more profitable to work in the local sawmill of Silas Griffith, or the logging operations of M. J. Hapgood, on Peru Mountain." Harvey, "The Swedes in Vermont," 23. The *Vermont Phoenix* reported in April 1891, "most of them remain on the farms where they were first located…and the younger men are at work on a lumber job in Peru." *Vermont Phoenix*, 17 April 1891. The Swedes' immediate employment at the Peru lumber mill is documented in the archives of the Landgrove Historical Society, and figured prominently in an exhibit it produced on them. Research by Karl Pfister of the Landgrove Historical Society records that, in addition to the Nyrens, Westines, Andersons, and Neilsons, "A fourth couple were very likely on the 1890 boat. Anders and Kardina Johanneson were married on September 6, 1891, and a daughter Christine, was born in Landgrove in June of 1892. However, they did not settle here."

82 Springfield *Republican*, 26 April 1890; St. Johnsbury *Caledonian Record*, 26 April 1890.

83 Springfield *Republican*, 30 May 1890.

84 Boston *Evening Transcript*, 5 August 1890.

85 Boston *Daily Advertiser*, 24 July 1890; St. Albans *Messenger*, 24 July 1890.

86 It was repeatedly reported in 1890 that the minister settled in with the Weston contingent, which made Landgrove the focus of Valentine's three colonies. It is uncertain who exactly he was, and if not drawn from one of the five families— Neilson, Nyren, Westine, Swenson, and Anderson—he did not stay long.

87 Boston *Daily Journal*, 24 July 1890.

88 St. Johnsbury *Caledonian Record*, 25 July 1890; St. Albans *Messenger*, 24 July 1890; Springfield *Republican*, 26 July 1890. Valentine told the St. Albans *Messenger* in August that at that very moment three families destined for Weston, three for Wilmington, and two more families were already on their way from Sweden. St. Albans *Messenger*, 1 August 1890.

89 St. Albans *Messenger*, 24 July 1890.

90 Ibid., 19 May 1890.

91 Kansas City (MO) *Star*, 24 July 1890; Portland *Morning Oregonian*, 22 July 1890; Baltimore *Sun*, 23 July 1890.

92 Boston *Daily Advertiser*, 24 July 1890; Boston *Daily Journal*, 24 July 1890.

93 Cincinnati *Commercial-Gazette*, 20 July 1890.

94 Boston *Evening Journal*, 12 July 1890.

95 Boston *Daily Journal*, 24 July 1890.

96 St. Johnsbury *Caledonian Record*, 20 January 20 1890.

97 "Attractions In and Around Burlington" (Glens Falls, NY: C. H. Possons, 1890).

98 Boston *Evening Transcript*, 24 Jul 1890

99 The quoted speaker was H. K. Slayton. Bass, ed., *Report of the Nineteenth Annual Meeting of the Vermont Dairymen's Association*, 88.

100 *Passenger Lists of Vessels Arriving at Philadelphia, Pennsylvania, 1883-1945*. Micropublication T840. RG085. Rolls # 1-181. National Archives and Records Administration, Washington, DC.

101 *Vermont Phoenix*, 12 September 1890.

102 Boston *Evening Transcript*, 4 November 1904.

103 Brenham (TX) *Weekly Banner*, 18 September 1890.

104 Rozwenc, *Agricultural Policies in Vermont*, 68. Grange master Alpha Messer said at a Grange meeting that he had "no abiding faith in immigration from Sweden or any other foreign country as a direct means of permanent settlement for these farms." Graffagnino, *Vermont in the Victorian Age*, 120.

105 Burlington *Free Press*, 26 November 1890.

106 *Report of the Commissioner*, 25.

107 Ibid., 35-39.

108 The bill, H49, was submitted by Representative Taylor of Cornwall on October 9. The special committee was established the next day.

109 Edwin C. Rozwenc, "The Group Basis of Vermont Farm Politics, 1870-1945," *Vermont History* 25 (Fall 1957): 268-87.

110 Burlington *Free Press*, 1 September 1904.

111 Montpelier *Argus and Patriot*, 24 September 1890.

112 Bennington *Banner*, 27 November 1890.

113 *Deerfield Valley Times*, 12 December 1890.

114 *Vermont Phoenix*, 2 January 1891.

115 Burlington *Clipper*, 26 January 1891.

Chapter 3

1 Brattleboro *Vermont Phoenix*, 5 May 1893.

2 Londonderry (VT) *Sifter*, 12 May 1893.

3 Vermont Legislative Directory, 1892 (Montpelier, VT: Watchman Publishing Company, 1892); Lewis C. Aldrich, *History of Bennington County, Vt.* (Syracuse, NY: D. Mason & Co., Publishers, 1889), 498.

4 U.S. Department of the Interior, Census Office, Fifteenth Census, 1930, Landgrove, Bennington County, Vermont.

5 Jennie Westine's birth date was 19 January 1891. U.S. Department of the Interior, Census Office, Twelfth Census, 1900, Landgrove, Bennington County, Vermont.

6 Federal Census, Year: *1900*; Census Place: *Orange, Franklin, Massachusetts*; Roll *649*; Page *6A*; Enumeration District: *0494*; Family History Library microfilm: *1240649*.

7 Harry Neilson's 1937 marriage certificate lists his birthplace as Jamaica, as do his draft cards for both world wars.

8 St. Albans (VT) *Messenger*, 15 December 1921.

9 Boston *Globe*, 3 April 1891; St. Albans *Messenger*, 9 April 1891. The *Messenger* later retracted this statement, writing that an investigation by Governor Page had revealed that Norton's Swedes were "getting along quite well." St. Albans *Messenger*, 21 May 1891.

10 St. Albans *Messenger*, 19 June 1891.

11 *Vermont Phoenix*, 27 March 1891.

12 Boston *Transcript*, 5 November 1904.

13 St. Albans *Messenger*, 24 August 1891.

14 Montpelier (VT) *Argus and Patriot*, 17 December 1891.

15 For example, the education policy of Governor Carroll Page, who entered office in 1891, sought to reorganize the school system around a fear that unassimilated foreigners who came to Vermont threatened to plunge the state into anarchy. John A. Sautter, "Equity and History: Vermont's Education Revolution of the Early 1890s," *Vermont History* 76 (Winter/Spring 2008): 5.

16 *Report of the Twenty-First Annual Meeting of the Vermont Dairymen's Association* (Montpelier, VT: Press of the Watchman Publishing Co., 1891), 98; Hamilton Child, ed., *Gazetteer and Business Directory of Windham County, Vt., 1724-1884* (Syracuse, NY: Journal Office, 1884), 304.

17 Bennington (VT) *Banner*, 26 June 1891.

18 Burlington (VT) *Clipper*, 25 June 1891.

19 Montpelier *Argus and Patriot*, 20 May 1891.

20 James P. McKinney, *The Industrial Advantages of the State of Vermont* (Rochester,

NY: Commerce Publishing Company, 1890), 13-14.

21 Blake Harrison, *The View from Vermont: Tourism and the Making of a Rural American Landscape* (Burlington, VT: University of Vermont Press/Hanover, NH: University Press of New England, 2006), 34.

22 *Journal of the House of the State of Vermont* (Montpelier, VT: Argus and Patriot Job Printing House, 1891), 44-45.

23 *Men and Women of America: A Biographical Dictionary of Contemporaries* (New York: L. R. Haersley & Company, 1910), 779.

24 Ira K. Batchelder, *Reunion Celebration, Together with an Historical Sketch of Peru, Bennington County* (Brattleboro, VT: Phoenix Job Print, 1891), 6; Aldrich, *History of Bennington County*, 461.

25 Bennington (VT) *Banner*, 14 July 1891.

26 St. Albans *Messenger*, 24 August 1891.

27 *Vermont Phoenix*, 2 October 1891.

28 Ibid., 27 March 1891

29 St. Albans *Messenger*, 24 August 1891.

30 Announced in the *Vermont Phoenix*, 27 March 1891; "Summer Resorts," *Report of the State Board of Agriculture*, 1891, 164-67.

31 Springfield (MA) *Republican*, 12 September 1891.

32 E. Melanie Dupuis and Paul Vandergeest, eds., *Creating the Countryside: The Politics of Rural and Environmental Discourse* (Philadelphia: Temple University Press, 1996), 265. *Thirteenth Vermont Agricultural Report by the State Board of Agriculture, for the Year 1893* (Burlington, VT: Free Press Printers and Publishers, 1893), 28; *The Resources and Attractions of Vermont: With a List of Desirable Homes for Sale* (Montpelier, VT: Watchman Press, 1891), 78.

33 Boston *Transcript*, 5 November 1904.

34 Jacob G. Ullery, comp., *Men of Vermont: An Illustrated Biographical History of Vermonters and Sons of Vermont* (Brattleboro, VT: Transcript Publishing Company, 1894), 372.

35 Victor I. Spear, *Vermont: A Glimpse of Its Scenery and Industries* (Montpelier, VT: Vermont State Board of Agriculture, 1893).

36 "Farm Management," *Thirteenth Vermont Agricultural Report*.

37 Victor I. Spear, *Report on Summer Travel for 1894* (Montpelier, VT: Watchman Press, 1894), 7.

38 Boston *Evening Transcript*, 4 November 1904.

39 *The Industries and Wealth of the Principal Points of Vermont* (New York: American Publishing and Engraving Company, 1891), 112.

40 Emphasizing the Vermont Development Association's reliance on specialized experts and professionals, the Burlington *Free Press* extolled in an editorial that "the names of the gentlemen who were given the management of the affairs of the organization are sufficient to ensure effective as well as energetic effort." Burlington *Free Press*, 14 March 1895.

41 Arthur F. Stone, *The Vermont of Today*, 4 vols. (New York: Lewis Historical Publishing Co., 1929), 2: 59.

42 U.S. Department of the Interior, Census Office, Twelfth Census, 1900, Landgrove, Bennington County, Vermont.

43 Karl Pfister collection, Landgrove Historical Society, Landgrove, Vermont.

44 Londonderry *Sifter*, 27 September 1895.

45 U.S. Department of the Interior, Census Office, Thirteenth Census, 1910, Landgrove, Bennington County, Vermont.

46 John J. Duffy, Samuel B. Hand, and Ralph H. Orth, eds., *The Vermont Encyclopedia* (Hanover, NH: University Press of New England, 2003), 196.

47 The marble business had gravitated to the towns of Proctor and Rutland to Dorset's north, where higher-quality marble was located. Tyler Resch, *Dorset: In the Shadow of the Marble Mountain* (West Kennebunk, ME: Published for the Dorset Historical Society by Phoenix Publishing, 1989), 145.

48 Richard M. Campbell, *Dorset, Vermont, as a Summer Home* (Danby, VT: Mirror Printing, 1898).

49 Resch, *Dorset*, 197.

50 Jane Stern, *Elegant Comfort Food from Dorset Inn* (Dorset, VT: Rutledge Hill Press, 2005), 6.

51 St. Albans *Messenger*, 25 March 1895.

52 Vermont Tribune, *Ludlow and Her Neighbors, Being a Special Souvenir Edition of the Vermont Tribune* (Ludlow, VT: Vermont Tribune Office, 1899), 41.

53 Burlington *Free Press*, 23 December 1897.

54 Both Carl Nyren and Anna Neilson appear in the 1900 census as residents of their parents' homes, and also of the boardinghouse on Mount Tabor. U.S. Department of the Interior, Census Office, Twelfth Census, 1900, Mount Tabor, Rutland County, Vermont.

55 Ibid., Landgrove, Bennington County, Vermont.

56 Ibid.

57 Addie Tifft's 1899 birth certificate lists Eddie Tifft's job as lumberman.

58 Sara Gregg writes in *Managing the Mountains*, "Agricultural production in the mountains continued to decline [after the 1890s]. As upland pastures returned to forest, the land sprouted stands of white pines. By 1900 the concentration of high-value pine ranging in age from 20 to 60 years set off a renewed logging boom in northern New England...During the early twentieth century, the hilltowns' restricted economy and changing settlement patterns drew attention to the crucial interdependence of farm and forest...Because many upland farmers depended on an income from their farm woodlots, families were often forced to give up their farms once local timber resources were depleted. J. Russell Smith observed this transformation in progress in the early twentieth century: these people had been living on small farms which produced a part of the family support, the rest being obtained from work in the forest in the winter." Sara Gregg, *Managing the Mountains: Land Use Planning, the New Deal, and the Creation of a Federal Landscape in Appalachia* (New Haven, CT: Yale University Press, 2013), 113-15.

59 Ralph Moffitt, interview by Samuel R. Ogden, 1967. The explosion was on December 16, 1900, according to Ogden, *The Cheese that Changed Many Lives; or, A senti-*

mental history of a tiny town high in the Green Mountains (Landgrove, VT: Just-So Press, 1978), 83.

60 *Report of the Commissioner of Fish and Game* (Montpelier, VT: Vermont Fish and Game Commission, 1902), 24.

61 See Paul M. Searls, *Two Vermonts: Geography and Identity, 1865-1910* (Durham, NH: University of New Hampshire Press; Hanover, NH: University Press of New England, 2006), 117-30, for a more thorough discussion of this topic.

62 See Town of Londonderry, "About Londonderry," http://londonderryvt.org/community/arts-historical/about-londonderry/.

63 Robert C. Jones, *Railroads of Vermont*, 2 vols. (Shelburne, VT: New England Press, 1993), 2: 53.

64 *Distinguished Successful Americans of Our Day* (Chicago: Successful Americans, 1911), 558.

65 Hazel Anderson marriage certificate, *Vermont Marriage Records, 1909-2008*; User Box Number: *PR-01560*; Roll Number: *S-30644*; Archive Number: *M-1953467*, Vermont State Archives and Records Administration (VSARA), Middlesex.

66 Carl Tifft death certificate, *Vermont Death Records, 1909-2008*; User Box Number: *PR-02132*; Roll Number: *S-31439*; Archive Number: *PR-1490-1491*, VSARA.

67 John Neilson's daughter Bula (sometimes written as "Beda") died at age 15 of meningitis in 1904. State of Vermont, Vermont Vital Records, 1871–1908. New England Historic Genealogical Society, Boston, Massachusetts.

68 *Lebanon, Grafton, New Hampshire*; Roll: 946; Page: 4A; Enumeration District: 0063; Family History Library microfilm: 1240946. United States of America, Bureau of the Census. *Twelfth Census of the United States, 1900* (Washington, DC: National Archives and Records Administration, 1900), T623, 1854 rolls.

69 Bennington *Banner*, 11 July 1904.

70 Burlington *Free Press*, 1 September 1904; "The Protectionist," August 1904 (Boston: Home Market Club), 202.

71 Boston *Evening Transcript*, 4 November 1904.

72 Bennington *Banner*, 28 August 1904.

73 *Vermont Life* 24 (Autumn 1969): 7.

74 Ogden, *The Cheese that Changed Many Lives*, 7-8.

CHAPTER 4

1 Burlington (VT) *Free Press*, 6 August 1907.

2 Bennington (VT) *Banner*, 27 May 1907.

3 May's marriage certificate lists her birthplace as "Vermland, Sweden." State of Vermont. Vermont Vital Records, 1871–1908. New England Historic Genealogical Society, Boston, Massachusetts.

4 Londonderry (VT) *Sifter*, 30 May 1907.

5 U.S. Department of the Interior, Census Office, Thirteenth Census, 1910, Dorset, Bennington County, Vermont.

6 In the sort of dizzying familial relations that were common in the area, Richard Reed was the son of Ebenezer Reed and Louise Lillie, who Ebenezer had married after the death of his first wife, Mary Tifft. Two of Ebenezer's brothers had also married daughters of Rufus Tifft, who was married to Jane Lillie, whose brother Stewart had married Rufus's sister Hannah, producing Louise. Louise and Ebenezer had a daughter Harriet in 1859, and 25 years later she married Dorset teamster Willard Tifft, the brother of John Tifft. Agnes Beebe's mother, Calista Hazelton, was the sister of Sarah Hazelton, had who married Moses Tifft, John's uncle. Willard Tifft death certificate, Vermont Death Records, 1909-2008; User Box Number: PR-01923; Roll Number S-30891; Archive Number: M-2051998, Vermont State Archives and Records Administration (VSARA), Middlesex.

7 U.S. Department of the Interior, Census Office, Thirteenth Census, 1910, Pawlet, Rutland County, Vermont.

8 Ibid., Londonderry, Windham County, Vermont.

9 Manchester (VT) *Journal*, 12 September 1907.

10 Samuel R. Ogden, *The Cheese that Changed Many Lives; or, A sentimental history of a tiny town high in the Green Mountains* (Landgrove, VT: Just-So Press, 1978), 81; *Journal of the House of Representatives of the State of Vermont, Biennial Session, 1906* (St. Albans, VT: St. Albans Messenger Company Print, 1907), 150.

11 Michael Sherman, et. al., *Freedom and Unity: A History of Vermont* (Barre, VT: Vermont Historical Society, 2004), 376; Richard W. Judd, *Second Nature: An Environmental History of New England* (Amherst, MA: University of Massachusetts Press, 2014), 116-19.

12 Bristol (VT) *Herald*, 10 June 1909; *Freedom and Unity*, 377-79; Sara Gregg, *Managing the Mountains: Land Use Planning, the New Deal, and the Creation of a Federal Landscape in Appalachia* (New Haven, CT: Yale University Press, 2013), 55.

13 Reprinted in the Wilmington (VT) *Deerfield Valley Times*, 18 June 1909.

14 Rutland (VT) *Herald*, 22 March 1980; Burlington *Free Press*, 16 July 1933.

15 Ogden, *The Cheese that Changed Many Lives*, 64-65.

16 Bennington *Banner*, 14 July 1909.

17 Samuel R. Ogden, *This Country Life* (New York: A. S. Barnes and Company, 1946), 10-14.

18 Frank L. Greene, *Vermont, the Green Mountain State: Past, Present, Prospective* (Montpelier, VT: Vermont Commission to the Jamestown Tercentennial Exposition, 1907).

19 Among other initiatives, Proctor championed the reorganization of Vermont's courts, the reformation of utility and railroad regulation, and progressive forestry policies. Proctor urged the establishment of a body to regulate telephone, telegraph, electric light, gas, and other public service companies. At his urging the state's Railroad Commission took on the responsibility of regulating public service companies like electric lighting and gas, and was renamed the Public Service Commission. Vermont historian Walter Crockett wrote in 1921 that, "no legislative session in recent years…passed as many important measures as that of 1906," see Samuel B. Hand, *The Star that Set: The Vermont Republican Party, 1854-1974* (Lan-

ham, MD: Lexington Books, 2002), 81, 118, 181; William Doyle, *The Vermont Political Tradition and Those Who Helped Make It* (Barre, VT: The Author, 1984), 150; John J. Duffy, Samuel B. Hand, and Ralph H. Orth, eds., *The Vermont Encyclopedia* (Hanover, NH: University Press of New England, 2003), 241; Sherman, et. al., *Freedom and Unity*, 363.

20 Winston A. Flint, *The Progressive Movement in Vermont* (Washington, DC: The American Council on Public Affairs, 1941), 41.

21 Bennington *Banner*, 15 July 1911.

22 Sherman, et. al., *Freedom and Unity*, 370.

23 Bennington *Banner*, 25 April 1911.

24 *Agriculture of Vermont: First Annual Report of the Commissioner of Agriculture of the State of Vermont* (Montpelier, VT: Capital City Press, 1909), 7.

25 Perry H. Merrill, *History of Forestry in Vermont, 1909-1959* (Montpelier, VT: Vermont Historical Society, 1959), 3.

26 *Agriculture of Vermont*, 173: Hawes wrote, "as the Act creating the position of State Forester was only passed late in the session, and the appointment was not made until the middle of February...but a bare beginning in the work has thus far been made...The beginnings of forestry which are now being made in this country are necessarily crude...reckless cutting resulted, as in Vermont, in a temporary utilization for agriculture of much land that should never have been cleared."

27 Vermont State Board of Agriculture, *Beautiful Vermont: Unsurpassed as a Residence or Playground; for the Summer Resident; the Summer Visitor; the Tourist; the Capitalist and the Workingman* (Woodstock, VT: State Board of Agriculture, 1907).

28 Ellen Stroud, *Nature Next Door* (Seattle: University of Washington Press, 2012), 81.

29 New York *Sun*, 7 September 1913.

30 Ogden, *The Cheese that Changed Many Lives*, 14; Chicago *Inter-Ocean*, 25 September 1910.

31 Burlington *Free Press*, 23 September 1909.

32 Bennington *Banner*, 27 November 1911; Burlington *Free Press*, 28 November 1911.

33 Brooklyn *Daily Eagle*, 26 July 1914.

34 Almon C. Judd, *The Ideal Tour* (Waterbury, CT: Almon Judd, 1911).

35 Burlington *Free Press*, 27 July 1908.

36 "Former Presidents of the University of Vermont," www.uvm.edu/president/formerpresidents/?Page=bailey.html; John Beckley, et al., *Thank you Guy Bailey* (self-published, 1976), 8.

37 St. Johnsbury (VT) *Caledonian Record*, 16 November 1910; Brattleboro *Vermont Phoenix*, 9 December 1910.

38 Stroud, *Nature Next Door*, 81; Christopher M. Klyza and Stephen C. Trombulak, *The Story of Vermont* (Hanover, NH: University Press of New England, 1999), 108.

39 The legislation creating the Bureau of Publicity invested it with the responsibility "to promote the further development of the natural resources of the state by the collections, preparation, publication and distribution of reliable information and statics touching its natural and industrial advantages."

40 Reprinted in the Bennington *Banner*, 5 May 1911.

41 Montpelier *Vermont Watchman*, 5 May 1910.

42 H. H. Chadwick, *The Vermont Bureau of Publicity: Its History, Expenditures and Activities* (Montpelier, VT: Vermont Bureau of Publicity, 1934), 5.

43 Vermont Bureau of Publicity, *Vermont: Designed by the Creator for the Playground of the Continent* (Montpelier, VT: Capital City Press, 1911).

44 Guy Bailey and Orlando Martin, *Homeseekers' Guide to Vermont Farms* (St. Albans, VT: St. Albans Messenger Company, 1911).

45 Bennington *Banner*, 15 May 1911.

46 Article from the *Vermont Watchman*, reprinted in the Montpelier (VT) *Morning Journal*, 19 July 1912; Burlington *Free Press*, 2 May 1912.

47 Montpelier (VT) *Journal*, 26 July 1912.

48 In addition, "Vermont hotels and boarding houses have increased in number within the last year." Bennington *Banner*, 16 May 1912.

49 Burlington *Free Press*, 22 February 1912.

50 Greater Vermont Association, *Constitution and By-Laws* (Essex Junction, VT: Greater Vermont Association, 1912), 4. There is a description of the GVA in Arthur F. Stone, *The Vermont of Today: With its Historic Background, Attractions and People*, 4 vols. (New York: Lewis Historical Publishing Company, 1929), 1: 855.

51 "The Greater Vermont Association," *The New England Magazine* 47 (March 1912): 250.

52 Greater Vermont Association, *The Salient Features of Vermont as a Vacation State* (Essex Junction, VT: Greater Vermont Association, 1913).

53 *The Vermonter* 15 (January 1910): 114; Vermont Bureau of Publicity, *Vermont: Designed by the Creator for the Playground of the Continent* (Montpelier, VT: Capital City Press, 1911).

54 Louis J. Paris, *The Long Trail* (Brandon, VT: the Brandon Inn, 1914), 13.

55 Chadwick, *The Vermont Bureau of Publicity*, 1. The appropriation remained at $10,000 a year until 1922.

56 Bennington *Banner*, 12 October 1912.

57 *Who's Who Among North American Authors*, vol. 4, 1929-1930 (Los Angeles: Golden Syndicate Publishing Company, 1930), 249; Frank L. Fish, *Horace Ward Bailey: Vermonter* (Rutland, VT: The Tuttle Company, 1914).

58 *Vermont Summer Resorts* (Montpelier, VT: The Bureau of Publicity, 1912).

59 Chadwick, *The Vermont Bureau of Publicity*, 5.

60 Dorman B. E. Kent, "One Thousand Men," *Proceedings of the Vermont Historical Society for the Years 1913-1914* (Vermont Historical Society, 1915), 152.

61 Barre (VT) *Times*, 16 August 1913.

62 Burlington *Free Press*, 17 April 1913.

63 Vermont Secretary of State, *Vermont Farms: Some Facts and Figures Concerning the Agricultural Resources and Opportunities of the Green Mountain State* (St. Johnsbury, VT: The Caledonian Company, 1913); Stroud, *Nature Next Door*, 85.

64 Vermont Bureau of Publicity, *Industrial Vermont: The Mineral, Manufacturing, and Water Power Resources of the Green Mountain State* (Montpelier, VT: Capital City Press, 1914), 3.

65 Ogden, *The Cheese that Changed Many Lives*, 43.

66 Thomas D. McDevitt, "George Schmitt: Pioneer Aviator," *Rutland Historical Society Quarterly* 15 (1985): 47.

67 U.S. Department of the Interior, Census Office, Thirteenth Census, 1910, Londonderry, Windham County, Vermont.

68 Ibid.

69 Vermont Planning Council, *Vision and Choice: Vermont's Future* (Montpelier, VT: Vermont Planning Council, 1968), 25.

70 Sherman, et. al., *Freedom and Unity*, 379; Merrill, *History of Forestry*, 16.

71 Tyler Resch, *Dorset: In the Shadow of the Marble Mountain* (West Kennebunk, ME: Published for the Dorset Historical Society by Phoenix Publishing, 1989), 144-52.

72 *Vermont Phoenix*, 19 July 1912.

73 *Deerfield Valley Times*, 10 January 1890.

74 Vermont Marriage Records, 1909-2003, 30 January 1910. Vermont State Archives and Records Administration, Middlesex.

75 Fontaine Martin, *The Landgrove Meetinghouse: A Cross Section of Landgrove, Vermont, History* (Landgrove, VT: F. Martin, 1981), 130.

76 Bennington *Banner*, 19 June 1912.

77 Brattleboro (VT) *Reformer*, 21 April 1914

78 Bennington *Banner*, 21 April 1914.

79 Burlington *Free Press*, 19 December 1914; Barton (VT) *Orleans County Monitor*, 23 December 1914.

80 Bennington *Banner*, 20 February 1915.

81 *Proceedings of the Seventh Annual Meeting of the National Child Labor Committee* (New York: The American Academy of Political and Social Science, 1911), 184; Flint, *The Progressive Movement in Vermont*, 75; Sherman, et. al., *Freedom and Unity*, 367.

82 In 1912 a State Board of Education was created, and the Carnegie Foundation was commissioned to study the state's rural schools. The foundation's report two years later found the state's schools to be, on the whole, in deplorable condition, often in dilapidated buildings with ill-prepared teachers and an inadequate curriculum. Sherman, et. al., *Freedom and Unity*, 372.

83 Kemp R. Flint, *Poor Relief in Vermont* (Northfield, VT: Norwich University, 1916), 4. Comments on the report can be found in Stone, *The Vermont of Today* 1: 675. Mason Stone, "The Rural Schools," in *Agriculture of Vermont*, 48.

84 Mortimer R. Proctor and Roderic Olzendam, *The Green Mountain Tour: Vermont, the Unspoiled Land* (Rutland, VT: Tuttle Company, 1915), 6; Vermont Bureau of Publicity, *The Lake Region of Western Vermont* (Morrisville, VT: Vermont Bureau of Publicity, 1918); Vermont Bureau of Publicity, *The Lake Region of Eastern Vermont* (Essex Junction, VT: Vermont Bureau of Publicity, 1917).

85 Bennington *Banner*, 16 May 1912.

86 For example, an article titled "Vermont for Vermonters" appeared in a 1910 issue of *The Vermonter* magazine. *The Vermonter*, 15 (1910): 88-89.

87 Montpelier *Morning Journal*, 11 December 1913. Even that phrase could be em-

ployed to opposite ends, as the Bennington *Banner* did in 1913: Believing that in places "where there were half a dozen summer people ten years ago, today there are hundreds," the *Banner* recommended the state "seize on every opportunity to advertise our advantages. Our slogan should be 'Vermont for Vermonters.'" Bennington *Banner*, 3 May 1913.

88 *The Vermonter* 20 (June 1915): 9.

89 Burlington *Free Press*, 30 June 1915.

90 Bennington *Banner*, 15 October 1915.

91 Walter H. Crockett, *Vermont: Its Resources and Opportunities* (Rutland, VT: Tuttle Co., 1916), 3.

92 Brattleboro (VT) *Daily Reformer*, 29 March 1916.

93 Brattleboro *Reformer*, 15 April 1916; *Landgrove Town Annual Report for 1916*, 37.

94 *Vermont Phoenix*, 14 December 1916.

95 *Proceedings of the Twenty-Second Annual Meeting of the Vermont Maple Sugar Makers' Association* (St. Albans, VT: St. Albans Messenger Co. Print, 1915), 34.

96 Brattleboro *Reformer*, 26 March 1917.

97 Londonderry *Sifter*, 22 December 1916.

98 Nell I. Painter, *Standing at Armageddon* (New York: W. W. Norton, 1989), 321-22.

99 Middlebury (VT) *Register*, 30 March 1917.

100 Londonderry *Sifter*, 8 April 1917.

Chapter 5

1 See Robert Dorman, *Revolt of the Provinces: The Regionalist Movement in America, 1920-1945* (Chapel Hill, NC: University of North Carolina Press, 1993), 81-144; Warren Susman, *Culture as History: The Transformation of American Society in the Twentieth Century* (New York: Pantheon Books, 1972), 123-49; Michele Hilmes, *Radio Reader: Essays in the Cultural History of Radio* (New York: Routledge, 2001), 68-83.

2 Burlington (VT) *Free Press*, 17 March 1921

3 His cousin and brother-in-law Julius Westine was living in Danby and working for the Bellows Falls Ice Company in Mount Tabor. Brattleboro *Vermont Phoenix*, 27 July 1917.

4 Ibid., 29 July 1917. In 1918, for example, Willie Westine was paid $3.40 for 17 hours of roadwork, while Harry Neilson performed seven hours of shoveling. *Landgrove Town Report for 1918.*

5 *Vermont Phoenix*, 9 November 1917.

6 Manchester (VT) *Journal*, 3 October 1918; Vermont Birth Records, 1909-2003. Vermont State Archives and Records Administration (VSARA), Middlesex.

7 *Vermont Phoenix*, 26 October, 14 December 1917; Manchester *Journal*, 3 July 1919; United States, Selective Service System. *World War I Selective Service System Draft Registration Cards, 1917-1918*. Washington, D.C.: National Archives and Records Administration (NARA). M1509, 4,582 rolls.

8 Bennington (VT) *Banner*, 23 August, 1 September 1917, 24 July 1918; Brattleboro (VT) *Reformer*, 18 July 1918.

9 *Vermont Phoenix*, 10 January 1919.

10 For example, see Vermont Bureau of Publicity, *Summer Homes in Vermont, Cottage Sites and Farms for Sale* (Montpelier, VT: Capital City Press, 1917).

11 Bennington *Banner*, 7 September 1917.

12 Burlington *Free Press*, 19 June 1918.

13 Ibid., 15 January 1935, 6 August 1942.

14 Bennington *Banner*, 5 March 1970.

15 Samuel R. Ogden, *The Cheese that Changed Many Lives; or, A sentimental history of a tiny town high in the Green Mountains* (Landgrove, VT: Just-So Press, 1978), 33.

16 Michael Sherman, et. al, *Freedom and Unity: A History of Vermont* (Barre, VT: Vermont Historical Society, 2004), 408-409.

17 Ibid., 408-409, 415-16.

18 *Vermont Magazine*, January-February 2014.

19 Manchester *Journal*, 25 March 1920; Brattleboro (VT) *Daily Reformer*, 8 May 1920. Neilson purchased the house from Frank Smithkin, a Russian immigrant.

20 Brattleboro *Daily Reformer*, 8 May 1920; Manchester *Journal*, 13 March 1919.

21 U.S. Department of the Interior, Census Office, Fourteenth Census, 1920, Pawlet, Rutland County, Vermont.

22 The Andersons' ties to these families grew with the marriage of Hazel Anderson in 1923 to Cecil Twyne. Twyne was Alonzo Butler's nephew and had been raised by his grandmother, Agnes Beebe Butler, and her third husband, John Tifft. Tifft was 19 years younger than Agnes and was a cousin of Eddie Tifft, Lottie Nyren's husband.

23 St. Albans (VT) *Messenger*, 15 December 1921.

24 Burlington (VT) *Weekly Free Press*, 18 September 1919.

25 St. Johnsbury (VT) *Caledonian Record*, 21 August 1919.

26 Ibid., 30 September 1914; Guildhall (VT) *Essex County Herald*, 1 December 1916.

27 In 1919 Crockett issued a new volume extolling Vermont's beauty titled *The Green Mountains of Vermont*, see Burlington *Free Press*, 28 June 1919.

28 *Essex County Herald*, 25 June 1919.

29 St. Johnsbury *Caledonian Record*, 20 June 1920.

30 New York *Tribune*, 30 May 1920; *The Sun and New York Herald*, 30 May 1920.

31 Burlington *Free Press*, 5 October 1920.

32 In *The View from Vermont*, Blake Harrison writes that, "Automobiles granted American travelers a new degree of spontaneity in their travel decisions and a new degree of freedom to explore areas farther from the confines of railroad lines." Blake Harrison, *The View from Vermont: Tourism and the Making of a Rural American Landscape* (Burlington, VT: University of Vermont Press/Hanover, NH: University Press of New England, 2006), 54.

33 *New York Times*, 4 June 1921.

34 Sara Gregg, *Managing the Mountains: Land Use Planning, the New Deal, and the Creation of a Federal Landscape in Appalachia* (New Haven, CT: Yale University

Press, 2013), 142; *The Routledge History of Rural America* (New York: Routledge, 2016), 15.

35 Paul M. Searls, *Two Vermonts: Geography and Identity, 1865–1910* (Durham, NH: University of New Hampshire Press; Hanover, NH: University Press of New England, 2006), 23-30.

36 Brooklyn (NY) *Eagle*, 20 June 1923.

37 Crockett cheerfully summed up the year by saying that the Bureau of Publicity "has never been so frequently queried as to the attractions and advantages of Vermont as at the present time." Barre (VT) *Times*, 20 December 1920.

38 Bennington *Banner*, 30 August 1921

39 Vermont Bureau of Publicity, *Motor Tours in Vermont* (Montpelier, VT: Capital City Press, 1921). One newspaper wrote, "If motorists and potential motorists should chance to see the new booklet, *Vermont Motor Tours*, put out by the Vermont publicity bureau, they would find much in the booklet to attract them to the Green Mountain state for a vacation and perhaps for a permanent residence." Barre (VT) *Daily Times*, 5 July 1921.

40 Burlington *Free Press*, 29 August 1921

41 *Essex County Herald*, 30 May 1917.

42 Barre *Times*, 22 October 1920.

43 Reprinted in the Morrisville (VT) *News and Citizen*, 11 May 1921.

44 Philadelphia *Evening Ledger*, 15 June 1921.

45 Brattleboro *Daily Reformer*, 30 August 1921.

46 Manchester *Journal* 22 September 1921.

47 Harrison, *The View from Vermont*, 141.

48 Nutting also warned that Vermont "was to a considerable extent becoming a new French Canadian province." Wallace Nutting, *Vermont Beautiful: Illustrated By the Author with Three Hundred and Four Photographs Covering All the Counties in Vermont* (New York: Old America Company, 1922), 273.

49 Burlington *Free Press*, 22 June 1923.

50 Ibid., 12 May 1922; Barre *Times*, 1 May 1922.

51 Bennington *Banner*, 15 May 1922; Middlebury (VT) *Register*, 12 October 1922.

52 H. H. Chadwick, *The Vermont Bureau of Publicity: Its History, Expenditures and Activities* (Montpelier, VT: Vermont Bureau of Publicity, 1934), 1.

53 Burlington *Free Press*, 28 July 1922.

54 Brooklyn (NY) *Daily Eagle*, 8 June 1924.

55 Zephine Humphrey, "The New Crop," *Outlook* 134 (July, 11 1923).

56 Burlington *Free Press*, 20 October 1923, 3 June 1930.

57 Zephine Humphrey, "The New Crop," *Outlook* 134 (11 July 1923), 381.

58 The decline of the timber industry between 1900 and 1930 occurred across New England, driven by technological changes. Meanwhile, the amount of Vermont employed as farmland declined in the same period, even as the size of farms increased. See Robert E. Pike, *Tall Trees, Tough Men* (New York: W. W. Norton, 1967), 262-63; Sherman, et. al., *Freedom and Unity*, 407-408.

59 Ogden, *The Cheese That Changed Many Lives*, 73.

60 In 1927 the value of summer homes in the state was reported to be over $25 million, with the largest amount in Bennington County. The value of summer homes in Dorset alone was at least $450,000. The value of such land in Landgrove, meanwhile, was only $800. Burlington *Free Press*, 7 December 1927.

61 Ibid., 21 August 1923.

62 Within days of the humble inauguration ceremony in Plymouth, the editor of the *Vermont Phoenix* wrote that "the world would look in vain for a finer or more impressive illustration of the genuine democracy of America's Government...than in the picture of Calvin Coolidge...inducted into office at the home of his father in a neat little farm house nestling among the Green Mountains." *Vermont Phoenix,* 6 August 1923.

63 Burlington *Free Press*, 8 August 1923.

64 Sherman, et. al., *Freedom and Unity*, 393.

65 Burlington *Free Press*, 18 January 1922.

66 Ibid., 21 February, 24 February 1925.

67 Ibid., 8 July 1926.

68 Ibid., 25 July 1938.

69 Author interview with Robert and Helen Tifft, Arlington, Vermont, June 22, 2014.

70 Author interview with Lillian Fellows-Abbott, July 11, 2014; Burlington *Free Press*, 23 August 1926, 31 May 1928.

71 Fourteenth Census, U.S. Department of the Interior, 1920, Sandgate, Bennington County, Vermont. (NARA microfilm publication T625, 2076 rolls). Records of the Bureau of the Census, Record Group 29. NARA, Washington, D.C.

72 Gregg, *Managing the Mountains*, 142; Sherman, et. al., *Freedom and Unity*, 408-409.

73 Richard M. Judd, *The New Deal in Vermont: Its Impact and Aftermath* (New York: Garland Publishing, 1979), 23-24.

74 Charles W. Johnson, *The Nature of Vermont* (Hanover, NH: University Press of New England, 1998), 58.

75 Burlington *Free Press*, 20 July 1937.

76 Ibid., 10 February 1932.

77 Ibid., 26 August 1982; David E. Conrad, *The Land We Cared For* (USDA-Forest Service, Region 9, 1997), 76; Christopher M. Klyza and Stephen C. Trombulak, *The Story of Vermont* (Hanover, NH: University Press of New England, 1999), 74.

78 H. H. Chadwick, *Vermont's Tourist Business: A Study Covering Ten Years* (Publicity Service, Department of Natural Resources, 1944), 8.

79 Burlington *Free Press*, 3 December 1925; Arthur F. Stone, *The Vermont of Today: With its Historic Background, Attractions and People*, 4 vols. (New York: Lewis Historical Publishing Company, 1929), 1: 263.

80 Stone, ibid., 856.

81 Early in the year there were proposals for something to be called the Council for Vermont Progress because, one newspaper wrote, "Throughout Vermont there seems to be an unrest due to a consciousness that we are not playing fast enough the game of State improvement and development." Burlington *Free Press*, 27 May 1925.

82 Ibid., 7 September 1925.

83 Ibid., 13 January 1926.

84 Ibid., 24 July 1925, 8 July 1926.

85 North Adams (MA) *Transcript*, 13 November 1925.

86 Burlington *Free Press*, 23 February, 1 March 1926.

87 Ibid., 18 January 1928.

88 *The Vermont Review*, July-August 1926.

89 Klyza and Trombulak, *The Story of Vermont*, 99; Conrad, *The Land We Cared For*, 76.

90 Author interview with Sally Ogden, January 14, 2014; Burlington *Free Press*, 4 April 1942.

91 Bennington *Banner*, 27 December 1971.

92 Burlington *Free Press*, 22 August 2004.

93 Ogden, *The Cheese That Changed Many Lives*, 66.

94 Burlington *Free Press*, 12 April 1924.

95 Ibid., 8 August 1924.

96 Ibid., 22 August 1924.

97 Louisville (KY) *Courier Journal*, 7 June 1925; Chicago *Daily Tribune*, 20 June 1926; St. Louis *Post-Dispatch* 13 June 1926; Detroit *Free Press*, 13 June 1925.

98 Brooklyn *Daily Eagle*, 29 June 1924.

99 Chadwick, *The Vermont Bureau of Publicity*, 4.

100 Burlington *Free Press*, 8 July 1926. The Green Mountain Club took a similarly elitist attitude toward its patrons in those years. In 1923 the New York section of the GMC decided it would no longer choose members based just on their interest in hiking, but instead "must necessarily stress selective factors in additions to our membership." The club as a whole decided that its problem was how to increase membership "without attracting undesirables," defined not only by class by also ethnicity: Jews were excluded. Hal Goldman, "'A Desirable Class of People': The Leadership of the Green Mountain Club and Social Exclusivity, 1920-1936," *Vermont History* 65 (Summer/Fall 1997): 131-52.

101 Chadwick, *The Vermont Bureau of Publicity*, 3.

102 Burlington *Free Press*, 27 January 1926.

103 Ibid., 8 July 1926.

104 Louisville *Courier-Journal*, 12 May 1926.

105 Brooklyn *Daily Eagle*, 12, 19 June 1927.

106 Perry H. Merrill, *The Making of a Forester: An Autobiographical History* (Perry H. Merrill, 1983), 63-64.

107 Burlington *Free Press*, 18 April 1927.

108 Ibid., 27 March 1929.

109 Such was the tourism boom in the 1920s that a group of New York businessmen organized the Summer Homes in Vermont Corporation in 1927. The company published *Your Summer Home in Vermont*, which had a similar format to the Bureau of Publicity's homes-for-sale publications. Published on behalf of "those who seek country life," it claimed the corporation employed over one hundred representatives eager to act as sales agents. The Richford (VT) *Journal* wrote that the corpo-

ration's founders were driven by the belief that "the tenement dweller is sick and tired of his life and is just ready to own a cozy little cottage back in the country." The *Journal* thought it wonderful that "each year brings an increasing number of outsiders without our borders who invest their money in real estate and two weeks or a month in the summer in good health." Richford *Journal*, 28 March 1927. The company went bankrupt in 1930 but remains a testament to the direction of the use of Vermont's landscape. *Your Summer Home in Vermont* (New York: Summer Homes in Vermont Corporation, 1927); Burlington *Free Press*, 18 April 1930

110 See Nancy Gallagher, *Breeding Better Vermonters: The Eugenics Project in the Green Mountain State* (Hanover, NH: University Press of New England, 1999).

111 Chadwick, *The Vermont Bureau of Publicity*, 22.

112 Bennington *Banner*, 14 December 1962.

113 Dona Brown, *Back to the Land: The Enduring Dream of Self-Sufficiency in Modern America* (Madison, WI: University of Wisconsin Press, 2011), 185-86; Nicholas Clifford, "Take Back Vermont—in 1929: Vrest Orton and Green Mountain Independence," *Vermont Commons* 17 (2007).

114 Burlington *Free Press*, 5 June 1929.

115 Ibid.

116 Ibid., 23 September 1929.

117 Author interview with Leslie Westine, September 16, 2013.

118 Fontaine Martin, *The Landgrove Meetinghouse: A Cross Section of Landgrove, Vermont, History* (Landgrove, VT: F. Martin, 1981), 132.

119 Brattleboro *Reformer*, 18 September 1929; Ogden, *The Cheese that Changed Many Lives*, 75.

120 *Rutland, Vermont City Directory* (Springfield, MA: H. A. Manning Co., 1928).

121 Martin, *The Landgrove Meetinghouse*, 133.

122 Ogden, *The Cheese that Changed Many Lives*, 66-72.

123 Burlington *Free Press*, 11 April 1947.

124 Ogden, *The Cheese that Changed Many Lives*, 78.

125 *Vermont Phoenix*, 18 August, 22 December 1916.

126 Bennington *Banner*, 12 February 1919.

127 Ogden, *The Cheese That Changed Many Lives*, 64-65.

CHAPTER 6

1 Samuel R. Ogden, *The Cheese that Changed Many Lives; or, A sentimental history of a tiny town high in the Green Mountains* (Landgrove, VT: Just-So Press, 1978), 79; Burlington (VT) *Free Press*, 22 August 2004.

2 Burlington *Free Press*, 26 January 1939.

3 Ibid., 11 April 1947.

4 Samuel R. Ogden, *This Country Life* (New York: A. S. Barnes and Company, 1946), 32-35.

5 Ogden, *The Cheese that Changed Many Lives*, 94.

6 Burlington *Free Press*, 11 April 1947.

7 Ogden, *The Cheese that Changed Many Lives*, 76.

8 Dona Brown, *Back to the Land: The Enduring Dream of Self-Sufficiency in Modern America* (Madison, WI: University of Wisconsin Press, 2011), 143.

9 When the food was brought out, Ogden wrote, "we all had fun as though at a picnic." *The Cheese that Changed Many Lives*, 84.

10 Ogden, *This Country Life*, 35.

11 Fontaine Martin, *The Landgrove Meetinghouse: A Cross Section of Landgrove, Vermont, History* (Landgrove, VT: F. Martin, 1981), 136; Ogden, *The Cheese that Changed Many Lives*, 95.

12 Burlington *Free Press*, 21 November 1931.

13 Bennington (VT) *Banner*, 5 March 1970.

14 Manchester (VT) *Journal*, 23 January 2015; Swarthmore College *Bulletin* 10 (1911).

15 Michael Sherman, et. al., *Freedom and Unity: A History of Vermont* (Barre, VT: Vermont Historical Society, 2004), 432.

16 Edwin Rozwenc, *Agricultural Policies in Vermont, 1860-1945* (Montpelier, VT: Vermont Historical Society, 1981), 163-66.

17 Richard M. Judd, *The New Deal in Vermont: Its Impact and Aftermath* (New York: Garland Pub., 1979), 27.

18 Sara Gregg, *Managing the Mountains: Land Use Planning, the New Deal, and the Creation of a Federal Landscape in Appalachia* (New Haven, CT: Yale University Press, 2013), 158.

19 Burlington *Free Press*, 1 September 1933. According to the *Free Press*, the three Vermont towns with no unemployment were Glastenbury, Somerset, and Landgrove, the first two possessing even fewer residents than Landgrove.

20 Gregg, *Managing the Mountains*, 159.

21 Nancy Gallagher, *Breeding Better Vermonters: The Eugenics Project in the Green Mountain State* (Hanover, NH: University Press of New England, 1999), 161.

22 Gregg, *Managing the Mountains*, 61. As the director of the commission later said, "the purpose of the Vermont Commission on Country Life was to encourage Vermont people to study their own country life problems and develop a plan for progress." Burlington *Free Press*, 22 August 1959.

23 Vermont Commission on Country Life, *Rural Vermont: A Program for the Future, By Two Hundred Vermonters* (Burlington, VT: Vermont Commission on Country Life, 1931), 148.

24 Ibid., 117-33.

25 Burlington *Free Press*, 1 September 1931.

26 Ibid., 9 December 1931.

27 H. H. Chadwick, *Vermont's Tourist Business: A Study Covering Ten Years, 1934-43* (Burlington, VT: Free Press Printing Company, 1944), 11; Richford (VT) *Journal Gazette*, 16 July 1931.

28 Vermont Bureau of Publicity, *Vermont Farms and Summer Homes for Sale* (St. Albans, VT: Messenger Press, 1929, 1931, 1932, 1934, 1942, 1943); H. H. Chadwick,

Vermont Tours (Montpelier, VT: Vermont Bureau of Publicity, 1933).

29 Dorothy Canfield Fisher, *Vermont Summer Homes* (Montpelier, VT: The Bureau of Publicity, 1932), 6; C. Clare Hinrichs. "Consuming Images: Making and Marketing Vermont as Distinctive Rural Place," in E. Melanie DuPuis and Paul Vandergeest, eds., *Creating the Countryside: The Politics of Rural and Environmental Discourse* (Philadelphia: Temple University Press, 1996), 265-66.

30 Vermont Bureau of Publicity, *Unspoiled Vermont*, (Montpelier, VT: The Bureau of Publicity, 1933); Brandon (VT) *Union*, 4 August 1933.

31 Brandon (VT) *Journal*, 21 November 1934.

32 H. H. Chadwick, *The Vermont Bureau of Publicity: Its History, Expenditures and Activities* (Montpelier, VT: Vermont Bureau of Publicity, 1934), 5.

33 Chadwick, *Vermont's Tourist Business*, 8.

34 Burlington *Free Press*, 25 June, 24 November 1934.

35 Vermont Commission on Country Life, *Rural Vermont*, 107-15.

36 Burlington *Free Press*, 10 February 1934.

37 Sherman, et. al., *Freedom and Unity*, 464-65; Gregg, *Managing the Mountains*, 154-55; Perry H. Merrill, *History of Forestry in Vermont, 1909-1959* (Montpelier, VT: Vermont Historical Society, 1959), 50; David E. Conrad, *The Land We Cared For* (USDA-Forest Service, Region 9, 1997), 76.

38 Burlington *Free Press*, 4 June 1933, 6 April 1936.

39 Ibid., 5 June 1933.

40 Merrill gave a speech to that effect in 1933. Ibid., 15 May 1934.

41 Perry H. Merrill, *Vermont Skiing: A Brief History of Downhill and Cross Country Skiing*, (Montpelier, VT: the author, 1987), 4-5.

42 Burlington *Free Press*, 12 June 1934.

43 Ibid., 17 July 1935.

44 Ibid., 18 April, 5 August 1935, 17 June 1936.

45 Blake Harrison, *The View from Vermont: Tourism and the Making of a Rural American Landscape* (Burlington, VT: University of Vermont Press/Hanover, NH: University Press of New England, 2006), 124.

46 Burlington *Free Press*, 1 August 1933.

47 Bennington *Banner*, 4 October 1933.

48 Burlington *Free Press*, 8 November 1933.

49 Ibid., 3 October 1933.

50 Ibid., 15 May, 21 June 1934; Vermont State Planning Board, *Graphic Survey: A First Step in State Planning for Vermont* (Montpelier, VT: Vermont State Planning Board, 1935), i-iii.

51 Hannah Silverstein, "No Parking: Vermont Rejects the Green Mountain Parkway," *Vermont History* 63 (Summer 1995): 133-57.

52 Bennington *Banner*, 14 December 1962.

53 Burlington *Free Press*, 22 August 2004.

54 Ibid., 20 August 1942.

55 Ibid., 26 January 1939

56 Ibid., 14 October 1932.

57 Rutland (VT) *Herald*, 17 June 1985.

58 Bennington *Banner*, 23 September 1966.

59 Ibid., 14 December 1962.

60 Burlington *Free Press*, 12 January 1921, 16 January 1935.

61 Ibid., 17 February 1935. Speaking in favor of an increased fee for fishing and hunting licenses, Ogden argued that "the increased fee would enable the planting of more fish and the construction of more rearing pools which benefits would more than offset the extra amount asked from the sportsmen."

62 Bennington *Banner*, 4 October 1961.

63 Perry H. Merrill, *The Making of a Forester: An Autobiographical History* (Montpelier, VT: Perry H. Merrill, 1984), 72.

64 Burlington *Free Press*, 11 June 1935; Chadwick, *Vermont's Tourist Business*, 25.

65 Vermont State Planning Board, *Graphic Survey*, xv.

66 Ibid., 43-44.

67 Ibid., 54; Chadwick, *Vermont's Tourist Business*, 38-39.

68 Burlington *Free Press*, 31 July 1931, 23 February 1937; Chadwick, *Vermont's Tourist Business*, 24.

69 In his history of the Vermont marble industry, Mike Austin calls the strike "one of the most bitter strikes Vermont has ever witnessed." Mike Austin, *Stories from Vermont's Marble Valley* (Charleston, SC: The History Press, 2010), 143.

70 Rutland *Herald*, 22 February 1936.

71 Bryan Degnan, "Unspoiled Vermont," *Commonweal* 30 (October 1936): 15.

72 Austin, *Stories from Vermont's Marble Valley*, 144.

73 Douglas S. Lertola and Mary H. Fregosi, "The Vermont Marble Company Strike of 1935-36," *Rutland Historical Society Quarterly* 32 (2002): 1-24.

74 Isabell L. Agrell, *Sinclair Lewis Remembered* (Self-published, 1996), 241.

75 The Landgrove Community Club Committee, *Landgrove, 1930 to 1980* (The Community Club Committee, 1980), 16; Bennington *Banner*, 29 July 1967.

76 Ogden, *This Country Life*, 118.

77 *Landgrove, 1930-1980*, 17.

78 Author interview with Priscilla Grayson, 14 January 2014.

79 Burlington *Free Press*, 24 November 1934; Marilyn Stout, "Small Beginnings: The First Rope Tow in Vermont," *Historic Roots* 3 (December 1998): 9-15.

80 Bennington *Banner*, 4 October 1961, 2 March 1977; Jules Older, *Ski Vermont! A Complete Guide to the Best Vermont Skiing* (Post Mills, VT: Chelsea Green Publishing, 1991), 12, 16. Blake Harrison, "The Technological Turn: Skiing and Landscape Change in Vermont, 1930-1970," *Vermont History* 71 (Summer/Fall 2003): 212-13.

81 Pat Harty, "The Story of Bromley Mountain," *Vermont Life* 7 (Winter 1952-1953): 20.

82 Ogden, *The Cheese that Changed Many Lives*, 88.

83 Burlington *Free Press*, 26 January 1939.

84 Ibid., 29 January 1937.

85 Bennington *Banner*, 4 January 1962.

86 An example is in the Burlington *Free Press*, 7 January 1937.

87 Dr. Alan Carter is credited as the main founder, conductor, and music director in the Burlington *Free Press*, 2 October 1972.

88 He quickly upheld that progressive reputation by appearing at a labor banquet in the spring of 1937. He told attendees that the government of Vermont belonged as much to organized labor as to anyone else, a particularly poignant statement in the aftermath of the marble strike.

89 George D. Aiken "Inaugural Address," https://www.sec.state.vt.us/media/48485/Aiken1937.pdf.

90 Burlington *Free Press*, 5 March 1937.

91 Ibid., 11 February 1937.

92 Ibid., 5 March 1937.

93 Ibid., 29 March, 3 April 1937.

94 Ibid., 24 March 1938.

95 Ibid.

96 Ibid., 25 July 1938.

97 Ibid., 26 July 1938.

98 Ibid., 26 January 1939

99 Ibid., 12 November 1938.

100 Ibid., 12 April 1939.

101 Bennington *Banner*, 4 April 1939.

102 Burlington *Free Press*, 11 March 1939.

103 Ibid., 6 May 1938.

104 Ibid., 22 February 1939.

105 Ibid., 15 March 1939.

106 Harrison, *The View from Vermont*, 111; Burlington *Free Press*, 29 January 1940.

107 Burlington *Free Press*, 8 April 1939.

108 Ibid., 29 June 1939.

109 Ibid., 18 November 1991.

110 Ibid., 4 April 1940.

111 Ibid., 15 November 1940.

112 Landgrove Community Club Committee, *Landgrove 1930 to 1980*, 25.

113 Charles E. Crane, *Let Me Show You Vermont* (New York: Alfred A. Knopf, 1937), 137. Sam Ogden was an advisor on Crane's chapter "Summer-Homing in Vermont," and among his advice was to go to small farms off of main roads and inquire about purchasing them, even if there was no "For Sale" sign, since "they may be had for a price which seems low to the outsider, high to the owner." *Let Me Show You Vermont*, 138.

114 Fisher, *Vermont Summer Homes*, 18.

115 Bennington *Banner*, 29 July 1967.

116 Sherman, et. al., *Freedom and Unity*, 461.

117 Burlington *Free Press*, 13 April 1939.

118 Chadwick, *Vermont's Tourist Business*, 37.

119 Burlington *Free Press*, 19 September 1941.

120 Rutland *Herald*, 15 September 1941.

121 Bennington *Banner*, 14, 25 September 1941; St. Johnsbury (VT) *Caledonian-Record*, 19 September 1941.

122 United States, Selective Service System. Selective Service Registration Cards, World War II: Fourth Registration. Records of the Selective Service System, Record Group Number 147. National Archives and Records Administration, Washington, DC.

123 Samuel R. Ogden, *How to Grow Food for your Family* (New York: A. S. Barnes, 1942).

124 Samuel B. Hand, *The Star that Set: The Vermont Republican Party, 1854–1974* (Lanham, MD: Lexington Books, 2002), 136.

125 Burlington *Free Press*, 7 August 1942.

126 Ibid., 19 August 1942.

127 *Life* 13 (24 August 1942): 31.

128 Burlington *Free Press*, 29 August 1942.

129 Ibid., 11 August 1942; Brattleboro (VT) *Reformer*, 22 August 1942.

130 Bennington *Banner*, 22 August 1942.

131 Burlington *Free Press*, 1 September 1942.

132 Bennington *Banner*, 2 September 1942.

133 Hand, *The Star that Set*, 170-71.

134 Brattleboro *Reformer*, 11 September 1942.

135 Burlington *Free Press*, 21 September 1942.

136 Brattleboro *Reformer*, 22 October 1942; Burlington *Free Press*, 27 October 1943.

137 Burlington *Free Press*, 21 October 1942.

Chapter 7

1 Burlington (VT) *Free Press*, 18 May 1950.

2 Michael Sherman, et. al., *Freedom and Unity: A History of Vermont* (Barre, VT: Vermont Historical Society, 2004), 480-81.

3 It is impossible to fully verify that Rockwell used Carl Nyren as a model, but both a niece, Lillian Fellows-Abbott, and a grand-nephew of Nyren, Robert Tifft, who were not acquainted with each other, claim it is true.

4 Burlington *Free Press*, 19 February 1943.

5 Ibid., 27 March 1943.

6 H. H. Chadwick, *Vermont's Tourist Business: A Study Covering Ten Years, 1934–43* (Publicity Service, Department of Natural Resources, 1944), 25; Burlington *Free Press*, 3 April 1943.

7 Burlington *Free Press*, 14 March 1944.

8 Ibid., 22 March 1945.

9 Ibid., 30 May, 11 June 1945.

10 Ibid., 30 March 1945; C. Clare Hinrichs, "Consuming Images: Making and Marketing Vermont as a Distinctive Rural Place," in E. Melanie DuPuis and Paul Vandergeest, eds., *Creating the Countryside: The Politics of Rural and Environmental Discourse* (Philadelphia: Temple University Press, 1996), 267-68.

11 Burlington *Free Press*, 11 June 1945.

12 Ibid., 19 September 1945.

13 Ibid., 20 December 1945, 28 November 1946.

14 Rutland (VT) *Herald*, 9 September 1946.

15 Burlington *Free Press*, 6 August 1946.

16 Ibid., 4 September 1946.

17 Ibid., 3 April 1946.

18 Ibid., 5 April 1946.

19 Ibid., 16 August 1946.

20 Vermont Industrial Relations Council, *Vermont Industrial Relations Council Handbook* (Montpelier, VT: The Vermont Industrial Relations Council, 1946), 6.

21 Bennington (VT) *Banner*, 5 September 5 1946.

22 Burlington *Free Press*, 12 September 1946.

23 Ogden wrote in *This Country Life*, "Within the past several months many returning service men have come to our house to get help and advice about living in the country." Samuel R. Ogden, *This Country Life* (New York: A. S. Barnes, 1946), 74; succeeding quotes are on v, 9, 23, 28.

24 See, for example, the Freeport (IL) *Freeport Journal-Standard*, 22 January 1947; Pittsburgh *Press*, 1 December 1946.

25 Burlington *Free Press*, 11 October 1946.

26 Ibid., 15 November, 18 December 1946.

27 Ibid., 1 January 1947.

28 "Inaugural Address of Ernest W. Gibson," 1947, available at https://www.sec.state. vt.us/media/48710/Gibson1947.pdf.

29 Ibid., 15 January, 1947; Bennington *Banner*, 25 October 1968.

30 Burlington *Free Press*, 16 January, 26 April 1947.

31 Ibid., 3 April 1947.

32 Ibid., 12 March 1947.

33 Earle Newton, *The Vermont Story: A History of the People of the Green Mountain State, 1749-1949* (Montpelier, VT: Vermont Historical Society, 1949), 234.

34 Burlington *Free Press*, 20 March, 21 March 1947.

35 The Bennington *Banner* called the Vermont State Water Conservation Board, "Ogden's own brainchild." Bennington *Banner*, 4 October, 27 March 1947.

36 Burlington *Free Press*, 30 December 1946, 23 April, 20 October 1947.

37 Ibid., 7 June 1947.

38 Ibid., 20 October 1947.

39 The Development Commission established at this time an industrial development division, "The basic function" of which "was to attract new industries to the state

and encourage existing ones to expand. Aiming for this target, the Commission's industrial staff is now at work on the accumulation of information on existing space available for manufacturing purposes and potential manufacturing sites." Ibid.

40 *Vermont Life* 1 (Summer 1947): 4-7. In 1948 the Development Commission released "Financial Statistics of State, County and Local Government in Vermont 1932-1946," a 441-page survey of the state with industrial development as the hopeful product of its information. "Financial Statistics of State, County and Local Government in Vermont 1932-1946" (Montpelier, VT: The Development Commission, 1948).

41 Of these films, one can be viewed online: *Background for Living*, https://archive.org/details/BackgroundForLiving_460.

42 Burlington *Free Press*, 17 November 1948.

43 Perry H. Merrill, *Vermont Skiing: A Brief History of Downhill and Cross Country Skiing* (Montpelier, VT: the author, 1987), 18

44 Jeffrey R. Leich, "New Hampshire and the Emergence of an American Ski Industry," New England Ski Museum, http://newenglandskimuseum.org/new-hampshire-and-the-emergence-of-an-american-ski-industry/, June 4, 2014.

45 Burlington *Free Press*, 7 April 1949, 2 March 1950.

46 Ibid., 7 December 1948, 7 April 1949. Ogden at the time was at the head of the Development Commission's tracking of ski income. The 1949 season was terrible, with little snow, bringing home the fact that the sport was at the mercy of weather conditions. "Unfortunately, nothing can be done about a poor ski season," Ogden remarked at its end, while suggesting that care be taken to locate new ski centers as favorably as possible. Vermont's five major ski centers as listed by Ogden were the Dutch Hill and Hogback areas near Bennington and Brattleboro, Big Bromley, Snow Valley at Manchester, and Pico near Rutland. Ibid., 2 March 1950.

47 Ibid., 16 September 1949.

48 Ibid., 27 September 1949.

49 Ibid., 31 March 1950.

50 Newton, *The Vermont Story*, 242.

51 Burlington *Free Press*, 3 September 1947, 16 October 1948.

52 Ibid., 25 October 1952.

53 From a manuscript in the private collection of Duncan Ogden.

54 *The American Home* 37 (May 1947): 24-26.

55 *New York Times*, 29 April 2012. In *The Vermont Story*, Earle Newton wrote approvingly that Ogden had "for ten years adroitly and tastefully built and remodeled houses, re-established schools, encouraged local crafts, and engaged in local politics." Newton, *The Vermont Story*, 242.

56 Burlington *Free Press*, 11 April 1947.

57 Vrest Orton founded the Vermont County Store in 1946 as "almost an exact replica of his father's store in Calais, stocking it with food and specialized goods that had largely disappeared from modern stores." *New York Times*, 5 December 1986.

58 Mary Moore, "The Rowen Forge," *Craft Horizons* 10 (Summer 1950): 6-9.

59 *Yankee* 18 (September 1952), 18-21.

60 *Manning's Bellows Falls Directory*, 25 (Springfield, VT: H. A. Manning and Company, 1954).

61 *Manning's Bellows Falls Directory*, 19 (Springfield, VT: H. A. Manning and Company, 1948).

62 Vermont Planning Council, *Vision and Choice: Vermont's Future* (Montpelier, VT: Vermont Planning Council, 1968).

63 Samuel B. Hand, *The Star that Set: The Vermont Republican Party, 1854-1974* (Lanham, MD: Lexington Books, 2002), 217.

64 Sherman, et. al., *Freedom and Unity*, 518; Harold A. Meeks, *Time and Change in Vermont* (Chester, CT: Globe Pequot Press, 1989), 303-305.

65 Sherman, et. al., *Freedom and Unity*, 618-19.

66 Michael Sherman, Jennie G. Versteeg, Samuel B. Hand, and Paul S. Gillies, "The Character of Vermont: Twentieth-Anniversary Reflections," Center for Research on Vermont Occasional Paper Series, Paper 5 (1996).

67 Scott and Helen Nearing, *Living the Good Life* (New York: Schocken Books, 1970), 195,

68 Ibid., 168.

69 "The Wisdom of Helen and Scott Nearing," *Mother Earth News* 61 (January/February 1980), http://www.motherearthnews.com/homesteading-and-livestock/helen-and-scott-nearing-zmaz80jfzraw.aspx.

70 Dorothy Canfield Fisher, *Vermont Tradition: The Biography of an Outlook on Life* (New York: Little Brown and Co., 1953), 16.

71 Burlington *Free Press*, 25 June 1962.

72 Ibid., 13 January 1951; Bennington *Banner*, 29 June 1962.

73 Burlington *Free Press*, 28 February 1951.

74 Ibid., 11 March, 6 April 1951.

75 Frank Bryan, *Yankee Politics in Rural Vermont* (Hanover, NH: University Press of New England, 1974), 81.

76 Or at least so he wrote on a copy of the photograph that is in the possession of his son Duncan.

77 Rutland *Herald*, 6 May 1970; Merrill, *Vermont Skiing*, 18-19.

78 Bennington *Banner*, 21 January 1967.

79 Sherman, et. al. *Freedom and Unity*, 523-24.

80 Burlington *Free Press*, 29 December 1956.

81 Ibid., 12 June 1956.

82 Ibid., 26 January 1957.

83 Ibid., 26 April 1957.

84 Rutland *Daily Herald*, 11 October 1957.

85 Senator George Aiken expressed pleasure at the appointment, recalling his own appointment of Ogden to various boards and commissions. Ibid., 31 July 1957.

86 Samuel Ogden's son Duncan wrote in a personal, unpublished history of Landgrove that, "The end [for Stony Hill Farm] came in the late 1950s when new state regulations required dairy farms to install bulk milk tanks. The Codys could not

afford this expense and along with other marginal hill farms were driven out of business." Duncan Ogden described Lester Cody as "a mountain man, good with horses, at logging operations, and helped my father with village restoration projects."

87 Vermont Planning Council, *Vision and Choice*, 25.

88 Bennington *Banner*, 5 October 1955.

89 Author interview with Robert Tifft, 26 June, 2014.

90 Vermont Death Records, 1909-2008; User Box Number: PR-02116; Roll Number: S-31395; Archive Number: PR-1402-1403. Vermont State Archives and Records Administration, Middlesex.

Chapter 8

1 Landgrove was something of a model for others by this time, if not explicitly. Some 25 miles away from Landgrove, in the town of Grafton, New York financier Dean Mathey launched a project in the early 1960s to "restore and preserve the beauty of the past" by buying as many houses in town as possible and renovating them, with the result that within decades, according to the organization Mathey founded, it was "difficult to find a house in Grafton that is not neat and trim and very much as though it were all prettied up to have a picture taken." Wilf Copping, *A Vermont Renaissance: Grafton and the Windham Foundation* (Grafton, VT: The Windham Foundation, 1978), 7-8.

2 Bennington (VT) *Banner*, 4 October 1961.

3 Ibid., 18 October 1961.

4 Article reprinted in the Troy (NY) *Record*, 30 September 1961.

5 Bennington *Banner*, 27 September 1961.

6 Ibid., 19 October 1961.

7 Ibid., 14 December 1962.

8 Perry H. Merrill, *Vermont Skiing: A Brief History of Downhill and Cross Country Skiing* (Montpelier, VT: the author, 1987), 31.

9 Reprinted in the North Adams (MA) *Transcript*, 20 July 1956.

10 Rutland (VT) *Daily Herald*, 19 January 1962.

11 Ibid., 2 February 1962.

12 Bennington *Banner*, 8 February 1962

13 Ibid., 5 January 1962.

14 Ibid., 15 January 1960.

15 Vermont State Archives and Records Administration, Middlesex, Vermont: User Box Number: PR-02116, Roll Number: S-31397, Archive Number: PR-1406-1407; User Box Number: PR-01925, Roll Number: S-31296, Archive Number: PR-1188-1190; User Box Number: PR-01925, Roll Number: S-31300, Archive Number: PR-1196-1198; User Box Number: PR-02132, Roll Number: S-31448, Archive Number: PR-1508-1509.

16 Burlington (VT) *Free Press*, 25, 26 June 1962.

17 Brattleboro *Vermont Phoenix*, 2 November 1962.

18 Burlington *Free Press*, 1 February 1963.

19 Samuel B. Hand, Anthony Marro, and Stephen C. Terry, *Philip Hoff: How Red Turned Blue in the Green Mountain State* (Hanover, NH: University Press of New England, 2011), 50; Burlington *Free Press*, 18 May 1963.

20 *Report of Governor's Panel on Scenery and Historic Sites*, review panel, Samuel R. Ogden, chairman (Montpelier, VT: Central Planning Office, 1963); Bennington *Banner*, 4 February 1964.

21 Burlington *Free Press*, 30 March 1964.

22 Bennington *Banner*, 4 February 1964.

23 Michael Sherman, et. al., *Freedom and Unity: A History of Vermont* (Barre, VT: Vermont Historical Society, 2004), 513-14.

24 Bennington *Banner*, 15 March 1963.

25 Ibid., 28 June 1963, 25 October 1968.

26 Ibid., 14 February 1964.

27 Ibid., 2 April 1964.

28 Ibid., 23 August 1963.

29 Burlington *Free Press*, 16 December 1963.

30 Bennington *Banner*, 17 January 1964.

31 Burlington *Free Press*, 7 April 1964.

32 This letter is in the personal collection of Duncan Ogden.

33 Noel Perrin, "The Two Faces of Vermont," *Vermont Life* 19 (Winter 1964): 31-33; Blake Harrison, "Tracks Across Vermont: *Vermont Life* and the Landscape of Downhill Skiing, 1946-1970," *Journal of Sport History* 28 (Summer 2001): 265.

34 Hand, et. al., *Philip Hoff*, 58-61. Hoff made this point explicitly in the Vermont Public Television interview conducted by Christopher Graff in the series *The Governors*.

35 Samuel B. Hand, *The Star that Set: The Vermont Republican Party, 1854-1974* (Lanham, MD: Lexington Books, 2002), 256.

36 Bennington *Banner*, 31 July 1964.

37 Ibid., 3, 7 July 1964, 12 February, 26 November, 11 December 1965.

38 Ibid., 13 March 1964, 26 March 1965.

39 Ibid., 10 September 1965.

40 Burlington *Free Press*, 11 September 1965.

41 Bennington *Banner*, 27 April 1966.

42 Ibid., 28 April 1966.

43 Representative Emory Hebard of Glover added, "If they want to make it over like Connecticut, where they came from, why don't they stay in Connecticut?" Burlington *Free Press*, 6 March 1966.

44 Blake Harrison, *The View from Vermont: Tourism and the Making of a Rural American Landscape* (Burlington, VT: University of Vermont Press/Hanover, NH: University Press of New England, 2006), 204.

45 Ibid., 215-17; Sherman, et. al., *Freedom and Unity*, 513-14.

46 Bennington *Banner*, 26 August 1966, 16 July 1968.

47 Ibid., 9 August 1966.

48 Ibid., 31 January 1967.

49 Burlington *Free Press*, 18 August 1966.

50 On Ogden's speech at a legislative hearing, the Burlington *Free Press* reported, "Samuel Ogden of Landgrove, a known champion of unspoiled Vermont, said it is false to think more signs bring more tourists to a motel. 'Running a good shop will to that,' he said." Ibid., 26 January 1967.

51 Sherman, et. al., *Freedom and Unity*, 513-14.

52 Bennington *Banner*, 29 July 1967.

53 Newport News (VA) *Daily Press*, 24 September 1967.

54 North Adams *Transcript*, 6 May 1967.

55 Bennington *Banner*, "Winter in Vermont," 21 January 1967.

56 *Vermont Life* 22 (Summer 1968): 16; Burlington *Free Press*, 7 January 1972.

57 Bennington *Banner*, 12 March 1969.

58 Burlington *Free Press*, 30 September 1969.

59 Bennington *Banner*, 22 August 1969; Berkshire (MA) *Eagle*, 24 August 1969.

60 Burlington *Free Press*, 25, 30 January 1967. Calling the Land Use Commission "one of the most contentious issues" of the year, the Bennington *Banner* wrote, "There's no need to disguise the fact that this is a statewide zoning proposition, and zoning is a concept that's been most difficult to put across among independent-minded Vermonters. But one of the reasons for the statewide approach is that local communities just haven't, and obviously won't—do the job themselves…The real point is that Vermont can only retain its independent character, its status as someplace 'different' if it continues to look like Vermont. It can't do this if it looks like eastern Massachusetts, or overcrowded New Jersey or Long Island, or even like New Hampshire, where there are now probably more billboards, roadside signs and ugly strip developments than there are trees or mountains." Bennington *Banner*, 27 January 1967.

61 Bennington *Banner*, 12 August 1968.

62 Ibid., 10 February 1967.

63 Ibid., 6 October 1967, 22 March 1968, 24 October 1969.

64 Ibid., 26 February 1969.

65 Ibid., 12 January 1968.

66 Ibid., 27 June 1969.

67 Samuel R. Ogden, *America the Vanishing* (Brattleboro, VT: The Stephen Greene Press, 1969), v.

68 St. Louis *Post Dispatch*, 19 April 1970.

69 Bennington *Banner*, 7 February 1970.

70 Camden (NJ) *Courier-Post*, 1 April 1970; Burlington *Free Press*, 6 January 1970.

71 Harold A. Meeks, *Vermont's Land and Resources* (Shelburne, VT: New England Press, 1992), 288.

72 Deane C. Davis, *Deane C. Davis: An Autobiography* (Shelburne, VT: New England Press, 1991), 260, 262.

73 Bennington *Banner*, 8 September 1971.

74 Burlington *Free Press*, 25 October 1969.

75 Bennington *Banner*, 25 January 1971. This dilemma has been articulated very well by Joe Sherman in his book *Fast Lane on a Dirt Road*, in which he writes that the consequence of the interstate highways was, "from having been a remote world of small mill towns and hill farms only 30 years before, Vermont now found itself within a day's drive of 65 million people. Tax subsidies were needed to prop up agriculture as a livelihood and as a visual backdrop for tourism. The state was laced with a plethora of environmental and social programs that required steadily increasing revenues, along with a large bureaucracy to implement them. And looming over the state and the times was yet another painful paradox: Growth threatened Vermont's special sense of place, yet maintaining that sense of place, with its pastoral look, open spaces, and small towns, threatened to make Vermont elitist, an upscale gateway for the rich." Joe Sherman, *Fast Lane on a Dirt Road: A Contemporary History of Vermont* (White River Junction, VT: Chelsea Green Publishing Company, 2000), 178.

76 Bennington *Banner*, 12 August 1968.

77 Walter Hard wrote, "The basic problem is taxes. The farmers can't afford to pay their taxes because they are based on fair market value." Burlington *Free Press*, 14 August 1970; *Vermont Life* 25 (Autumn 1970): 8-10.

78 Ibid., 5 June 1970; Christopher M. Klyza and Stephen C. Trombulak, *The Story of Vermont* (Hanover, NH: University Press of New England, 1999), 122.

79 Burlington *Free Press*, 26 December 1972. See Frank Smallwood, *Free and Independent: The Initiation of a College Professor Into State Politics* (Brattleboro, VT: The Stephen Greene Press, 1976), 103-19.

80 Bennington *Banner*, 21 May 1971.

81 Duncan Ogden wrote in a letter to an acquaintance on June 27, 1985, "Mamie had a great deal of love for everyone and certainly Sam was never the same without her. The last few years were hard for Sam and those of us who were trying to understand what was happening to him."

82 Bennington *Banner*, 5 May 1972.

83 Ibid., 21 February, 12 May 1972.

84 Burlington *Free Press*, 2 October 1972.

85 See, for example, Catherine O. Foster, *The Organic Gardener* (New York: Vintage Books, 1972).

86 Bennington *Banner*, 24 November 1972.

87 The nurse who typed the article for Ogden wrote his son, "He has a tremor of his hands, hesitation of his speech, and he obviously, as he says, has a great deal of difficulty getting his thoughts together and making his mind work smoothly. He still tends to blame his family for not being attentive or realizing the depth of his grief." The letter is in the personal collection of Duncan Ogden.

88 *New York Times*, 23 January 1973.

89 Bennington *Banner*, 9 March 1973.

90 Samuel R. Ogden, *The Cheese that Changed Many Lives; or, A sentimental history of a tiny town high in the Green Mountains* (Landgrove, VT: Just-So Press, 1978), 113.

Conclusion

1   Rutland (VT) *Herald*, 28 June 1985.
2   For examples, see Bennington (VT) *Banner*, "Winter in Vermont," 21 January 1967; ibid., 11 November 1961. The Burlington (VT) *Free Press* reported in 1967, "Mr. Ogden was born in Elizabeth, N.J. and since 1929 has boasted 'I'm a Vermonter.'" Burlington *Free Press*, 25 March 1967.
3   Burlington *Free Press*, 22 August 2004.
4   *Vermont Magazine* 21 (September/October 2009): 17-19.

BIBLIOGRAPHY

PRIMARY SOURCES

Agriculture of Vermont: First Annual Report of the Commissioner of Agriculture of the State of Vermont. Montpelier, VT: Capital City Press, 1909.

Aiken, George D. "Inaugural Address," https://www.sec.state.vt.us/media/48485/Aiken1937.pdf

"Attractions In and Around Burlington." Glens Falls, NY: C. H. Possons, 1890.

Auld, Joseph. *Picturesque Burlington: A Handbook of Burlington, Vermont, and Lake Champlain.* Burlington, VT: Free Press Association, 1893.

Bailey, Guy, and Orlando Martin. *Homeseekers' Guide to Vermont Farms.* St. Albans, VT: St. Albans Messenger Company, 1911.

Bass, E. L., ed. *Report of the Nineteenth Annual Meeting of the Vermont Dairymen's Association.* Montpelier, VT: The Watchman Publishing Company, 1889.

Batchelder, Ira K. *Reunion Celebration, Together with an Historical Sketch of Peru, Bennington County.* Brattleboro, VT: Phoenix Job Print, 1891.

Campbell, Richard M. *Dorset, Vermont, as a Summer Home.* Danby, VT: Mirror Printing, 1898.

Chadwick, H. H. *The Vermont Bureau of Publicity: Its History, Expenditures and Activities.* Montpelier, VT: Vermont Bureau of Publicity, 1934.

——. *Vermont's Tourist Business: A Study Covering Ten Years, 1934-43.* Publicity Service, Department of Natural Resources, 1944.

——. *Vermont Tours.* Montpelier, VT: Vermont Bureau of Publicity, 1933.

Chase, Frederick. "Is Agriculture Declining in New England?" *New England Magazine* 2 (1890).

Child, Hamilton, ed. *Gazetteer and Business Directory of Windham County, Vt., 1724-1884.* Syracuse, NY: Journal Office, 1884.

Crane, Charles E. *Let Me Show You Vermont.* New York: Alfred A. Knopf, 1937.

Distinguished Successful Americans of Our Day. Chicago: Successful Americans, 1911.

Fish, Frank L. *Horace Ward Bailey: Vermonter.* Rutland, VT: The Tuttle Company, 1914.

Fisher, Dorothy Canfield. *Vermont Summer Homes.* Montpelier, VT: The Bureau of Publicity, 1932.

————. *Vermont Tradition: The Biography of an Outlook on Life*. New York: Little Brown and Co., 1953.

Greater Vermont Association. *Constitution and By-Laws*. Essex Junction, VT: Greater Vermont Association, 1912.

————. *The Salient Features of Vermont as a Vacation State*. Essex Junction, VT: Greater Vermont Association, 1913.

Greene, Frank L. *Vermont, the Green Mountain State: Past, Present, Prospective*. Montpelier, VT: Vermont Commission to the Jamestown Tercentennial Exposition, 1907.

Journal of the House of Representatives of the State of Vermont (multiple volumes).

Journal of the Senate of the State of Vermont (multiple volumes).

Judd, Almon C. *The Ideal Tour*. Waterbury, CT: Almon Judd, 1911.

Kent, Dorman B. E. "One Thousand Men." *Proceedings of the Vermont Historical Society for the Years 1913-1914*. N.p.: Vermont Historical Society, 1915.

Landgrove Town Report (multiple issues).

Manning's Bellows Falls Directory. Springfield, VT: H. A. Manning and Company, 1948, 1952, 1954.

John G. McCullough papers. Bennington Museum, Bennington, Vermont.

McKinney, James P. *The Industrial Advantages of the State of Vermont*. Rochester, NY: Commerce Publishing Company, 1890.

Men and Women of America: A Biographical Dictionary of Contemporaries. New York: L. R. Haersley & Company, 1910.

Nordgren, John G., "Nordgren & Bergstrom, hufvudagenter for Bay State Companiets land i Nebraska och Wyoming," 1888.

Nutting, Wallace. *Vermont Beautiful: Illustrated By the Author with Three Hundred and Four Photographs Covering All the Counties in Vermont*. New York: Old America Company, 1922.

Ogden, Samuel R. *America the Vanishing*. Brattleboro, VT: The Stephen Greene Press, 1969.

————. *How to Grow Food for your Family*. New York: A. S. Barnes, 1942.

————. *This Country Life*. New York: A. S. Barnes and Company, 1946.

Paris, Louis J. *The Long Trail*. Brandon, VT: the Brandon Inn, 1914.

Passenger Lists of Vessels Arriving at Philadelphia, Pennsylvania, 1883-1945. Micropublication T840. RG085. Rolls # 1-181. National Archives and Records Administration, Washington, DC.

Karl Pfister collection, Landgrove Historical Society, Landgrove, Vermont.

Possons, C. H. *Vermont: Its Resources and Industries*. Glens Falls, NY: C. H. Possons, 1889.

Proceedings of the Seventh Annual Meeting of the National Child Labor Committee. New York: The American Academy of Political and Social Science, 1911.

Proceedings of the Twenty-Second Annual Meeting of the Vermont Maple Sugar Makers' Association. St. Albans, VT: St. Albans Messenger Co. Print, 1915.

Proceedings of the Vermont Historical Society, 1903-1904. St. Albans, VT: Vermont Historical Society, 1904.

Proctor, Mortimer R. and Roderic M. Olzendam. *The Green Mountain Tour: Vermont, the Unspoiled Land*. Essex Junction, VT: Vermont Bureau of Publicity, 1915.

"The Protectionist," August 1904. Boston: Home Market Club.

Putnam, J. H. "The Depopulation of Our Rural Districts: Cause, and Some Suggestions in Regard to a Remedy." *Report of the Vermont Board of Agriculture*. Montpelier, VT: J. & J. M. Poland, 1878.

Report of the Commissioner of Agricultural and Manufacturing Interests of the State of Vermont. Rutland, VT: The Tuttle Company, Official State Printers, 1890.

Report of the Commissioner of Fish and Game. Montpelier, VT: Vermont Fish and Game Commission, 1902.

Report of Governor's Panel on Scenery and Historic Sites. Review panel, Samuel R. Ogden, chairman. Montpelier, VT: Central Planning Office, 1963.

Report of the Twenty-First Annual Meeting of the Vermont Dairymen's Association. Montpelier, VT: Press of the Watchman Publishing Co., 1891.

The Resources and Attractions of Vermont: With a List of Desirable Homes for Sale. Montpelier, VT: Watchman Press, 1891.

Rutland, Vermont City Directory. Springfield, MA: H. A. Manning Co., 1928.

Spear, Victor I. *Report on Summer Travel for 1894*. Montpelier, VT: Watchman Press, 1894.

———. *Vermont: A Glimpse of Its Scenery and Industries*. Montpelier, VT: Vermont State Board of Agriculture, 1893.

Stebbins, Rufus P. *An Historical Address, Delivered at the Centennial Celebration of the Incorporation of the Town of Wilbraham*, 15 June 1863. Boston: G. C. Rand and Avery, 1863.

State of Vermont. Vermont Vital Records. New England Historic Genealogical Society, Boston, Massachusetts.

Summer Homes in Vermont Corporation. *Your Summer Home in Vermont*. New York: Summer Homes in Vermont Corporation, 1927.

United States, Selective Service System. *World War I Selective Service System Draft Registration Cards, 1917–1918*. Washington, DC: National Archives and Records Administration (NARA).

United States, Selective Service System. Selective Service Registration Cards, World War II: Fourth Registration. Records of the Selective Service System. National Archives and Records Administration, Washington, DC.

U.S. Commission of Immigration. "Passenger List of Steamship British Princess from Liverpool," August 5, 1890.

U.S. Department of the Interior, Census Office, Seventh Census, 1850. Bennington County, Vermont.

———, Eighth Census, 1860. Bennington County, Vermont

———, Tenth Census, 1880. Bennington County, Vermont

———, Twelfth Census, 1900. Bennington County, Rutland County, Vermont.

———, Thirteenth Census, 1910. Bennington County, Vermont

———, Fourteenth Census, 1920. Bennington County, Vermont.

———, Fifteenth Census, 1930. Bennington County, Vermont.

Valentine, Alonzo B. "Swedish Immigration." *The Quill* 1 (September 1890).

Vermont Bureau of Publicity. *The Lake Region of Eastern Vermont*. Essex Junction, VT: Vermont Bureau of Publicity, 1917.

———. *The Lake Region of Western Vermont*. Morrisville, VT: Vermont Bureau of Publicity, 1917.

——— *Motor Tours in Vermont*. Montpelier, VT: Capital City Press, 1921.

———. *Summer Homes in Vermont, Cottage Sites and Farms for Sale.* Montpelier, VT: Capital City Press, 1917.

———. *Unspoiled Vermont.* Montpelier, VT: The Bureau of Publicity, 1933.

———. *Vermont: Designed by the Creator for the Playground of the Continent.* Montpelier, VT: Capital City Press, 1911.

———. *Vermont Farms and Homes for Sale.* Montpelier, VT: The Bureau of Publicity, 1920.

———. *Vermont Farms and Summer Homes for Sale.* St. Albans, VT: Messenger Press, 1929, 1931, 1932, 1934, 1942, 1943.

———. *Vermont, the Land of Green Mountains.* Essex Junction, VT: Office of the Secretary of State, 1913.

———. *Vermont Summer Resorts.* Montpelier, VT: The Bureau of Publicity, 1912.

———. *Where to Stop When in Vermont: Directory of Hotels and Boarding Houses.* Essex Junction, VT: Vermont Bureau of Publicity, 1913.

———. *Where Vermont Leads.* Montpelier, VT: Vermont Bureau of Publicity, 1928.

Vermont Commission on Country Life, *Rural Vermont: A Program for the Future, By Two Hundred Vermonters.* Burlington, VT: Vermont Commission on Country Life, 1931.

Vermont Development Commission. "Economic Aspects of Recreational Development in Stowe, Vermont: Survey and Analysis." Montpelier, VT: Research Division.

———. "Financial Statistics of State, County and Local Government in Vermont 1932-1946." Montpelier, VT: The Development Commission, 1948.

———. *Report of the Vermont Development Commission for Biennial Ending June 30, 1948.* Montpelier, VT: Vermont Development Commission, 1948.

Vermont Birth Records. Vermont State Archives and Records Administration. Middlesex, Vermont.

Vermont Death Records. Vermont State Archives and Records Administration. Middlesex, Vermont.

Vermont Industrial Relations Council. *Vermont Industrial Relations Council Handbook.* Montpelier, VT: The Vermont Industrial Relations Council, 1946.

Vermont Legislative Directory, 1892. Montpelier, VT: Watchman Publishing Company, 1892.

Vermont Marriage Records. Vermont State Archives and Records Administration. Middlesex, Vermont.

Vermont Office of Secretary of State. "Official Highway Map of the State of Vermont." Montpelier, VT: Vermont Secretary of State, 1924.

The Vermont Planning Council. *Vision and Choice: Vermont's Future.* Montpelier, VT: Vermont Planning Council, 1968.

Vermont Publicity Service. "Vermont Winter Sports." Montpelier, VT: Vermont Publicity Service, 1947.

Vermont Secretary of State. *Vermont Farms: Some Facts and Figures Concerning the Agricultural Resources and Opportunities of the Green Mountain State.* St. Johnsbury, VT: The Caledonian Company, 1913.

Vermont State Board of Agriculture. *Beautiful Vermont: Unsurpassed as a Residence or Playground; for the Summer Resident; the Summer Visitor; the Tourist; the Capitalist and the Workingman.* Woodstock, VT: State Board of Agriculture, 1907.

———. *Eleventh Vermont Agricultural Report by the State Board of Agriculture, for the Years 1889-1890*. Montpelier, VT: Argus and Patriot Print, 1890.

———. *Thirteenth Vermont Agricultural Report by the State Board of Agriculture, for the Year 1893*. Burlington, VT: Free Press Printers and Publishers, 1893.

Vermont State Planning Board. *Graphic Survey: A First Step in State Planning for Vermont*. Montpelier, VT: Vermont State Planning Board, 1935.

Vermont Tribune. *Ludlow and Her Neighbors, Being a Special Souvenir Edition of the Vermont Tribune*. Ludlow, VT: Vermont Tribune Office, 1899.

Who's Who Among North American Authors, vol. 4, 1929-1930. Los Angeles: Golden Syndicate Publishing Company, 1930.

NEWSPAPERS AND PERIODICALS

The American Home
Baltimore *Sun*
Barre (VT) *Times*
Barton (VT) *Orleans County Monitor*
Bennington (VT) *Banner,*
Boston *Daily Advertiser*
Boston *Daily Journal*
Boston *Evening Journal*
Boston *Evening Transcript*
Boston *Globe*
Brandon (VT) *Union*
Brattleboro (VT) *Daily Reformer*
Brattleboro *Vermont Phoenix*
Brenham (TX) *Weekly Banner*
Bristol (VT) *Herald*
Brooklyn (NY) *Daily Eagle*
Burlington (VT) *Clipper*
Burlington (VT) *Free Press*
Burlington (VT) *Weekly Free Press*
Burlington Independent
Chicago *Daily Tribune*
Chicago *Inter-Ocean*
Cincinnati *Commercial Gazette*
Cleveland *Plain Dealer*
Commonweal
Craft Horizons
Dallas *Morning News*
Detroit *Free Press*
Fort Worth *Weekly Gazette*
Freeport (IL) *Freeport Journal-Standard*
Grand Forks (ND) *Herald*
Greymouth, New Zealand, *Grey River Argus*
Guildhall (VT) *Essex County Herald*

Kansas City (MO) *Star*
Life
Londonderry (VT) *Sifter*
Louisville (KY) *Courier Journal*
Ludlow *Vermont Tribune*
Macon (GA) *Telegraph*
Manchester (VT) *Journal*
Middlebury (VT) *Register*
Montpelier (VT) *Argus and Patriot*
Montpelier *Vermont Watchman*
Morrisville (VT) *News and Citizen*
The New England Magazine
New Haven (CT) *Register*
New York *Herald-Tribune*
New York Times
New York *Sun*
Newport News (VA) *Daily Press*
North Adams (MA) *Transcript*
Outlook
Philadelphia *Evening Ledger*
Pittsburgh *Daily Post*
Portland *Morning Oregonian*
Providence (RI) *Journal*
Richford (VT) *Journal*
Rutland (VT) *Herald*
St. Albans (VT) *Messenger*
St. Johnsbury (VT) *Caledonian Record*
St. Louis *Post-Dispatch*
St. Paul (MN) *Daily Globe*
San Francisco *Bulletin*
Springfield (MA) *Republican*
Topeka (KS) *Capital*
Troy (NY) *Weekly Budget*
Vermont Life
Vermont Magazine
The Vermont Review
The Vermonter
Wheeling (WV) *Daily Register*
Wilmington (VT) *Deerfield Valley Times*
Yankee

Books

Agrell, Isabell L. *Sinclair Lewis Remembered.* Self-published, 1996.
Aldrich, Lewis C. *History of Bennington County.* Syracuse, NY: D. Mason & Co.,
    Publishers, 1889.
Andersson, Ingvar. *A History of Sweden.* New York: Prager, 1956.

Arnold, Thomas W. *Two Hundred Years and Counting: Vermont Community Census Totals, 1791 to 1980.* Burlington, VT: Center for Rural Studies, University of Vermont.

Austin, Mike. *Stories from Vermont's Marble Valley.* Charleston, SC: The History Press, 2010.

Barron, Hal S. *Those Who Stayed Behind: Rural Society in Nineteenth-Century New England.* Cambridge: Cambridge University Press, 1984.

Beckley, John, et al. *Thank you Guy Bailey.* Self-published, 1976.

Brown, Dona. *Back to the Land: The Enduring Dream of Self-Sufficiency in Modern America.* Madison, WI: University of Wisconsin Press, 2011.

———. *Inventing New England.* Washington, DC: Smithsonian Books, 1997.

Bryan, Frank. *Yankee Politics in Rural Vermont.* Hanover, NH: University Press of New England, 1974.

Conforti, Joseph. *Imagining New England.* Chapel Hill, NC: University of North Carolina Press, 2001.

Conrad, David E. *The Land We Cared For.* USDA-Forest Service, Region 9, 1997.

Copping, Wilf. *A Vermont Renaissance: Grafton and the Windham Foundation.* Grafton, VT: The Windham Foundation, 1978.

Crockett, Walter H. *Vermont, the Green Mountain State,* 5 vols. New York: Century History Company, 1921-23.

Cutter, William R. *New England Families Genealogical and Memorial,* vol. 3. New York: n.p., 1915.

Davis, Deane C. *Deane C. Davis: An Autobiography.* Shelburne, VT: New England Press, 1991.

Dorman, Robert. *Revolt of the Provinces: The Regionalist Movement in America, 1920-1945.* Chapel Hill, NC: University of North Carolina Press, 1993.

Doyle, William. *The Vermont Political Tradition and Those Who Helped Make It.* Barre, VT: The Author, 1984.

Duffy, John J., Samuel B. Hand, and Ralph H. Orth, eds., *The Vermont Encyclopedia.* Hanover, NH: University Press of New England, 2003.

DuPuis, E. Melanie, and Paul Vandergeest, eds. *Creating the Countryside: The Politics of Rural and Environmental Discourse.* Philadelphia: Temple University Press, 1996.

Flint, Kemp R. *Poor Relief in Vermont.* Northfield, VT: Norwich University, 1916.

Flint, Winston A. *The Progressive Movement in Vermont.* Washington, DC: The American Council on Public Affairs, 1941.

Foster, Catherine O. *The Organic Gardener.* New York: Vintage Books, 1972.

Gallagher, Nancy. *Breeding Better Vermonters: The Eugenics Project in the Green Mountain State.* Hanover, NH: University Press of New England, 1999.

Graffagnino, J. Kevin. *Vermont in the Victorian Age: Continuity and Change in the Green Mountain State, 1850-1900.* Bennington and Shelburne, VT: Vermont Heritage Press and Shelburne Museum, 1985.

Gregg, Sara. *Managing the Mountains: Land Use Planning, the New Deal, and the Creation of a Federal Landscape in Appalachia.* New Haven, CT: Yale University Press, 2013.

Hand, Samuel B. *The Star that Set: The Vermont Republican Party, 1854-1974.* Lanham, MD: Lexington Books, 2002.

———, Anthony Marro, and Stephen C. Terry. *Philip Hoff: How Red Turned Blue in the Green Mountain State.* Hanover, NH: University Press of New England, 2011.

Harrison, Blake. *The View from Vermont: Tourism and the Making of a Rural American Landscape.* Burlington, VT: University of Vermont Press/Hanover, NH: University Press of New England, 2006.

Hilmes, Michele. *Radio Reader: Essays in the Cultural History of Radio.* New York: Routledge, 2001.

Jackson, Erica K. *Scandinavians in Chicago: The Origins of White Privilege in Modern America.* Champaign, IL: University of Illinois Press, 2018.

Jacobson, Matthew F. *Whiteness of a Different Color: European Immigrants and the Alchemy of Race.* Cambridge, MA: Harvard University Press, 1999.

Johnson, Charles W. *The Nature of Vermont.* Hanover, NH: University Press of New England, 1998.

Jones, Robert C. *Railroads of Vermont,* 2 vols. Shelburne, VT: New England Press, 1993.

Judd, Richard M. *The New Deal in Vermont: Its Impact and Aftermath.* New York: Garland Publishing, 1979.

Judd, Richard W. *Common Lands, Common People: The Origins of Conservation in Northern New England.* Cambridge, MA: Harvard University Press, 2000.

———. *Second Nature: An Environmental History of New England.* Amherst, MA: University of Massachusetts Press, 2014.

Klyza, Christopher M. and Stephen C. Trombulak. *The Story of Vermont: A Natural and Cultural History.* Hanover, NH: University Press of New England, 1999.

The Landgrove Community Club Committee, *Landgrove, 1930 to 1980.* The Community Club Committee, 1980.

Martin, Fontaine. *The Landgrove Meetinghouse: A Cross Section of Landgrove, Vermont, History.* Landgrove, VT: F. Martin, 1981.

Meeks, Harold A. *Time and Change in Vermont.* Chester, CT: Globe Pequot Press, 1989.

———. *Vermont's Land and Resources.* Shelburne, VT: New England Press, 1992.

Merrill, Perry H. *History of Forestry in Vermont, 1909-1959.* Montpelier, VT: Vermont Historical Society, 1959.

———. *The Making of a Forester: An Autobiographical History.* Perry H. Merrill, 1983.

———. *Roosevelt's Forest Army: A History of the Civilian Conservation Corps, 1933-1942.* Montpelier, VT: The Author, 1984.

———. *Vermont Skiing: A Brief History of Downhill and Cross Country Skiing.* Montpelier, VT: the author, 1987.

———. *Vermont Under Four Flags: A History of the Green Mountain State.* Montpelier, VT: The Author, 1975.

Morrissey, Charles T. *Vermont, a Bicentennial History.* New York: W. W. Norton & Co., 1981.

Nearing, Scott and Helen. *Living the Good Life.* New York: Schocken Books, 1970.

Newton, Earle. *The Vermont Story: A History of the People of the Green Mountain State, 1749-1949.* Montpelier, VT: Vermont Historical Society, 1949.

Ogden, Samuel R. *The Cheese that Changed Many Lives; or, A sentimental history of a tiny town high in the Green Mountains.* Landgrove, VT: Just-So Press, 1978.

Older, Jules. *Ski Vermont! A Complete Guide to the Best Vermont Skiing.* Post Mills, VT: Chelsea Green Publishing, 1991.

Painter, Nell I. *Standing at Armageddon.* New York: W. W. Norton, 1989.

Pike, Robert E. *Tall Trees, Tough Men.* New York: W. W. Norton, 1967.

Potash, P. Jeffrey. *Vermont's Burned-Over District: Patterns of Community Development and Religious Identity, 1761-1850*. Brooklyn, NY: Carlson Publishing, 1991.

Resch, Tyler. *Dorset: In the Shadow of the Marble Mountain*. West Kennebunk, ME: Published for the Dorset Historical Society by Phoenix Publishing, 1989.

Rolando, Victor R. *200 Years of Soot and Sweat: The History and Archaeology of Vermont's Iron, Charcoal, and Lime Industries*. Burlington, VT: Vermont Archaeological Society, 1992, available at http://www.vtarchaeology.org/wp-content/uploads /200_years_ch6_optimized.pdf.

Roth, Randolph. *The Democratic Dilemma*. New York: Cambridge University Press, 1987.

Rozwenc, Edwin. *Agricultural Policies in Vermont, 1860-1945*. Montpelier, VT: Vermont Historical Society, 1981.

Russell, Howard S. A. *A Long Deep Furrow: Three Centuries of Farming in New England*. Hanover, NH: University Press of New England, 1976.

Scott, Franklin D. *Sweden: The Nation's History*. Carbondale, IL: Southern Illinois University Press, 1988.

Searls, Paul M. *Two Vermonts: Geography and Identity, 1865-1910*. Durham, NH: University of New Hampshire Press; Hanover, NH: University Press of New England, 2006.

Sherman, Joe. *Fast Lane on a Dirt Road: A Contemporary History of Vermont*. White River Junction, VT: Chelsea Green Publishing Company, 2000.

Sherman, Michael, et al. *Freedom and Unity: A History of Vermont*. Barre, VT: Vermont Historical Society, 2004.

Smallwood, Frank. *Free and Independent: The Initiation of a College Professor into State Politics*. Brattleboro, VT: The Stephen Greene Press, 1976.

Stern, Jane. *Elegant Comfort Food from Dorset Inn*. Dorset, VT: Rutledge Hill Press, 2005.

Stone, Arthur F. *The Vermont of Today: With its Historical Background, Attractions, and People*. 4 vols. New York: Lewis Historical Publishing Co., 1929.

Stroud, Ellen. *Nature Next Door*. Seattle: University of Washington Press, 2012.

Susman, Warren. *Culture as History: The Transformation of American Society in the Twentieth Century*. New York: Pantheon Books, 1972.

Temin, Peter. *Engines of Enterprise: An Economic History of New England*. Cambridge, MA: Harvard University Press, 2000.

Ullery, Jacob G., comp. *Men of Vermont: An Illustrated Biographical History of Vermonters and Sons of Vermont*. Brattleboro, VT: Transcript Publishing Company, 1894.

Wilson, Harold F. *The Hill Country of Northern New England*. Montpelier, VT: Vermont Historical Society, 1947.

Wood, Grace E. P. *History of the Town of Wells, Vermont*. Wells, VT: self-published, 1955.

ARTICLES

Barron, Hal S. "The Impact of Rural Depopulation on the Local Economy: Chelsea, Vermont, 1840-1880." *Agricultural History* 54 (1980): 318-35.

Brown, Dona. "Vermont as a Way of Life." *Vermont History* 85 (Winter/Spring 2017): 43-64.

Clifford, Nicholas. "Take Back Vermont—in 1929: Vrest Orton and Green Mountain Independence." *Vermont Commons* 17 (2007).

"Former Presidents of the University of Vermont," www.uvm.edu/president
/formerpresidents/?Page=bailey.html.

Goldman, Hal. "'A Desirable Class of People': The Leadership of the Green Mountain
Club and Social Exclusivity, 1920-1936." *Vermont History* 65 (Summer/Fall 1997):
131-52.

Harrison, Blake. "The Technological Turn: Skiing and Landscape Change in Vermont,
1930-1970." *Vermont History* 71 (Summer/Fall 2003): 212-13.

———. "Tracks Across Vermont: *Vermont Life* and the Landscape of Downhill Skiing,
1946-1970." *Journal of Sport History* 28 (Summer 2001): 265.

Harty, Pat. "The Story of Bromley Mountain," *Vermont Life* 7 (Winter 1952-1953): 20.

Harvey, Dorothy M. "The Swedes in Vermont." American Swedish Historical Foundation *Yearbook* (1960): 23-43.

Leich, Jeffrey R. "New Hampshire and the Emergence of an American Ski Industry,"
New England Ski Museum, http://newenglandskimuseum.org/new-hampshire-
and-the-emergence-of-an-american-ski-industry/, June 4, 2014.

Lertola, Douglas S. and Mary H. Fregosi. "The Vermont Marble Company Strike of
1935-36." *Rutland Historical Society Quarterly* 32 (2002): 1-24.

Lund, John. "Vermont Nativism: William Paul Dillingham and U.S. Immigration
Legislation." *Vermont History* 63 (Winter 1995): 15-29.

McDevitt, Thomas D. "George Schmitt: Pioneer Aviator." *Rutland Historical Society
Quarterly* 15 (1985): 47.

Moore, Mary. "The Rowen Forge." *Craft Horizons* 10 (Summer 1950): 6-9.

Perrin, Noel. "The Two Faces of Vermont." *Vermont Life* 19 (Winter 1964): 31-33.

Rebek, Andrea. "The Selling of Vermont: From Agriculture to Tourism, 1860-
1910." *Vermont History* 44 (Winter 1976): 14-27.

Rozwenc, Edwin C. "The Group Basis of Vermont Farm Politics, 1870-1945." *Vermont
History* 25 (Fall 1957): 268-87.

Sautter, John A. "Equity and History: Vermont's Education Revolution of the Early
1890s," *Vermont History* 76 (Winter/Spring 2008): 1-18.

Sherman, Michael, Jennie G. Versteeg, Samuel B. Hand, and Paul S. Gillies. "The
Character of Vermont: Twentieth-Anniversary Reflections." Center for Research
on Vermont Occasional Paper Series, Paper 5 (1996).

Silverstein, Hannah. "No Parking: Vermont Rejects the Green Mountain Parkway."
Vermont History 63 (Summer 1995): 133-57.

Stout, Marilyn. "Small Beginnings: The First Rope Tow in Vermont." *Historic Roots* 3
(December 1998): 9-15.

Town of Londonderry, "About Londonderry," http://londonderryvt.org/community/
arts-historical/about-londonderry/.

Tremblay, Raymond H., et al. "Projections of Dairy Farm Numbers in Vermont."
Vermont Agricultural Station Bulletin. Burlington, VT: University of Vermont
Agricultural Experiment Station, 1968.

"The Wisdom of Helen and Scott Nearing," *Mother Earth News* 61 (January/February
1980), http://www.motherearthnews.com/homesteading-and-livestock/helen-
and-scott-nearing-zmaz8ojfzraw.aspx.

INDEX

Note: Endnote information is indicated by n and note number following the page number.

"abandoned" farms: evolution of use of, 28, 64; French Canadian immigrants attracted to, 50; media on, 222n35; reputational damage from description of, 26–27, 32, 39, 100, 109; Swedish immigrants recruited to fill, 18–19, 24–29, 32–35, 39–43, 50–51, 63–65, 109–10, 217n1; tourism attracted by, 39–40, 52–53, 65, 75, 90, 103, 106, 109, 132, 134, 152
Act 250, 206–8
"An Act to Aid the Town of Landgrove in the Payment of Its Indebtedness," 69–70
Addison County, Vermont: population of, 218n5; Swedish immigrants in, 160
advertising: billboard or roadside, 62, 133, 150, 168, 198–99, 250n50, 250n60; farms for sale, 34, 53, 54, 55, 82, 110; Swedish immigration program banned from, 8, 21, 34; Swedish immigration program media coverage as, 27, 49, 53; tourism promotion through, 76, 78, 79–80, 82–83, 88, 101–6, 110, 116–18, 133–34, 197–98, 200; VCCL media coverage as free, 133. *See also* promotion
affordability: preservation endangering, 2, 206–7; Tiffts and local families challenges of, 108, 214; Vermont land's perceived, 33, 102, 123–24
African American immigrants, 22
agriculture. *See* farming and agriculture
Aiken, George D., 147–51, 155–56, 163, 243n88, 247n85
alcohol, 61
"All-Vermont Program," 115
The American Home magazine, 173

American Woolen Mill, 175
America the Vanishing (Ogden), 205
Anderson family, 68–69, 84, 86, 96, 99, 131, 155
Anderson, Agnes (later Brown), 56, 155, 189
Anderson, Carl, 30, 84, 96, 99, 175
Anderson, Celia, 99
Anderson, Charles, 44, 84, 144, 200, 210
Anderson, Cora (née Wilkins), 68, 99
Anderson, Donald, 210
Anderson, Edwin: children and descendants of, 47, 56–57; community and lifestyle of, 47, 60; death of, 84; occupations of, 35–36, 45, 110; recruitment to Vermont of, 30, 31, 35–36
Anderson, Ellen, 56, 144, 175, 200
Anderson, Emma: children and descendants of, 47, 56–57, 84; community and lifestyle of, 47, 60, 99; death of, 144; death of spouse, 84; occupations of, 60, 84, 122; recruitment to Vermont of, 30, 31
Anderson, Esther (later Carey), 56, 84, 144, 175, 200
Anderson, Harry, 47, 68, 84, 99, 159
Anderson, Hazel (later Twyne), 62, 68, 175, 200, 235n22
Anderson, Hilma (later Butler). *See* Butler, Hilma (née Anderson)
Anderson, Norman, 159
Anderson, Robert, 210
Arlington, Vermont: Rockwell models from, 160; Swedish immigrants in, 154, 160, 183–84, 189, 210; tourism and summer homes in, 143
Arvika, Sweden, 29
Ascutney ski area, 180
Automobile Club of America, 76–77
automobiles: highways and roads for (*see*